FROM THE AMERICAN DRAMA

FROM THE
AMERICAN DRAMA

THE MODERN THEATRE SERIES

VOLUME FOUR

CAPTAIN JINKS OF THE HORSE MARINES

THE NEW YORK IDEA

PULLMAN CAR HIAWATHA

THE MAN WITH THE HEART IN THE HIGHLANDS

GUYS AND DOLLS

Edited By

ERIC BENTLEY

GLOUCESTER, MASS.

PETER SMITH

1974

The Anchor Books edition is the first publication of *The Modern Theatre, Volume 4: From the American Drama,* edited by Eric Bentley.

Anchor Books edition: 1956

Library of Congress Catalog Card Number 55–7979
Copyright ©, 1956, by Eric Bentley
Reprinted, 1974, by Permission of
Doubleday & Co., Inc.
ISBN: 0-8446-1657-5

ACKNOWLEDGMENTS

Captain Jinks of the Horse Marines was first brought to my attention by Mr. William Becker. *The New York Idea* was recommended by Mr. Edmund Wilson; I also have a happy memory of a production of it at the University of Minnesota Theatre. What especially commended *Pullman Car Hiawatha* to me was a production by Mr. Alan Schneider at the Neighborhood Playhouse. *My Heart's in the Highlands* is so famous an American play it seemed a pity that the shorter (and better?) work from which it derives had never been widely available; Mr. Saroyan himself supplied the necessary co-operation. The task of securing anthology rights to a recent and unpublished Broadway hit like *Guys and Dolls* is a formidable one; I should never have been able to see it through without the help of Mr. Allen Whitehead of Music Theatre Inc., Mr. Harold Orenstein of the Frank Music Corporation, and Mr. Jason Epstein, editor of Doubleday Anchor Books. Precise acknowledgment of permission to print is provided on the title page of each play.

E.B.

FOREWORD

It would of course have been possible to include American plays in the first three volumes of my Modern Theatre series; but surely many readers would prefer that the American drama be given a whole volume to itself. Such at any rate was the thought behind the present collection. Now, among the thousands and thousands of American plays, which five would do best service here? What a problem! There was obviously no foolproof solution to it. There was one class of plays, however, that would not do good service, namely, the plays which everyone interested in the subject already has in his library. For, while the European drama is to an alarming extent unavailable in English translation, inexpensive editions of American plays, separate or in collections, pour constantly from the presses. On the other hand, this is no place to reprint "America's lost plays" of the eighteenth and nineteenth centuries: such a collection would be too narrowly antiquarian in its appeal. Merit—the power to amuse and if possible to fascinate—must remain a chief desideratum. And—again, if possible—the five texts should form some sort of unity; each should gain from the co-presence of the others. Possibly, even, a view of the American theatre might be hinted at—a particular direction might be given, for what this is worth, an editor's blessing.

"What do they know of England who only England know?" To see America as a distinct phenomenon, one has to be non-American. For this book, a foreign-born editor has chosen a group of scripts which are inalienably—incurably, if you like—American. American dramatists have produced no profound masterpieces to set beside the profound masterpieces of American fiction. The American theatre has produced no *Moby Dick*, no *Scarlet Letter*, no *Portrait of a Lady*, nor even a *Great Gatsby*, a *Sun Also Rises*, an

As I Lay Dying, but at its best it has a quality—a flavor, a tang, a gusto, a verve, a flamboyance—not present in the contemporary drama of other countries. I believe that any European who has seen a few American comedies— even in translation and acted by Europeans—will vouch for this statement. Further evidence is to be found in the circumstance that American plays are hard for British actors to act, while *Oklahoma!* or *Guys and Dolls* absolutely requires an American company. It isn't a matter of words but of a style of behavior, a way of moving and standing and sitting, folkways, mores, all the indescribable, concrete content of a national way of living. I recall, when I was an English undergraduate at Oxford, reading William Saroyan's first books of stories. Doubtless I overestimated them, but my point here is that they brought before my mind's eye a New World such as no born American has ever seen. When I later came to this country, I found that reality did not correspond to the images Mr. Saroyan had called up in my European mind any more than reality corresponds to the images which Hollywood supplies to European minds. Not that Mr. Saroyan's writing is open to the same objection as the average Hollywood film. I believe that what Mr. Saroyan said about America was true; it was I who did the distorting. I still value those early tales of Fresno and offer one in the present volume in theatre form precisely because it conveys "the American quality," however much that quality can be misunderstood. The paradox of my early experience of this author was that, though my interpretations were wrong, my sense that his writing was above all American was correct.

It is not unheard of for an American actor of only moderate standing over here to make a killing in London because the British public finds his vitality nothing short of prodigious. Or take the difference between the chorus of an American musical and that of a British one; I refer less to a difference in proficiency than to one of personality, poise, and gait—in a word, of life-rhythm. The phlegm that has stood the British in such good stead in more important affairs is wholly a disadvantage in this more frivolous field. And even in a dramatic script there is a lot to be said for American "zip," "zing," "zoom," and all the other virtues that begin with a z as against the mild little number from England with its gentle ironical tone and its nice touches of humorous Anglo-Saxon characterization. But there is no need to cry down any other "way" in order to cry up this one. My contention is that the famous tempo of American productions, the famous energy of American playing (especially in light comedy and musicals) is an integral part of American culture and an organic product of American life. My choice of plays in this book is in line with this contention.

In a collection intended to represent the American drama as fully as possible, I should naturally have included O'Neill, Odets, Miller, Williams—the usual roster of names. Here, in my allotted space of some four hundred small pages, I have preferred to pick five items, perhaps not less distinguished but assuredly less likely to be in any non-specialist's library. They show the American theatre at its liveliest; they move with the swing of the American life-rhythm. Two of them (the Wilder and the Saroyan) take off into a characteristically American realm of fantasy: the word *zany* says about as much about the type as can be said in four letters. Two of the plays are realistic or at any rate would have been considered so when they were new; this is no raw naturalism, however, but a bland, humorous, and intelligent form of reportage; one might call it genre painting except that painting is static while in the writing of Fitch and Mitchell there is all the diabolical drive of the great comic tradition.

The fifth item is not a play at all but the book of a musical comedy. The idea—no, the fact—behind my choice of *Guys and Dolls* was that musical comedy is today the most lively part of the American theatre. This is not to say that the majority of musical comedies are good ones or that all of the good ones have a book that would make good reading. *Guys and Dolls* is a special case. Possibly it is the best of all American musical comedies. Certainly

the milieu it presents and the language in which that milieu
is presented embody "the American quality" as impres-
sively as anything else in this book.

Great plays are not everything. Theatre is not defined
by a list of literary masterpieces divided one from another, as they are, by great stretches of time. Theatre is a
living tradition of entertainment, unbroken now in western history for at least a thousand years. When we see
Beatrice Lillie on the stage or W. C. Fields on the screen,
we feel we are one with the ages, and I think we are
right to feel so, for behind these artists is the music hall,
and behind the music hall the musico-comic theatre of the
eighteenth century, and behind that theatre the *commedia
dell' arte,* and behind the *commedia dell' arte* Roman
comedy and the New Comedy of Greece . . . I believe
that the authors represented in this book have the pecu-
liarly American quality at its most vivid and, in addition,
belong to the great community of the theatre, here and
everywhere.

Eric Bentley

CONTENTS

FOREWORD BY ERIC BENTLEY vii

Captain Jinks of the Horse Marines 1
by CLYDE FITCH

The New York Idea 121
by LANGDON MITCHELL

Pullman Car Hiawatha 249
by THORNTON WILDER

The Man with the Heart in the Highlands 267
by WILLIAM SAROYAN

Guys and Dolls, after Damon Runyon 283
by JO SWERLING, ABE BURROWS
and FRANK LOESSER

NOTES 383

CAPTAIN JINKS

OF THE

HORSE MARINES

A Fantastic Comedy in Three Acts
by

CLYDE FITCH

PERSONS
CONCERNED IN THE PLAY

CAPTAIN ROBERT CARROLTON JINKS

CHARLES LA MARTINE

AUGUSTUS BLEEKER VAN VORKENBURG

Professor BELLIARTI

The HERALD *Reporter*

The TRIBUNE *Reporter*

The TIMES *Reporter*

The SUN *Reporter*

The CLIPPER *Representative*

A Newsboy

An Official Detective

A Sailor

A Policeman

A Telegraph Boy

Sailors, Domestics, and New Yorkers

MADAME TRENTONI (AURELIA JOHNSON)

MRS. GREENBOROUGH

MRS. JINKS

MRS. STONINGTON

MISS MERRIAM

1st Ballet Lady (MISS PETTITOES)

2nd Ballet Lady

3rd Ballet Lady

4th Ballet Lady (FRAULEIN HOCHSPITZ)

5th Ballet Lady

6th Ballet Lady (MRS. MAGGITT)

7th Ballet Lady

MARY: MADAME TRENTONI'S *Maid*

SCENE: *New York*   TIME: *Early Seventies*

ACT ONE

The landing dock of the Cunard Line. Late in the morn-
ing. The side of the vessel is seen on the left, with the
passengers' gangplank coming down to the center of the
stage. Across the river at the back is seen Hoboken with
the Stevens house on the hill. It is a gray, misty day, with
a drizzling rain which flatters the Jersey shore. The para-
phernalia of a landing stage is littered about, and some
small groups of luggage arrived on the steamer have not
yet been removed. A SAILOR *stands at the top of the gang-*
plank keeping a bored guard. There is a NEWSBOY *selling*
the Herald, Tribune, Times, Sun, Express, *and* Clipper.
A tired STEWARD *now and then passes in sight on the boat.*
A POLICEMAN *walks in and out on the dock. It is raining*
and everyone enters with a wet umbrella. The NEWSBOY
sitting on a barrel is whistling "Captain Jinks" and kicking
his heels against the barrel; he offers the POLICEMAN, *each*
time he passes him, a different paper. All the passengers
except MADAME TRENTONI *have long ago left the boat.*
Several truckmen and loafers are more or less busy on the
premises.

PETER, *whistling, interrupts himself as the* POLICEMAN *passes.*
Herald?

The POLICEMAN *pays no attention to the boy at any time.*
PETER *always continues whistling at once when he gets*
no answer and continues the tune exactly where he left
it off. The POLICEMAN *repasses.*

Tri-bune? Express?

He continues whistling. The POLICEMAN *repasses.*
Times?

Continues whistling. POLICEMAN *repasses.*

World? Clipper?

Continues whistling as the POLICEMAN *passes out of sight.*

The TRIBUNE REPORTER *hurries in. He goes quickly to the gangplank and starts to walk up it. The* SAILOR *at the top calls down and stops him.*

THE SAILOR. Nobody ain't allowed on board.

The NEWSBOY *laughs and whistles pointedly, "Shoo Fly, don't bother me!"*

THE TRIBUNE REPORTER. Why not? I'm from the Tribune.

THE SAILOR. That don't make no difference, not if you was Boss Tweed from Tammany Hall!

THE TRIBUNE REPORTER. Madame Trentoni hasn't left the boat yet, has she?

THE SAILOR. There ain't no blamed Italyan on this yere boat!

THE TRIBUNE REPORTER. The young lady speaks English. I mean the great——

PETER, *stopping whistling to interrupt.* Say, Jack! He means the primy donner what the young Prince of Wales says is a A one-er.

THE SAILOR. Oh, you mean the opry singer! She'll be leaving soon now. There's a good deal o' motion in her cabin, and there's eight men ordered below a-struggling with her bag-gage.

THE TRIBUNE REPORTER, *eagerly, and with commendable zeal.* How much baggage has she?

THE SAILOR. I dunno.

The TRIBUNE REPORTER *comes back down the gangplank.*

PETER, *on the barrel.* Have the *Tri*-bune?

THE TRIBUNE REPORTER, *grandiloquently, feeling very much the importance of his position, especially as there is no other reporter there.* I AM the Tribune!

He opens his umbrella and places it on the floor to dry.

PETER, *who is uneducated.* Huh?

THE TRIBUNE REPORTER. *I* make the paper.

PETER. Where's your machine?

THE TRIBUNE REPORTER, *pointing to his forehead.* Here!

PETER. Gee! I guess you're off your nut, ain't you?

THE TRIBUNE REPORTER, *obtusely.* No, no, my boy. I'm a reporter.

PETER. All right, boss, but you ain't the only party what's after Miss Squeeler in there!

THE TRIBUNE REPORTER, *with supreme elegance.* Other gentlemen of the press, I presume?

PETER. Naw, it ain't no gentlemen—it's a big toff—a regular lardy-dah what's been down here twice already with a gang of dandies and a brass band! The band was real discouraged the second time—was playing "Hail, Columbia" for all she was worth!

THE TRIBUNE REPORTER. I know about that. The Herald man got on to it yesterday. Hello, Times!

As the TIMES REPORTER *comes on.*

THE TIMES REPORTER. Is she out yet?

THE TRIBUNE REPORTER. No. But look here, Captain Jinks has been here with his chums and a band in their uniforms straight from the Republican parade.

THE TIMES REPORTER. If those fellows get hold of her first, we boys won't have a chance at an interview.

THE TRIBUNE REPORTER. Are they coming back?

PETER. Well, the band was a-kickin', but I guess the swells'll be back, because they was full of bokays.

THE TRIBUNE REPORTER. They had a tug engaged to go over the bar to meet the boat tomorrow. Nobody ever dreamed she'd be in before. Think of crossing the ocean in fourteen days—it's a record-breaker! Mapleson calmly went on to Boston to come back tonight or he'd be fixing everything for us!

THE TIMES REPORTER. I tell you what, we'll go get the boys now, quick, so we can all have a fair show together, and leave this youngster to tell Captain Jinks and his crowd when they come back that the lady won't——

Interrupted.

PETER. She ain't no common *lady*, she's a opry singer what the Prince of Wales——

Interrupted.

THE TRIBUNE REPORTER. Yes, yes! Mapleson gave us that story weeks ago. You tell Captain Jinks that Madame Trentoni won't leave the boat till after lunch. Are you fly?

PETER. What's it worth?

THE TIMES REPORTER. What'll you take?

PETER. You make *me* an offer.

THE TRIBUNE REPORTER. We'll give you a quarter.

The NEWSBOY *gives the* TRIBUNE REPORTER *one look, and then, sticking his thumbs in the armholes of his waistcoat, he whistles "Shoo Fly, don't bother me!"*

Well, what's the matter?

PETER. You get someone else to do your job. I go to Sunday school, an' I don't tell lies for nothing.

THE TIMES REPORTER. We'll give you a dollar.

PETER. All right! Pay in advance?

THE TRIBUNE REPORTER. Not by a long shot! Collect on delivery—of the lie! I'll go after the men, Jimmie, and you hang around out of the way here—just to keep an eye on the boy and see he *does his work!*

Picking up his umbrella, he goes out onto the street.

PETER. Gee! Lyin' 's no work fur me—it's play! That there about going to Sunday school was a sample.

THE TIMES REPORTER. Look out! Here they come.

Goes outside by the boat.

Three men are heard singing "Captain Jinks of the Horse Marines," faintly, then more loudly as they approach and come on through the big doorway on the right. The

three men are CHARLIE, GUSSIE, *and* CAPTAIN JINKS. *They
are good-looking young dandies,* GUSSIE *being more of a
fop than the others,* CAPTAIN JINKS *himself having a superb
figure and a frank, handsome face. All he needs is one
lesson to make a fine man of him. The three march in arm
in arm,* CAPTAIN JINKS *in the center. They wear scarlet
uniforms and big bearskin caps. Each carries a bouquet
of the period, small, with a flounce of lace around it. Their
singing and marching is of course simply a joke among
themselves. The* POLICEMAN *meets them coming from the
opposite side.*

THE POLICEMAN. Here! Here! No visitors allowed on this yere
dock without a permission.

CAPTAIN JINKS. I say, Charlie—Gussie—who's got the permission?

*Each one begins with his right-hand pocket, and all look
through all their pockets in unison without success; then
CAPTAIN JINKS removes his hat and triumphantly takes
out a piece of paper.*

Here you are, Mr. Policeman!

THE POLICEMAN, *not taking the paper.* All right!

And passes on.

CAPTAIN JINKS, *to* PETER, *who sits whistling on the barrel.*
Well, Horace Greeley, any signs of the opera queen yet?

PETER. Nope. Where's the band?

CAPTAIN JINKS. The band has struck, so we did our best
without it.

PETER. Well, say, she ain't up yet—she ain't to leave the boat
for a couple of hours yet.

CAPTAIN JINKS. What a sell!   *The men are much dis-*
GUSSIE. What a bore!   *appointed, and all speak*
CHARLIE. What a damn shame!   *at once.*

CAPTAIN JINKS. Who told you?

PETER. Jack Tar up there.

At this moment TWO SAILORS *appear on the ship and struggle down the gangplank with a large trunk, which they place at one side, and return up the gangplank.*

CHARLIE. Well, come along, Captain Jinks. We can't hang around here all morning.

GUSSIE. Let's go uptown to Union Square and have a drink.

CAPTAIN JINKS. No, no, fellows, we might miss her; some other crowd'll get hold of her and spoil our fun.

CHARLIE. Everyone's on the *qui vive* to entertain her. We must fill her time for a week with engagements before she leaves this dock.

GUSSIE. Yes siree, by Jove, so everyone in town will see we have the inside track!

CAPTAIN JINKS, *indicating* PETER. Get rid of the kid.

CHARLIE. Go 'long, Horace Greeley! *Scoot!*

PETER. I can't.

CAPTAIN JINKS. Why not?

PETER. I got to sell my papers.

CAPTAIN JINKS. Sell them somewhere else.

PETER. Nope! I got to sell 'em here. If you want me to get out, you got to *buy* me out.

CAPTAIN JINKS. Well, how many papers have you?

PETER. A dollar and a half's worth.

CAPTAIN JINKS. What'll you take for them?

PETER. A dollar sixty!

CAPTAIN JINKS. No, you won't. Come along, boys, chip in fifty cents each.

He starts singing "Up in a Balloon, Boys." The others join in, diving into their waistcoat pockets, and each pitches half a dollar into CAPTAIN JINKS's *hat.*

TWO SAILORS *bring down another big trunk and, depositing it near the first, return to the ship.*

CAPTAIN JINKS, *to* PETER. Here you are!

   Giving the money.

   The men stop whistling. The NEWSBOY *with his cap on one side swaggers off whistling "Up in a Balloon, Boys," but steals immediately back and hides under the gang-plank.*

CAPTAIN JINKS. I say, I'll match you both to see who pays for the landau to take her away.

CHARLIE. In the name of all three of us?

CAPTAIN JINKS. Oh, yes; but match who pays!

   Each gets out his coin.

   You first, Charlie, match me!

   They throw the coins.

CHARLIE. Heads!

CAPTAIN JINKS. Good! Gussie!

   He and GUSSIE *throw.*

GUSSIE. Tails!

CAPTAIN JINKS. Bravo! You pay for the landau, Gussie. Thank you, old man.

   Shaking his hand.

CHARLIE, *also shaking his hand.* Thank you!

GUSSIE. Botheration!

   The SAILORS *bring down another trunk.*

CAPTAIN JINKS. Hello, Jack! Is that little Italian bird on board awake yet?

A SAILOR. Oh, yes; she's busy giving presents to all the deck hands.

   They go back onto the ship.

CAPTAIN JINKS. I'll tell you what I'll do, fellows. I'll bet you five hundred dollars——

   Interrupted.

CHARLIE. I haven't got it!

CAPTAIN JINKS, *laughing*. Well, Gussie'll lend it to you, won't you, Gussie?

CHARLIE. That's so. 'Course he will!

CAPTAIN JINKS. I'll bet you both five hundred that I'll make love to her.

CHARLIE, *laughing*. That's nothing. I'd make love to anything for five hundred dollars.

CAPTAIN JINKS, *laughing*. Go West! I mean I'll bet you five hundred dollars I'll get up a flirtation with her.

CHARLIE. Make it a thousand.

CAPTAIN JINKS. Will you lend Charlie a thousand, Gussie?

CHARLIE. Yes; of course he will!

CAPTAIN JINKS. All right. Good!

CHARLIE. Done!

They shake hands.

I think I ought to stand some chance with the fair lady— she may have broken the hearts of the blue bloods of Europe, but after all, my great-great-grandfather settled in Maryland, driven from France by the Huguenot troubles, and my family is connected with the royal blood of France. We haven't a cent left; still, I think I can hold my own.

CAPTAIN JINKS, *bored*. Oh, all right, Charlie.

GUSSIE. You're not the only lardy-dah here. My ancestor, the first Van Vorkenburg, came over with Peter Stuyvesant and was an early Dutch governor of New York. My family has always been mixed up with the government of the country. My father is a politician now, and so we've never had to work for our living.

CHARLIE. Give us a rest!

CAPTAIN JINKS. Hold on a minute. What's the matter with my family! I'm Captain Jinks of the Horse Marines, formerly of Richmond, Virginia; a member of one of those real old Southern families you read about, ruined by the

Civil War—only, as a matter of fact, we were dead broke before the war began! However, never mind! Now, you boys go and get the landau.

CHARLIE. Not if we know it. She might come out while we were gone, and that would give you an advantage. I'm not losing Gussie's thousand so easily! I intend to get up a flirtation with her myself.

GUSSIE. Well, so do I, by Jove!

CAPTAIN JINKS. Oh do you! Another five hundred that neither of you get your arm around her waist!

Shaking hands with both quickly.

And come on now, *we'll all three go* after the landau.

They link arms and go out singing "Walking down Broadway." As they go the NEWSBOY *climbs up from under the gangplank and, placing two fingers of his hand in his mouth, whistles a piercing signal twice—then waves his cap. The* TIMES REPORTER *runs in.*

THE TIMES REPORTER. Is she coming?

PETER. No; but I got sumthin' to tell you—I mean, to *sell* you!

The POLICEMAN *enters and gives the* SAILOR *a bit of chewing tobacco, which he takes and says "Thank ye" for.*

THE TIMES REPORTER. What is it?

PETER. Pst!

Motioning toward the SAILOR *and* POLICEMAN, *who will hear.*

THE SAILOR, *who stands by.* Hello, she's a comin' now, I guess. The old party's between decks with full sail on.

PETER. What do you say to this?

Motioning the TIMES REPORTER *to one side, where he whispers to him in dumb show all about the three men and their bet. Surprise, curiosity, and delight are shown by the* TIMES REPORTER. *Meanwhile an official, a* PRIVATE DETECTIVE *in plain clothes, has sauntered in and meets the* POLICEMAN, *who has started back toward the street.*

THE DETECTIVE, *in semi-confidential tone.* I understand there's a opry singer on board this here boat who's goin' to land this A.M. with costumes and jewelry and a cartload of stuff. Not off yet, eh?

THE POLICEMAN, *very supercilious.* Naw!

THE DETECTIVE. Well, there's a suspicion she may try to do a bit of smuggling, and I'm detailed special to see there's no bribing of our officials. I shall do the examination myself.

He opens his coat, showing the official badge on his breast. Just be on hand in case there's a little job for you.

THE POLICEMAN, *with a very different manner—most obsequious—touches his hat.* Yes, surr.

THE DETECTIVE. Be in ear shot, and if you hear me whistle twice like this

Whistling twice.

—why, come along.

THE POLICEMAN, *touching his hat.* Yes, surr.

He offers the DETECTIVE a piece of chewing tobacco.

THE DETECTIVE. Oh, thank you.

Takes a bite, and returns the plug.

The POLICEMAN passes out. Meanwhile the NEWSBOY and the TIMES REPORTER have finished.

THE TIMES REPORTER. Look here. Keep mum about this, and I'll make it worth your while. I've got to consult with Mr. Mapleson before I publish a thing like that, but if it ever *is* published, it's got to be *my* story! Why, I ought to get a rise of salary if I get that for my paper.

The DETECTIVE starts to go as four men enter hurriedly, breathless, running in, all with dripping umbrellas—the HERALD REPORTER, the SUN REPORTER, the TRIBUNE REPORTER, and the CLIPPER REPRESENTATIVE.

ALL THE REPORTERS. Off yet?

Almost knocking over the DETECTIVE.

THE DETECTIVE. Excuse me, gentlemen.

And exits.

THE TIMES REPORTER. No—but she's expected shortly. Where's the Express? The World?

THE CLIPPER REPRESENTATIVE. They're waiting at the Brevoort House with her maid and old Belliarti.

THE TRIBUNE REPORTER. Where's the bouquet?

THE SUN REPORTER. Here.

They all gather around him and unwrap a huge and beautiful bouquet, which is covered with five different newspapers—the latter soaking wet from the rain.

THE TRIBUNE REPORTER. We protected it from the rain with a representative sheet of each one of us, so as to show no partiality and have the bouquet represent in every way the United Press of New York!

The bouquet is in the shape of a cone whose base is nearly a yard in diameter. There are two tiers of red and white roses, alternating, and the structure is crowned by one important calla lily. A large bow with streamers of red, white, and blue ribbon adds a last gala and patriotic note!

MRS. GREENBOROUGH *appears on the ship and hesitates at the top of the gangplank.*

PETER, *aside to the* SAILOR. Come on, let's sell 'em. Here's the old lady—let's pretend she's the primy donny!

THE SAILOR, *chuckling.* You're a rum un!

He goes up the gangplank to help MRS. GREENBOROUGH.

PETER. Hi! Pst!

Whistles again between his fingers; the REPORTERS *all turn; the bouquet is unwrapped.*

Here she is!

MRS. GREENBOROUGH *comes down the gangplank. She is a pretty, middle-aged lady, kind, motherly, and a little foolish. She has one especial characteristic: she talks, whenever starting, in a steady stream but never finishes a speech, as no one will wait for her but either interrupts*

*or leaves her. When interrupted she invariably stops short
with a broad and sweet smile, good-naturedly accepting
what has become for her the inevitable. She is dressed
a few years behind the times but is somewhat prejudiced
against the quiet colors. All the* REPORTERS *drop their
umbrellas and rush to meet her. They reach the foot of
the gangplank just as she does, and, gathering all to the
right side, bow low and offer her the big bouquet.*

THE TIMES REPORTER. Welcome, madame, to our great country! The American Eagle, whose own high C carries from
the shores of the Atlantic to the Pacific's golden strand,
welcomes her sister songbird! And the press of New York
offer their united compliments and felicitations with the
accompanying bouquet.

*Giving the bouquet with a bow which he has copied from
one of Lester Wallack's. All the* REPORTERS *applaud.*

THE HERALD REPORTER. Bravo, Pat!

The NEWSBOY *on his barrel and the* SAILOR *at the top of
the gangplank are very much amused.* MRS. GREEN-
BOROUGH *is tremendously surprised, and, taking the bouquet, is followed to one side by all the* REPORTERS, *who
encircle her.*

MRS. GREENBOROUGH. My word! I never was so surprised in
all my life, nor so overpowered, nor so fluctuated either,
for I'm sure I'm speechless, I can't say a word! Only fancy,
this is the first booky I've had donated to me since my
old gentleman used to call me pretty pet names in the
gone-by days!

She continues talking a steady stream, but the TIMES *and
the* HERALD REPORTERS *come away from the others and
speak to each other aside.*

THE HERALD REPORTER. For heaven's sake, there must be some
mistake.

THE TIMES REPORTER. *She* eighteen years old? She's three
times eighteen!

THE HERALD REPORTER. Does Mapleson want to tell us the
Prince gave *grandma* an emerald bracelet?

PETER, *innocently.* Gee! I made a mistake. That ain't the party; that must be her mother.

THE TIMES REPORTER. Oh, it's the companion, of course! What idiots! Get back the bouquet!

THE HERALD REPORTER. How?

Calls.

Bill!

The TRIBUNE REPORTER *joins them.*

THE TRIBUNE REPORTER. She can't be——

Interrupted by

THE HERALD REPORTER. No, no, it's the chaperon—— Go on— get back the bouquet.

THE TRIBUNE REPORTER. What! Get it back? I can't. Here! Pete!

The SUN REPORTER *leaves* MRS. GREENBOROUGH *gladly.*

THE SUN REPORTER. Say, shorthand isn't quick enough to take down *her* conversation.

THE TRIBUNE REPORTER. Don't bother. It's the wrong party. Get back the bouquet.

THE SUN REPORTER. Ask for it, or grab it?

The CLIPPER REPRESENTATIVE *quickly joins them from* MRS. GREENBOROUGH, *who is still talking and raises her voice a little as they leave her, but seeing their backs toward her breaks off in the middle of a sentence, smiling, and smells her bouquet.*

THE SUN REPORTER, THE TIMES REPORTER, THE TRIBUNE RE-PORTER, *and* THE HERALD REPORTER, *all together.* We've made a mistake!

The NEWSBOY *whistles shrilly through his fingers to attract their attention, and they all turn quickly to look as* AURELIA *appears on the ship. She is quite the most lovely creature that ever came, like Venus Aphrodite, from the sea! Youth and beauty join in making her adorable; and a charming individuality, with a sense of humor bewilderingly attractive, makes her victory over mere man, irre-*

spective of age or station, child's play. Her modish bustle only accentuates the grace of her girlish figure. And even a "waterfall"* only seems to make a friendly background for her perfect brow and finely poised head. She carries in her arms a very small black-and-tan dog; she wears an ermine fur tippet and carries a muff. The REPORTERS *quickly draw up to one side.* AURELIA *stops at the top of the gangplank for a moment, looking around her and smiling, and then runs gaily down.*

AURELIA. Hip! hip! hurrah! Here we are at last on American soil—planks—never mind, *soil*—— e pluribus unum!

She stands by the foot of the gangplank. All the RE-PORTERS *raise their hats.*

MRS. GREENBOROUGH, *accustomed to* AURELIA'S *beauty and at present entirely self-absorbed.* Oh, Aurelia darling, do look at the beautiful booky these dear Americans have given me; did you ever see——

Interrupted.

AURELIA. No, I never did! Good morning, gentlemen!

All the REPORTERS *bow low.*

THE TIMES REPORTER, *stepping slightly forward.* Welcome, madame, to our great country! The American Eagle, whose own high C carries from the shores of the Atlantic to the Pacific's golden strand, welcomes her sister songbird! And the press of New York offer their united compliments and felicitations with the—with—with the bouquet which will arrive at your hotel this evening!

AURELIA. Thank you very much, I'm sure. Here, Mrs. Gee; please hold Camille.

Giving the small black-and-tan dog to MRS. GREEN-BOROUGH.

I call him "Camille" because "Marguerite Gautier" is so long, and I wanted to name him after my first great success. You are all the reporters, aren't you?

*I.e., a chignon.

Smiling ravishingly straight into every one of their faces.
They told me you'd be here.
She shakes hands all around with each one of them as she speaks.
I'm so glad; I'm dying to be interviewed!
Laughing.

THE HERALD REPORTER, *apropos of her walk.* We see you have the Saratoga Stride in England.

AURELIA. You mean my walk? With the Grecian Bend? Oh, but we call it the Brighton Dip. Yes, it's very fashionable with us!

THE TRIBUNE REPORTER. To what hotel do you go?

AURELIA. The Brevoort House on the Fifth Avenue at Eighth Street; I'm told that is best and not so far uptown as the Fifth Avenue Hotel on the Broadway.

THE TIMES REPORTER. And much nearer the New Academy of Music where you are to sing.

AURELIA. Did Mrs. Greenborough present herself?

MRS. GREENBOROUGH. No, I thought I'd better——
She stops short with a smile, interrupted.

AURELIA. Quite right. This is my aunt, gentlemen.
Elaborate bows.
Ballet girls and opera comique singers are obliged to have a mother, you know, but grand opera and Shakespeare can travel with an *aunt*.

MRS. GREENBOROUGH. Fancy, I haven't yet half thanked——
Smiles, interrupted.

AURELIA, *interrupting.* What lovely weather! I've always heard so much of your American climate.

THE TIMES REPORTER. But we call this very bad.

AURELIA. Not to me, I assure you, who sailed from *Liverpool*. I call it almost sunny! Only, dear me, very warm!
Taking off her furs and placing them on a trunk.
They told me it was so cold here!

THE HERALD REPORTER. And how do you like America?

AURELIA. Oh, I adore it! It's superb!

Looking about her at the little dock, and speaking in the stereotyped manner.

It's so enormous, so great a country! I'm amazed at its size!

Then, coming down to a more natural manner, she laughs.

Of course I've not seen very much yet. What town is that across the river over there? Is that Boston?

THE TIMES REPORTER. No, that's Hoboken!

AURELIA. Oh! A suburb, I presume.

THE TIMES REPORTER. Yes, of *Hamburg*.

AURELIA. I hope to see a great deal of your country. I'm mad to go to A. T. Stewart's shop, and to see Saratoga, which I've heard heaps about! And the very first morning I have free from a rehearsal I've promised myself I shall run over to Niagara Falls and back!

All the REPORTERS are following her with lightning rapidity, looking up now and then, smiling and nodding to her as she talks.

Mrs. Gee!

MRS. GREENBOROUGH. Yes, my love?

AURELIA. Do go see why they don't bring out the rest of my luggage!

To the REPORTERS.

There are forty-eight boxes.

MRS. GREENBOROUGH. Don't you want——

Interrupted.

AURELIA. Nothing, dear heart, please go.

MRS. GREENBOROUGH goes up the gangplank into the boat.
AURELIA continues to the REPORTERS.

Did you get that? I have *forty-eight boxes.*

THE TIMES REPORTER. That's a good many more even than Parepa-Rosa brought over!

AURELIA. Oh, but she depended entirely on her voice!

THE TRIBUNE REPORTER. What did you make your debut in?

AURELIA. *La Traviata;* has it been sung here yet?
Sitting on one of her trunks.

THE TIMES REPORTER. Oh yes, often, but we understood there was a probability of changing.

AURELIA, *in surprise.* Changing? Why?

THE TIMES REPORTER. Well—er—there have been several letters written to the Evening Post asking that you make your debut in a less risqué opera.

AURELIA. But it's my *great* success!

THE TIMES REPORTER. The Ladies' Anti-French Literature League is leading the movement. There's a great feeling against the *play.* Lots of people won't go to see it.

AURELIA. But how absurd—no one ever understands what an Italian opera is about! Oh dear, I hope I shall be a success! I'm awfully nervous. Oh, *please* like me!
The REPORTERS *stop scribbling a moment to throw up their hats and shout.*

ALL THE REPORTERS. We do!
Two SAILORS *bring more luggage and go back.*

AURELIA. I'm afraid you'll think me a very foolish young person, I do so want you to like me. You know I'm really an American!
All the REPORTERS *look up surprised.*

THE HERALD REPORTER. Really?

AURELIA. Yes, my father came from *Trenton,* New Jersey.
All the REPORTERS *drop their heads quickly to their tablets and go on taking notes at a furious rate.*
That's how I get my name—Trentoni—don't you see? I'm a *New Jersey* Italian! My real name is Johnson, but of course that wouldn't look at all well on the bills—"Miss Aurelia Johnson in *Semiramide!*" I haven't been in Amer-

ica since I was three years old, but really it does all look familiar! At least I wish it did!

THE TRIBUNE REPORTER, *as they all write.* You were taught singing in Italy?

AURELIA. Yes, my mother sang in the chorus with Titians, and the night I was born she represented a princess at a ball in the second act—so you see I am really of noble birth! I was left an orphan at three, and then my best friend, Signor Belliarti, took care of me like a father and mother both. You know Papa Belliarti?

THE HERALD REPORTER. Yes, we've heard the story. Your ballet master, I believe?

AURELIA. Yes, bless him! He's worn the same pattern of clothes for fifty years! Would as soon think of changing his affections as altering the cut of his coat. It was through his friendship with Arditi I had my chance with Mapleson in London, where I've sung principally the last two years.

THE TIMES REPORTER. Do you know the Royal Family?

AURELIA. Er—not intimately—that is to say—*personally*—but I know them very well—*by sight!* You see, they don't go to the opera since the death of the Prince Consort.

MRS. GREENBOROUGH *comes back down the gangplank.*
My dear young gentlemen! She's turned the heads——
Stops with a smile, interrupted.

AURELIA, *rising.* Please get out my pink dolman, this one is so warm.

MRS. GREENBOROUGH. But tell them how the elite——
Stops with a smile, interrupted, and goes to a large bundle of shawls, which she undoes and takes out the pink dolman.

AURELIA. Oh yes, the uppertendom have been entrancingly kind to me. But I'll tell you a secret: I want the big *crowd* to love me! I want to outdo Lydia Thompson! I want to win the hearts of the gallery boys!

PETER *throws his cap up in the air and shouts.* Hooray!

AURELIA, *seeing him.* What a nice boy! Mrs. Gee, give him a sixpence! Oh dear, how much is a sixpence?

THE TRIBUNE REPORTER. Twelve cents.

AURELIA. Then give him a twelve-cent piece; it's one of those little silver things, you know.

MRS. GREENBOROUGH *does so.*

SAILORS *bring down more luggage and again go back. A* TELEGRAPH BOY *enters with a telegram.*

TELEGRAPH BOY. Madame Trentoni?

ALL THE REPORTERS, *going to the boy.* Yes!

They go back in a body to AURELIA. *The* TIMES REPORTER *gives her the telegram.*

AURELIA, *opening it.* A wire! How entrancing!

TELEGRAPH BOY. Somebody sign?

The TRIBUNE REPORTER *grandiloquently signs and the* TELEGRAPH BOY *leaves.*

AURELIA. It's from Mapleson; he'll arrive at four! Didn't expect the ship in till tomorrow! Wasn't it superb, our trip! We broke the record for the Atlantic. A good omen for me. Only think, we crossed in *thirteen* days! It takes your breath away!

THE TRIBUNE REPORTER. We'll cross in less than ten days yet!

AURELIA. Oh dear, I shouldn't like to go so fast as that; it would make me dizzy!

MRS. GREENBOROUGH. Here is your dolman, my dear. I don't know if——

Interrupted.

The TIMES REPORTER *and* TRIBUNE REPORTER *both take hold of the dolman.*

AURELIA, *laughing.* No, wait! Let me see, there must be no partiality.

She offers her right arm to the HERALD REPORTER, *who pulls off that sleeve.*

Thank you!

She turns to the SUN REPORTER *and offers her left arm.*
He pulls off the left sleeve.

Thank you.

Taking the jacket from the SUN REPORTER *she gives it to*
the CLIPPER REPRESENTATIVE.

Will you give that to Mrs. Greenborough, please.

He does so, and MRS. GREENBOROUGH *puts it away among*
the straps. AURELIA, *turning to the* TRIBUNE REPORTER
and TIMES REPORTER, *who hold the dolman between them.*

Now together, gentlemen, please.

She turns her back upon them, and they place the dolman
on her shoulders; turning quickly again, she curtsies low
to all of the REPORTERS, *laughingly.*

Thank you all very much!

All the REPORTERS *take off their hats and bow.*

SAILORS *bring out more luggage.*

THE HERALD REPORTER. Are you interested at all in politics?

AURELIA. Oh yes, I *adore* politics! Don't all women?

THE HERALD REPORTER. We're having a pretty severe cam-
paign here between Grant and Greeley. I don't suppose
you remember the war?

AURELIA. Oh yes, I do, perfectly. Why, I was thirteen years
old.

THE TIMES REPORTER. Impossible! Mr. Mapleson says that you
are now only eighteen.

AURELIA. Does he!

She laughs.

Oh well, that's only *operatically* I'm eighteen, but *politi-*
cally I'm twenty-two! Of course I never approved of but
one kind of *slaves—men* slaves!

THE HERALD REPORTER. You have—

Looking about him.

—*five* here!

More bows.

AURELIA. Bravo! Now, you know an Englishman wouldn't
have thought of that till tonight, and then he'd have
mailed it to me on a postcard.

THE HERALD REPORTER. Who do you favor for president?

AURELIA, *smiling.* Oh, I don't know. Who do you?

THE HERALD REPORTER. Ah! But that's what we want to get
out of you.

AURELIA, *taking him one side and linking her arm confiden-
tially in his.* Now look here, let's keep this between ourselves. Who does your journal?

THE HERALD REPORTER, *rather flattered.* General Grant!

AURELIA. Of course!
She shakes hands with the REPORTER.
A great general, and I *adore* soldiers.

THE TRIBUNE REPORTER. No stealing a march!

THE HERALD REPORTER. Oh, that's all right!
He joins the others.

AURELIA, *taking the* TRIBUNE REPORTER *to one side.* What's
your paper?

THE TRIBUNE REPORTER. The Tribune, founded by the Demo-
cratic candidate for president, Horace Greeley.

AURELIA, *aside to the* TRIBUNE REPORTER. He founded a newspaper, did he? Then he's my man, for what would we
artists do without the press! I adore the press!
They rejoin the others.
SAILORS *bring on more luggage.*

A SAILOR. Will you have the livestock out, too, ma'am?

AURELIA. Oh, the darlings! Yes indeed.
The SAILORS *go back on to the ship.*
My other dogs.
To MRS. GREENBOROUGH.
But that's not all my luggage?

MRS. GREENBOROUGH. Papa Belliarti and your maid took your stage clothes with them to the hotel early this morning.

AURELIA *cries out.* Papa Belliarti was *here,* and I didn't see him!

MRS. GREENBOROUGH. You were asleep, and he wouldn't have you wakened.

AURELIA, *excitedly.* Dear old darling! When I haven't slept a wink all night. I was so excited knowing I'd see him this morning. Let's make haste. I'm afraid, gentlemen, I must ask you now to excuse me. Oh, but just wait a minute. Mrs. Gee, give me my camel's-hair shawl from the Queen—*from the Queen!*

Repeating with emphasis lest the REPORTERS *should not catch it, and watching them from the corner of her eye to see the effect, she throws off her dolman and takes from* MRS. GREENBOROUGH *the shawl.*

It is easier to wear during the examination. I—er—I presume you are all taking notes of my dress.

THE HERALD REPORTER, *smiling.* Well, we're doing our best.

AURELIA. Listen; I'll get Mrs. Gee to help you. Mrs. Gee, give me another hat, too; I'm tired of this one. Give me the *Empress Eugénie.*

To the REPORTERS.

The last bonnet she designed before her flight from the Tuileries! And it still holds its own.

MRS. GREENBOROUGH *brings it and* AURELIA *puts it on.*

MRS. GREENBOROUGH. Did you——

Interrupted.

AURELIA. Yes, dear heart; now go with these charming gentlemen and describe all the things I've worn, *outside* things,

Aside to her.

and just hint at silk linings and Valenciennes lace. I've been told they put everything in their awful papers over here!

MRS. GREENBOROUGH. I'm sure I'll be——
> *Interrupted.*

AURELIA, *pushing her toward the* REPORTERS. Of course, who wouldn't be *delighted,* in such alluring company! Good morning, gentlemen!

ALL THE REPORTERS, *bowing.* Good morning.
> *They go off to the street with* MRS. GREENBOROUGH, *she talking all the time, describing* AURELIA'S *dress, etc. The* HERALD REPORTER *hangs back.*

AURELIA, *to the* HERALD REPORTER, *smiling but kindly.* Don't mind interrupting the dear soul; she expects it, and besides it rests her. We never let her finish a sentence for fear she would die of loss of breath at the end.

THE HERALD REPORTER. Thank you very much. And allow me to promise you a brilliant success.
> *He starts to go.*

AURELIA, *hesitatingly.* Are *all* Reporters handsome?

THE HERALD REPORTER, *red but happy.* They would like to be in *your* eyes, Madame Trentoni.
> *He exits in a seventh heaven.*

AURELIA, *flicking her hand after him, calls.* Superb!
> *She turns to the* NEWSBOY.

Boy! Come here a minute! Now, between ourselves, tell me something! Which is the best paper here—which do you sell the most?

PETER. Lady, they all was second-class what was here; the only *real* paper in New York is The Fireside Companion.
> CAPTAIN JINKS, CHARLIE, *and* GUSSIE *are heard whistling "Captain Jinks" in the distance.*

Ma'am—there's some dandies here now to welcome you; hear 'em! There's been a political parade today and they're all togged out in their uniforms! And I tell yer, they're high steppers! A one-ers—blue-blooders, regular lardy-dahs!

*The whistling changes to singing, and the three enter
from the street singing "Captain Jinks." They stop short
in the middle of a word as they see* AURELIA, *who, pretending not to notice them, looks at a label on a trunk.
The* NEWSBOY *whistles "Up in a Balloon, Boys," and goes
behind a trunk.*

CAPTAIN JINKS. She's off!

GUSSIE. She's a bouquet!

CHARLIE. She's a whole floral emblem! I will certainly do a
little flirting here myself! Everything square now, fellows,
and the best man wins! Go along, Captain Jinks, introduce
your pals.

They step toward AURELIA, CAPTAIN JINKS *slightly ahead.
The* NEWSBOY *stops whistling.*

CAPTAIN JINKS. I beg your pardon, Madame Trentoni?

AURELIA, *turns.* Yes?

CAPTAIN JINKS. Pray allow us to welcome you to New York.
Your coming turns October into June, and we will not miss
the birds this winter, since you will be singing in the
Academy trees.

Offering his bouquet.

AURELIA, *takes his bouquet.* Thank you very much, but remember there are birds—and—*birds!*

CAPTAIN JINKS. May I present Mr. Charles La Martine?

CHARLIE, *bows and gives his bouquet.* Twice welcome,
madam!

CAPTAIN JINKS. And may I present Mr. Augustus Van Vorkenburg? Familiarly known as "Gussie," also "Mother's
Darling."

GUSSIE, *to* CAPTAIN JINKS. Shut up!

Bows and gives his bouquet.

Thrice welcome!

AURELIA. Thank you.

To CAPTAIN JINKS.

And now won't one of your friends present *you?*

CHARLIE. This is Captain Jinks of the Horse Marines!

AURELIA, *laughing.* Oh, yes; I've heard of him.

CAPTAIN JINKS, *embarrassed.* No, no—I am Robert Jinks, tremendously at your service.

AURELIA. It doesn't really make any difference because I never remember names, but you are all very kind. I fancy you are some more reporters.

GUSSIE, *offended.* Oh, I say, no!

AURELIA, *insinuatingly.* I thought you might be, they seem to be such *handsome* men!

CHARLIE. No.

CAPTAIN JINKS. No——

AURELIA. Oh, then you must be the *editors!*

CAPTAIN JINKS, *laughing.* No, no, madam, we won't deceive you. We are only three good-for-nothings who have engaged seats in the front row for your entire season.

AURELIA. If you want me to believe that, do put on your hats, for you don't look the parts at all!

CHARLIE. We want to know if there is anything in the world we could do for you?

GUSSIE. We would like to plan something for your amusement; would you tell us your hotel?

AURELIA, *after a second's pause.* The Fifth Avenue.

GUSSIE, *who is really an ass, ties a knot in his handkerchief so as to remember it.*

CAPTAIN JINKS. There is to be a croquet match day after tomorrow at the fashionable club; perhaps you would care to go; if so, we would be glad to arrange.

MRS. GREENBOROUGH *comes back from her walk, having evidently been shaken by the* REPORTERS *at an early stage of the game.*

AURELIA. You're very kind. I never could understand the game, but my chaperon adores it and would love to come, I'm sure.

CAPTAIN JINKS, *who has not seen* MRS. GREENBOROUGH. We should be charmed.

GUSSIE. It'll be very dressy!

AURELIA. Dear Mrs. Gee, I want to present to you three New York *gentlemen* who have most kindly come to welcome us—Mrs. Greenborough.

The three men bow, saying, "Madam," but with a note of poignant disappointment in their voices.

AURELIA. And they *want* you, dear, to go to a croquet match with them.

MRS. GREENBOROUGH, *overjoyed.* My word, and that will be a treat! Thank you very much, gentlemen! My love, here come your pets, what shall——

Interrupted, as the SAILORS *enter with two large dogs—a Newfoundland and a white spitz—and a very large cage containing a small live monkey. The* SECOND SAILOR *returns to the boat, after putting the monkey down beside the gangplank.*

AURELIA. Oh yes, the darlings.

Going to meet the SAILOR *with the dogs. She stops to speak to* MRS. GREENBOROUGH.

Did you tell the reporters about that beastly monkey?

MRS. GREENBOROUGH. Oh no, I forgot.

AURELIA. My dear, how careless of you! So long as Mapleson insists on my having the horrid thing, you should have said the Khedive of Egypt gave him to me; that would have sounded superbly.

She goes to the SAILOR *and takes the leader of the two dogs from him; the* SAILOR *goes back on to the boat.*

You blessed old dogs, you! The poor things must be mad for a little exercise. Oh! Mr.——?

In front of CHARLIE.

CHARLIE, *flattered at being especially addressed.* La Martine. *Bowing.*

AURELIA. You said you wanted to do something for me; will
you take Leonora for a walk?

CHARLIE. I beg your pardon?

AURELIA, *giving him the leader of the Newfoundland dog.*
This is Leonora, out of *Trovatore,* you know. Just a bit
of a stroll and back, say ten minutes?
Looking him straight in the eyes and smiling sweetly.

CHARLIE. With pleasure, if I mustn't go alone?

AURELIA. Certainly not.
She crosses to GUSSIE.
Mr. Dundreary——

GUSSIE, *bowing.* Augustus Bleeker Van Vorkenburg.

AURELIA. What a *grand* name! You'll go along and take Rosina
—*Barber of Seville—won't* you—*Gussie?*

GUSSIE. Ah! But Charlie and I are no company for each other.

AURELIA, *gaily.* I see! You want ladies' society. Mrs. Gee! Mrs.
Gee!
Taking her arm.
You want a little walk, too. Yes, you do! You'll never get
that extra ten pounds off if you lose a single morning.
Take Camille along!
Giving her the black-and-tan.
Now be off. Good-by, *darlings; that's* for the *dogs!*

CHARLIE, *turning.* Which pair?

AURELIA, *laughing.* Clever, very clever!
CHARLIE, GUSSIE, *and the three dogs and* MRS. GREENBOR-
OUGH *exit,* MRS. GREENBOROUGH *talking about how glad
she is for a glimpse of land.*

CAPTAIN JINKS. Have you saved the monkey for me?

AURELIA. Oh! I wish you would! *Will you? Take* him and lose
him. I'm afraid of him, you know.

CAPTAIN JINKS. Then why do you keep him?

AURELIA. It's Mapleson's idea. He thinks it makes me interesting. Though why a monkey should do that I don't know, and I'd sleep happier tonight if that wretched animal was out of the way.

CAPTAIN JINKS. Would you mind walking a few steps over in that direction and keeping your back turned?

AURELIA. What are you going to do?

She goes a few steps to the left and stands with her back turned.

CAPTAIN JINKS *goes to the* NEWSBOY, *who is enjoying himself with the monkey in the cage. At the same time the* SAILOR *comes out and down the gangplank and calls to* AURELIA.

THE SAILOR. Miss! Ma'am!

AURELIA, *with her back turned.* Do you mean me?

CAPTAIN JINKS. Don't turn, please, till I tell you.

The POLICEMAN *comes slowly along.*

THE SAILOR, *on the gangplank.* Don't you want me to get the inspector for yer, yer things is all out?

AURELIA. Oh yes, please do. I do want to get away.

THE POLICEMAN. All right, Jack, I'm passin'; I'll send him along.

THE SAILOR. Thanky'.

Exits on boat. POLICEMAN *walks on.*

PETER, *who has been told by* CAPTAIN JINKS *he may have the monkey for his own if he will take it away, jumps up with a wild howl of delight.* Hiyi! To keep!

CAPTAIN JINKS. Shh! Yes.

Whispering.

Hurry now, and quiet.

Motioning him off with the cage—the NEWSBOY *seizes it.*

AURELIA. May I turn now?

CAPTAIN JINKS. In two minutes.

The NEWSBOY, *rushing past the* POLICEMAN *with the cage, is at this moment nabbed by him.*

THE POLICEMAN. Here! Where are you going with that animal?

CAPTAIN JINKS. That's all right—it's my affair—have a drink? *Gives him a quarter. The* NEWSBOY *passes out with monkey.*

THE POLICEMAN. Thank ye, sir, you're a gentleman, sir. *Goes.*

CAPTAIN JINKS, *to* AURELIA. Now! The monkey's gone, and you saw nothing, know nothing, so you see you can't be blamed. Mapleson can complain in the papers and have the docks better policed.

AURELIA. Really, you've made yourself my friend for life!

CAPTAIN JINKS. I hope to be permitted to take the monkey's place, so far as being often in your company is concerned.

AURELIA. Don't you think you young men were rather impertinent, however?

CAPTAIN JINKS. Yes, now I've met you I think we were. Still, I hope you'll forgive us.

AURELIA. Oh, I will, *you.*

CAPTAIN JINKS. And I hope I'll deserve that. Please, isn't there anything I could do for you? I don't suppose you know many people here.

AURELIA. Not a soul.

CAPTAIN JINKS. And you must go about—there's lots to see. Please let me take you. I'm more or less of an idiot, I know, but so are most men——
Interrupted.

AURELIA. Yes, it's not much of a distinction.

CAPTAIN JINKS. I was going to add so far as *women* are concerned!

AURELIA. Oh! I beg your pardon.

CAPTAIN JINKS. Really, joking aside, I ask you—mayn't I call upon you at your hotel?

AURELIA. I'll think it over.

CAPTAIN JINKS. Today?

AURELIA. No, I shall spend today with my dear foster father. You know Professor Belliarti? He came over a month ago to drill the ballet. The first time we've been separated since I was three years old!

She has forgotten herself and is speaking with real feeling.

He's the sweetest, dearest, most unselfish old creature who has given me everything I have in the world——

She stops short, suddenly realizing what she is saying.

Oh, I beg your pardon for going on so!

CAPTAIN JINKS, *sympathetically.* You needn't beg my pardon, for I can match your old gentleman with a dear little old lady living on a plantation far away down in Virginia who's done her very *darndest* for me.

They look at each other a moment without speaking, with a mutual understanding of each other's nature.

AURELIA. You *may* come and see me—tomorrow.

She gives him her hand.

CAPTAIN JINKS, *taking her hand.* Thank you.

MRS. STONINGTON *and* MISS MERRIAM *come timidly from the street. They are of middle age, and dressed a trifle out of date.* MISS MERRIAM, *who is of a decidedly shrinking nature, is attired in a vivid shade of bottle green heavily laid upon black. A quantity of green fringe, however, hints at her heart being still young and her spirits capable of gaiety, a fact also abetted by a spotted net over her "waterfall."* MRS. STONINGTON, *more dominant and evidently the spokeswoman, favors a strict magenta in her apparel. Both are simple, good-hearted, kindly intentioned but misguided ladies, the vice-president and secretary of the Anti-French Literature League; they act quite without malice.* MISS MERRIAM *is deaf and dumb.*

MRS. STONINGTON. I beg pardon; can you tell me where to find Madame Trentoni?

AURELIA. *I* am Madame Trentoni.

MRS. STONINGTON. Oh, really!

She turns and with her fingers tells MISS MERRIAM *that this is* MADAME TRENTONI. *She then introduces her companion.*

This is Miss Merriam, the corresponding secretary.

MISS MERRIAM *bows smilingly.*

AURELIA. How do you do?

MRS. STONINGTON. And *I* am Mrs. Stonington, the vice-president of the Anti-French Literature League.

AURELIA. How do you do.

Aside to CAPTAIN JINKS.

I thought they had come to apply for places in the ballet!

While AURELIA *is speaking to* CAPTAIN JINKS, MISS MERRIAM *has talked on her fingers to* MRS. STONINGTON. AURELIA *turns before she finishes and shows her surprise at* MISS MERRIAM'S *behavior.*

MRS. STONINGTON. My friend says to tell you at once that she is deaf and dumb, but she will be able to understand perfectly what you say from the motion of your lips.

AURELIA, *rather satirically.* How interesting!

MRS. STONINGTON. I presume you have not had much experience in singing to deaf and dumb people—what I mean to say is that you don't understand the language.

AURELIA. Not at all. Will you sit down?

Motioning to some trunks. MRS. STONINGTON *and* MISS MERRIAM *sit.*

MRS. STONINGTON. Thank you.

She looks up at CAPTAIN JINKS.

Signor Trentoni, I presume?

CAPTAIN JINKS *bows in elaborate acquiescence.*

AURELIA, *laughing in spite of herself.* No, no! How dare you! This is—a *friend* of mine who has kindly come to welcome me.

CAPTAIN JINKS. Mr. Jinks.

Bowing. The two ladies bow back.

MRS. STONINGTON, *to* CAPTAIN JINKS. *Do* sit.

He does so on another trunk. He and AURELIA *are much amused.* MISS MERRIAM *nods her head and smiles acquiescence during all of* MRS. STONINGTON's *speeches.*

We read in the papers this morning you had arrived sooner than expected, and we decided to come right down and take the bull by the horns.

AURELIA. Meaning *me,* I presume?

Trying hard not to laugh.

MRS. STONINGTON. Er—yes——

She is interrupted by MISS MERRIAM, *who tugs at her arm and makes a few rapid movements with her fingers.*

MRS. STONINGTON. Yes dear, and just like you!

To AURELIA.

She's so sensitive! She thinks it would be politer to say take the cow by the horns.

AURELIA. What can I do for you?

MRS. STONINGTON. It is stated in the papers that you intend to make your debutt in a piece called *Traviatter,* which, I am given to understand by a number of the members of our League who have read the book, is the French drammer, *La Dame aux Camélias.*

AURELIA. The papers and the League members are quite right.

MRS. STONINGTON. I am told the heroine is a—young person— no better than she should be, in fact not so good.

MISS MERRIAM *tugs violently at* MRS. STONINGTON's *arm and makes a few rapid passes with her fingers.*

MRS. STONINGTON. Of course! I never thought.

To AURELIA.

Excuse me, but would your gentleman friend be so kind as to walk to the other end of the dock for a few minutes?

AURELIA. Certainly. My friend is a very gallant man, Mrs. Vice-President; I am sure he would jump off the dock, if a lady asked him.

CAPTAIN JINKS. Not by a long shot!

MRS. STONINGTON, *seriously.* But I shouldn't think of asking such a thing; he might get drowned.

CAPTAIN JINKS, *rising.* Shall I go?

AURELIA. Yes, please, just for a second or two.

CAPTAIN JINKS *withdraws outside by the boat.*

MRS. STONINGTON. Our mission is a very delicate one.

AURELIA. I think I should call it indelicate—

MRS. STONINGTON. Oh no! We want to ask you to make your debutt in some other opera. And we have here a petition to that effect, signed by over six hundred women and school children of Harlem, Brooklyn, and Jersey City—oh yes, and Williamsburg.

Handing to AURELIA *the paper.*

AURELIA. Thank you so much! What a splendid advertisement!

MRS. STONINGTON. We heard your voice was *most* beautiful, and a *great* many of us want to hear you who couldn't go to *that* opera.

AURELIA. But do you know, when you come right down to the stories of the opera, I don't think there's much choice between them.

MRS. STONINGTON. Oh dear me, yes!

MISS MERRIAM *nods her head quietly but firmly and with a sweet smile.*

AURELIA. Well, what one would you propose?

MRS. STONINGTON, *triumphantly. Faust!*

> MISS MERRIAM *looks transported as she recalls the angels of the final scene.*

AURELIA. Oh, but that isn't a goody-goody story by any means!

MRS. STONINGTON. My dear! It's a *sweet* opera! I remember the beautiful tableau, like the death of little Eva, at the end.

AURELIA. I suppose you didn't notice that Mephistopheles seems to have got Marguerite after all; for the angels always take up quite a different young lady—and seem perfectly unconscious of their mistake.

MRS. STONINGTON. Never mind, the story is so pure.

AURELIA. But do you know what happens between the second and third acts?

MRS. STONINGTON. On the stage?

AURELIA. Oh dear, no! In the story.

MRS. STONINGTON. Faust and Marguerite get married.

AURELIA. No, they don't; that's the trouble.

MRS. STONINGTON, *staggered. What!!!*

AURELIA. They *didn't!*

MRS. STONINGTON. Bless my soul!

> *She rises, aghast.* MISS MERRIAM *pulls* MRS. STONINGTON'S *arm and makes a few rapid signs.*

MRS. STONINGTON, *to* MISS MERRIAM. *I should say so!*
> *Kisses her gratefully.*
> *To* AURELIA.

She says she's glad we asked that young man to go away.

> MISS MERRIAM *again pulls* MRS. STONINGTON'S *elbow and motions.*

MRS. STONINGTON. You dear thing, how like you!
> *To* AURELIA.

She wants to know why you don't make your debutt in oratorier. Come along now, do!

MISS MERRIAM *tugs again at* MRS. STONINGTON'S *arm and makes a few more finger movements.*

Yes!

To AURELIA.

The women of America ask you to sing in oratorier!

CAPTAIN JINKS *is heard whistling "Champagne Charlie is My Name."*

AURELIA, *who can hardly restrain her laughter.* I'll tell you what I'll do; I'm willing if you can persuade my manager; you see, really, these things are entirely in the hands of Mr. Mapleson.

MRS. STONINGTON. We'll see him at once.

MISS MERRIAM *tugs* MRS. STONINGTON'S *elbow and motions.*

MRS. STONINGTON. Quite so!

To AURELIA.

She says men are so *easy* we shall consider it settled!

CAPTAIN JINKS *stops whistling to call.* I'm whistling so as not to hear. Must I take another trip?

AURELIA. No, come in!

CAPTAIN JINKS *returns.*

AURELIA, *to* MRS. STONINGTON. Mr. Mapleson arrives this afternoon from Boston and will stop at the New York Hotel.

MRS. STONINGTON. Thank you. If you should need some extra ladies in the chorus for the oratorier, I would come—I know most of them, having belonged to the Oratorier Society for many years. We wear white dresses with blue sashes across the left shoulder, which makes a very pretty effect.

MISS MERRIAM *tugs* MRS. STONINGTON'S *arm and makes a few motions.* MRS. STONINGTON *nods her head and turns to* AURELIA.

And Miss Merriam always goes with me; she fills up and makes the chorus look bigger.

AURELIA. All of that, of course, will be left with Mr. Mapleson.

CAPTAIN JINKS, *with difficulty restraining his laughter.* Do they have men singers in an oratorio?

MRS. STONINGTON. Oh dear me, yes, we have some very handsome gentlemen singers in the club!

CAPTAIN JINKS. I wish you'd just mention me to Mr. Mapleson as a candidate.

MRS. STONINGTON, *smiling apologetically.* I'm afraid I couldn't do that. Don't you think it would look rather bold my suggesting a young man and a perfect stranger?

MISS MERRIAM *tugs* MRS. STONINGTON'S *elbow and makes a few motions.*

Yes.

To AURELIA.

We won't keep you any longer; we're very much obliged to you I'm sure, and the League will signify their gratefulness by giving you an afternoon reception in the rooms of the Young Men's Christian Association. Good-by.

Bows.

MISS MERRIAM *also smiles and bows.*

AURELIA, *also bowing.* Good-by.

MRS. STONINGTON *takes* MISS MERRIAM'S *arm and they turn their backs to* AURELIA *a second to consult.* MRS. STONINGTON *motions a moment.* MISS MERRIAM *nods her head delightedly. They both turn and go to* AURELIA *with outstretched hands, very pleased with themselves for the gracious thing they think they are doing.*

MRS. STONINGTON. Good-by.

She and AURELIA *shake hands.* AURELIA *says good-by; then* MISS MERRIAM *and* AURELIA *shake hands and* AURELIA *again says good-by.*

MRS. STONINGTON, *to explain and excuse their cordiality.* She says we don't consider *singers* actresses.

AURELIA. Very few are!

MRS. STONINGTON *and* MISS MERRIAM *leave the dock in a manner of pleased satisfaction.*

AURELIA, *laughingly to* CAPTAIN JINKS. What do you think Mapleson will do with them?

CAPTAIN JINKS, *laughing.* "Men are so easy!"

AURELIA. Ah, but she, poor thing, was deaf and dumb, the only kind of woman who ever would have said that.

CAPTAIN JINKS. I should hate a silent woman in a house. It would be like a bird who couldn't sing, a rose that had no scent, a baby that couldn't cry, a piano never played upon.

AURELIA. Oh, I don't suppose there ever was a piano that didn't at least once do its worst with Rubenstein's "Melody in F!" Is this the inspector!

As the PRIVATE DETECTIVE *enters with the* POLICEMAN. *The* DETECTIVE *has a folded paper in his hand.*

CAPTAIN JINKS. I reckon he is.

The DETECTIVE *and* POLICEMAN *pass among the trunks, counting them.*

AURELIA. I'm so nervous about the customs; I wish the whole thing were over. We hear such awful tales at home about them. I haven't a thing dutiable, of course, not a thing! I've only forty-eight boxes anyway, and they contain only my few personal effects!

CAPTAIN JINKS. I'll see what I can do with him to make him lenient as possible.

THE DETECTIVE, *aside to the* POLICEMAN. Keep in hearing distance of my whistle—if they're going to try any bribing tricks it'll be soon now.

The POLICEMAN *passes on and the* DETECTIVE *approaches* AURELIA.

Madam Trentoni?

AURELIA. Yes, sir. I hope you're not going to disturb everything; the boxes were so *beautifully* packed!

THE DETECTIVE. I must do my duty, madam.

CAPTAIN JINKS. We expect you to do that, officer, only don't exaggerate it!

THE DETECTIVE. Your husband, madam?

CAPTAIN JINKS. That's not your business!

AURELIA, *to* CAPTAIN JINKS. Oh, don't make him angry!

To the DETECTIVE, *very sweetly but with some nervousness.*

It's a friend who came down to meet me. I had a splendid crossing! Do you like ocean traveling?

THE DETECTIVE. Never tried it. Would you prefer a woman examiner, ma'am?

AURELIA. Oh no, I think I'd rather have a man. Unless, of course, you're going to be personal! If you're going to look for violins in the flounces of my petticoats and diamonds in my bustle, I'd rather have a *lady*—a *perfect* lady!

THE DETECTIVE, *looking at her.* I don't consider there'll be any need for that.

AURELIA. There! I knew the minute I saw you, you were going to be sweet and nice and obliging, and I'm going to be equally so and help you all I can.

CHARLIE *and* GUSSIE *return from their walk with the two dogs, followed by* MRS. GREENBOROUGH, *who is talking, although a little breathless from having been evidently hurried in her walk. She is interrupted by* AURELIA.

MRS. GREENBOROUGH. My word, though, gentlemen, you do walk fast; it's more——

AURELIA. Come along, Mrs. Gee; we want the keys.

MRS. GREENBOROUGH, *joining her by the trunks.* Has the——
Interrupted.

AURELIA. Yes, this is the inspector.

MRS. GREENBOROUGH, *excitedly.* How do you do, sir! We haven't a thing, not a single solitary——
Interrupted.

AURELIA. I've told him, Mrs. Gee.

To the DETECTIVE.

By-the-bye, you will find a box of new-looking curls and a

couple of "waterfalls," but they've been worn heaps of times—*by me,* I mean, as well as by the lady who grew 'em!

MRS. GREENBOROUGH, *to* CAPTAIN JINKS. Would you hold Camille?

AURELIA, *smiling to* CAPTAIN JINKS *as he takes the dog.* You see, you are to have your chance after all!

AURELIA *and the* DETECTIVE *begin unlocking and arranging the trunks. The* DETECTIVE *shows that he is very suspicious of* AURELIA *and of* CAPTAIN JINKS. CAPTAIN JINKS *joins* CHARLIE *and* GUSSIE *at one side, while* MRS. GREENBOROUGH *opens the trunks.*

CHARLIE. Well?

CAPTAIN JINKS. Well, what?

CHARLIE. How did you get on?

CAPTAIN JINKS. How do you mean?

CHARLIE. Why, with Trentoni! You've had a tremendous advantage over us!

CAPTAIN JINKS. Oh! Oh yes, our bet. That's off; she's too good for that sort of thing.

CHARLIE. No you don't! Look here, our bet holds good—a thousand dollars to me if I win and another thousand if *you don't.*

CAPTAIN JINKS. Nothing of the sort; both bets are off—they were only a joke, and a poor one!

CHARLIE. Here, no sneaking, a bet's a bet!

CAPTAIN JINKS. Not when it's an insult to a lady! And I won't permit any action in regard to Madame Trentoni unworthy of the highest woman in the land.

CHARLIE. Who appointed you her protector? You've bet me one thousand dollars you'd make love to her.

CAPTAIN JINKS. Wait!

Gives the dog Camille to GUSSIE.

I haven't quite a thousand with me, but—

Takes card and writes.

I O U $1000 for bet in reference to Madame Trentoni. There you are; you understand? There's no bet about anybody's making love to the lady! *The bet is off!*

AURELIA. Captain Jinks! Will you please help us a moment?

GUSSIE. Here!

Offering back the dog.

CAPTAIN JINKS. No, *you* keep *Camille!*

He joins AURELIA.

GUSSIE, *to* CHARLIE. Are you going to let him off?

CHARLIE. No indeed! He's got to stand by his bet with me, and I intend to win. You must help me, Gussie!

GUSSIE. How, old fellow?

CHARLIE. I've been pumping the old lady on our walk, and she's even a bigger prize than I thought. She's rich as Crœsus and gets a salary for singing that would knock *you* off your feet, Gussie.

GUSSIE. Really! Dear me!

CHARLIE. Yes—Jinks doesn't know, and don't tell him. I'm not only going to win my bet with him, I'm going to *marry her!*

GUSSIE. By Jove! You *are* going it, aren't you?

CHARLIE. You help me, and when I've married the lady, I'll pay you all I owe you.

GUSSIE. Thanks, old fellow. But suppose Captain Jinks——

CHARLIE. He'd never *marry* her; he belongs to two of the most stuck-up families, north or south, in the country! But if he tries to interfere with me in any way, we'll cook his goose for him all the same.

GUSSIE. How? He's such an attractive dog! Don't you think so?

CHARLIE. If he gets on the inside track I'll show him up to her —say he made a bet with us to marry her on account of her money and show his I O U for proof.

GUSSIE. But he *didn't* bet that.

CHARLIE. What's the odds! You're no Georgie Washington! And you must back me up or lose every cent I owe you.

GUSSIE. I suppose I mustn't let myself make a deep impression on her for fear of interfering with *you*.

CHARLIE, *amused*. Oh, you can try your luck! Come along now.

They join the others.

Can we be of any assistance?

AURELIA. Oh, you are—a very great deal with the dogs! I'm really awfully obliged to you. Come along, I'll walk with you to the end of the dock—it's stopped raining, hasn't it?

She turns to go with the two men. The DETECTIVE *has just begun to pitch out the contents of a trunk rather roughly on to the floor.* MRS. GREENBOROUGH *screams, which stops* AURELIA.

MRS. GREENBOROUGH. Oh! Aurelia! Look what he's doing!

CAPTAIN JINKS. Say, old man, is that necessary? Go on, hurry up, get through and come out and have a drink with me.

THE DETECTIVE, *looking at* CAPTAIN JINKS *very suspiciously.* No, thank you.

AURELIA. If you ruin my clothes I shall sue the city—I warn you of that! Do you take me for an Irish dressmaker with a French name smuggling in her winter models! My dear man, go on! Play hide-and-seek in every box if you like! Climb down all the corners, use my hats for tenpins, empty out the shoes, scatter my lingerie to the winds! *Jump* on every stitch I own! And then they call this a *free* country!! Captain Jinks, I leave not my honor but something much more fragile; I leave my *wardrobe* in your hands! Now, gentlemen.

And turning, she goes out with CHARLIE *and* GUSSIE.

MRS. GREENBOROUGH. You old ogre, you!

THE DETECTIVE. I don't take no interest in woman's clothes— I'm just doing my duty.

He throws open a hatbox with three hats in it and then begins to empty another trunk. MRS. GREENBOROUGH *is busy trying to repack after him.*

MRS. GREENBOROUGH. My word! It's a cruel shame! One would think you expected passengers to swim across the Atlantic, like that Lady Godiva, without a stitch on their backs! Another thing, I'm sure it's a great pity, seeing that you're going to display Madame Trentoni's entire wardrobe, we didn't ask those nice young men who gave me a bouquet to stay and take notes for their papers.

The DETECTIVE *goes to a certain trunk.* MRS. GREEN-BOROUGH *sees him and rises, crying out.*

No! No! You mustn't open that; I really do object now!

THE DETECTIVE, *very suspicious.* Oh, you especially object now!

His hand is on the lid.

Kindly give me the key!

MRS. GREENBOROUGH *sits on the trunk.* I won't! I appeal to your delicacy as a—as a—*gentleman.* That contains her—her—linen garments and Valenciennes lace.

THE DETECTIVE, *still suspicious.* Sounds very pretty—I must trouble you for the key.

MRS. GREENBOROUGH *gives it to him.* Toad!

The DETECTIVE *unlocks and opens the trunk.* PROFESSOR BELLIARTI *and* MARY, AURELIA'S *maid, enter from the street.*

Oh, Professor Belliarti, I'm so pleased you've come back! This dreadful man is making such an exposé of all Aurelia's clothes.

The POLICEMAN *strolls in again.*

PROFESSOR BELLIARTI. That can't be helped, my dear Mrs. Greenborough. Where is Aurelia?

AURELIA, *speaking most joyfully from the outside.* I hear a voice! I hear a voice I *love!*

She rushes in and across the stage into BELLIARTI'S *arms, throwing her own about his neck.*

MARY *has gone to the trunks and is putting them in order.*
She is joined by the POLICEMAN, *who helps her lock one*
of the trunks, the keys being in all the locks. When this is
done they stand on one side and talk, both enjoying
themselves very much. MARY *is pretty and the* POLICEMAN
is appreciative. The DETECTIVE *is searching through the*
trunks.

PROFESSOR BELLIARTI, *with a voice broken with happy emo-*
tion and holding AURELIA *close in his arms.* God bless my
little girl, God bless my little Taglioni! Glad to see her
old crow of a father, eh? Bless your pretty eyes, my Fanny
Elssler, my little singing bird!

AURELIA. Oh, Papa Belliarti! Oh, Papa Belliarti! Oh! Oh! Oh!

Gives him three big hugs.

I *am* so glad to see you!

Half crying, half laughing with joy.

It was awful disembarking here without a soul to meet
me—a soul I loved; for it's home I've come to after all,
isn't it? You've always taught me this *was home!*

Then with a little change of manner.

I did my best, but I'm afraid I've made dreadful mistakes
already and said the wrong things! But I don't care now
I've got you!

Choking up again.

I tried to be gay, but to tell the truth I'm so homesick,
and all I want is to have a good cry *here* in your arms!

Breaking down.

CAPTAIN JINKS *stands watching the* DETECTIVE *closely.*

The DETECTIVE *notices this.* CAPTAIN JINKS *gets out his*
purse and deliberately chooses a few bills and doubles
them up, doing it so the DETECTIVE *will see. The* DE-
TECTIVE *does see. Only the* POLICEMAN *is blind because*
he has MARY *in his eyes.*

PROFESSOR BELLIARTI. That'll be all right now—we have
beautiful rooms for you, and they are full of flowers that
have been sent, and the rain is over.

AURELIA. And so is mine.

Wiping her eyes.

There! See, the sun's out!

Smiling up at him and holding his hand and linking their arms together.

It really is you! And you are well! Tell me you are well! Of course you are, and as fat as ever!

BELLIARTI *being slender as a reed.*

You dear old darling you! Come, let me introduce to you these gentlemen who have very courteously come to welcome me. Gentlemen, I want to present to you my best friend and foster father, Professor Belliarti—a *great artist* in dancing, I can tell you that too.

PROFESSOR BELLIARTI, *with a quaint old-fashioned bow.* Gentlemen!

CAPTAIN JINKS. Honored sir.

CHARLIE, *at same time, bowing.* Very pleased.

GUSSIE. Delighted.

AURELIA, *to* BELLIARTI. And now I want you to see my cabin, how nice it was. Come along into the boat!

She leads him toward the gangplank. She sees MARY *and the* POLICEMAN. AURELIA *exchanges an amused glance with* BELLIARTI.

AURELIA. Mary!

MARY *doesn't hear.*

Mary!!

MARY. Yes, madam?

She blushes.

The POLICEMAN *slides out the big door suddenly.*

AURELIA. I only want to remind you, Mary, you are not in London! And let me warn you—as a *friend*, Mary—that the policemen here are *not English!*

PROFESSOR BELLIARTI. No, they are *Irish*, Mary, so look out for blarney!

AURELIA. And incidentally, Mary, you had better go on with the packing.

PROFESSOR BELLIARTI, *to the* DETECTIVE. You don't need to keep Madame Trentoni if the maid stays?

THE DETECTIVE. No, sir.

AURELIA. Delightful. Then we can go at once! Come and see my cabin first.

PROFESSOR BELLIARTI. Will one of you gentlemen kindly call a hack?

CAPTAIN JINKS, CHARLIE, *and* GUSSIE. Oh! Please take my *landau! My landau's* at your disposal.

AURELIA, *laughing on the gangplank.* But I can't go in the landau of all three!

CAPTAIN JINKS. Oh yes, you can, it's the *same* landau!

AURELIA. Then I accept with pleasure.

PAPA BELLIARTI *disappears on the ship.*

CHARLIE. I'll tell the driver to back in.

Goes out to the street.

GUSSIE *helps* MRS. GREENBOROUGH *with a trunk strap.*

AURELIA, *on the gangplank.* Oh, Captain Jinks.

CAPTAIN JINKS, *going up to her.* Yes?

AURELIA. Not tomorrow!

CAPTAIN JINKS, *tremendously disappointed.* No?

AURELIA. No! This afternoon at four.

Gives him her hand, which he kisses. She also goes on board and out of sight.

CAPTAIN JINKS. This afternoon at four!

After dreaming a moment, he pulls himself together and beckons to the DETECTIVE.

One minute!

Motioning him to one side with him. The DETECTIVE *goes, expecting what is going to happen.*

Look here, now, it's all right—the lady's all right, and you and I are all right. We understand each other, don't we?

THE DETECTIVE. I rather think we do, sir!

CHARLIE *returns.*

CAPTAIN JINKS. Good! Rush her things through now and don't bother her any more!

Giving him the bills.

THE DETECTIVE. Thank you.

Taking them. He blows his whistle twice as agreed on. The POLICEMAN *quickly enters.*

Officer, I give this man in charge for bribing a United States official.

General consternation.

CAPTAIN JINKS, *dumfounded.* But——

THE POLICEMAN, *linking his arm in* CAPTAIN JINKS's. Come along! Don't make no trouble now! Come along quietly!

The POLICEMAN *exits with* CAPTAIN JINKS. GUSSIE *and* CHARLIE *are delighted. The maid is surprised. The* DETECTIVE *is satisfied.*

AURELIA, *coming back from the boat.* Wasn't it charming, really? And only think, only thirteen days crossing.

PAPA BELLIARTI *follows her.*

CHARLIE. The landau's ready!

A large landau backs on from the street.

AURELIA. Oh, a superb turnout! Come along, Mrs. Gee!

And she gets in with MRS. GREENBOROUGH *and* BELLIARTI, *the two men helping them, and all talking at once. The bouquets are put in too.*

Really, gentlemen, you've been superbly kind! Really, I shan't forget it—you know, you're very attractive!

GUSSIE. Which one of us is most so?

AURELIA, *leaning out and over the side of the carriage.*

Impossible to say, you're all so perfectly charming! But where is Captain Jinks?

CHARLIE. Oh, he was called away suddenly, *by most important business!*

AURELIA. Tell him not to forget this afternoon at four!

CHARLIE. This afternoon at four.

PROFESSOR BELLIARTI, *to the driver.* The Brevoort House.

The landau starts off.

AURELIA. Good-by, good-by!

ALL. Good-by! Good-by!

MRS. GREENBOROUGH *throws back a bouquet which* CHARLIE *catches, and as the landau passes out of sight, with laughter and good-bys, the curtain falls.*

ACT TWO

A fortnight later. MADAME TRENTONI's *private parlor in the Brevoort House; a large room with double folding doors at the back which lead into another and larger room. There are two windows on the left side and a door and mantel on the right. The walls are tinted a light, cold, ugly violet, with a deep crimson velvet paper border. The furniture is gilt and upholstered with crimson satin with heavy red rope worsted fringe. It is comfortable and warm, especially in the summer and is not plain but hideous. At the windows are lace curtains with heavy satin lambrequins. There is a piano, open, by the windows, in one of which is a very small basket, with a very large handle, full of roses. There is a marble-topped center table bearing a Bible, a guide to the city, and a silver-plated card receiver. An oval-framed steel engraving called "Autumn" (a young lady most inappropriately dressed for that season of the year, with curvature of the spine, and balancing a prize bunch of grapes on the top of her bare shoulder) hangs on one wall, and on another its companion picture called "Spring" (another young lady, only this one evidently a blonde, also sure of the weather and her health, dressed in a veil and a large bunch of buttercups). On the mantel are some dreadful vases with nice little bouquets in them, and several photographs and some cards. The stage is empty. The hall door at the back near the double doors opens, and a hotel* SERVANT *shows in* CHARLES LA MARTINE *and* AUGUSTUS VAN VORKENBURG. *The* SERVANT *carries a small silver tray.*

SERVANT. What names shall I say to Madame Trentoni, gentlemen?

CHARLIE. Simply say two gentlemen.

He whistles "Champagne Charlie," saunters to a window,

and pulling aside the lace curtains looks out as the SERV-
ANT *exits.*

GUSSIE. She's *in* of course! I know that.

CHARLIE. Yes, so do I, but I'll bet you she won't receive us;
she'll send word she's out!

GUSSIE, *sitting on the sofa and tracing the cabbage roses on
the carpet with his cane.* I don't see how she dares again.
You don't see Captain Jinks coming up the avenue, do
you?

CHARLIE. No.

GUSSIE. Oh, but he isn't likely to *miss* a day!

CHARLIE. You're sure it's been every day?

GUSSIE. Yes, or oftener!

CHARLIE *sits on the piano stool and spins himself around.*
And they're seen constantly everywhere together. Last
night it was at Niblo's Garden to see *The Black Crook!*
And they're nearly every day at Maillard's or Delmonico's.

GUSSIE. Well, that'll have to let up a bit after tonight, when
she's begun singing.

CHARLIE. You bet. There's not a seat to be had for love or
money! They say there's not been such excitement in New
York over a debut since Jenny Lind.

GUSSIE. Has she been "at home" one single time *you've* called?

CHARLIE. Not one. And you?

GUSSIE. No.

CHARLIE. That's all right! Well, it'll end now, if she sees us
today. Don't you fail to back me up in everything!

GUSSIE. I'll do my best. Only, just as I've learned one lie, you
change it; it's very confusing.

The SERVANT *re-enters.*

CHARLIE. *Sh! !*

THE SERVANT. Madame Trentoni cannot say whether she is in
or not unless you send up your cards.

They give the SERVANT *their cards, and he again exits.*

GUSSIE, *examining the photographs on the mantel.* Who bailed Jinks out of jail that day she landed?

CHARLIE. Mapleson.

GUSSIE. Why did *he?*

CHARLIE. Oh, he always liked Captain Jinks! He likes all us good-looking fellows who make things hum at the Academy. *He* was a bully clever chap, that customs detective!

GUSSIE, *looking through the cards in the card receiver.* When does Jinks' case come up in court?

CHARLIE. Today.

GUSSIE. Today?

CHARLIE. Yes, this afternoon.

GUSSIE. What time?

CHARLIE. Two o'clock.

GUSSIE. Two o'clock. Good! It'll ruin his chance with Trentoni.

CHARLIE. Don't be an ass! Didn't he get into the scrape to save her inconvenience! It will make a hero of him in her eyes.

GUSSIE *whistles.* I didn't think of that! Probably he has told her all about it already.

CHARLIE. Go West, Fitznoodle! He's too damned modest. Besides, he's clever enough to see that if he told her about it, it would sound infernally like brag and spoil the effect. By the way, you'll have to lend me another hundred.

GUSSIE. By Jove! That makes a good deal, you know.

CHARLIE. Yes, but I must keep up appearances to catch Trentoni. So you must fork over *more* if you want to get the *rest* back.

GUSSIE. What do you want this hundred for?

CHARLIE. For a new Prince Albert and a swallow-tail suit. Look here; if she sees us now, this is what I am going to say to her.

GUSSIE. What?

CHARLIE. That Jinks bet us he would marry her and would pay his bet out of *her* money.

GUSSIE. But he can deny that.

CHARLIE. Let him, we're two to one!

GUSSIE. But still——

CHARLIE, *interrupting*. He made *a* bet, didn't he? He'll acknowledge that—I never heard him lie in his life; besides, I have his I O U to prove it. And I intend to arrange things so that he won't know really what he's owning up to. *Sh!*

The SERVANT *re-enters.*

THE SERVANT. Madame Trentoni regrets she is out!

He places their two cards on top of the card receiver. There is a knock on the hall door. The SERVANT *goes to open it.*

CHARLIE. Jinks, I'll bet you!

The SERVANT *opens the door and* CAPTAIN JINKS *enters.*

CAPTAIN JINKS. Madame Trentoni?

Sees the two other men; he is not pleased and bows coolly to them. How are you!

CHARLIE. Madame Trentoni is *out;* we've just sent up our cards.

CAPTAIN JINKS, *giving one of his cards to the* SERVANT. Oh, well, perhaps you didn't have *trumps!* Try this one!

THE SERVANT. Yes, sir.

He goes out.

CHARLIE. Well, have you worked it up—your flirtation?

CAPTAIN JINKS, *very quietly.* No.

CHARLIE. Then what are you doing here?

CAPTAIN JINKS, *firmly.* That's my affair.

CHARLIE. If you think you are going to marry this lady——

CAPTAIN JINKS, *still quietly but with tension.* That's *her* affair.

CHARLIE. I'll be damned if you do!

CAPTAIN JINKS. You will be if I *don't,* if it's thanks to *your* interference.

CHARLIE. Have you asked her yet?

CAPTAIN JINKS. Not often enough.

CHARLIE. Have you any reason to believe she will accept you?

CAPTAIN JINKS. None of your business.

CHARLIE, *getting angry and speaking louder.* Yes, it is—the business of all three of us!

CAPTAIN JINKS, *also getting angry, and less contained.* Look here, don't you dare mention that damned *wager!*

CHARLIE. You made it!

CAPTAIN JINKS. I called it off! I lost, if you like, and you have my note; in a week it will be paid up. I know when I made that bet appearances were against me, but this woman has taught me I'm not a fool nor a blackguard after all. As a fact, I haven't asked her to be my wife yet; but I've come to do so *now,* because *this morning* I got some work to do, an *honest job,* not very elegant—it wouldn't suit either of you—but it'll earn me a living, and thank God it puts me in a position to ask the woman I love to be my wife.

The SERVANT *comes back.*

THE SERVANT, *to* CAPTAIN JINKS. Madame Trentoni will be down in a few minutes.

He exits.

CAPTAIN JINKS. Thank you.

CHARLIE. Huh!

CAPTAIN JINKS *goes to the piano and with the forefinger of his right hand picks out "I'm Captain Jinks of the Horse Marines," playing it with a sort of triumphant force.*

CHARLIE, *to* GUSSIE. Come along; we might as well take our cards back.

And going to the card receiver they take their cards and put them back in their cases.

We may have to economize! Oh! By Jove! I have one of
my clever ideas.

The SERVANT *goes to the hall door and, opening it, stands
ready to show out* CHARLIE *and* GUSSIE.

CHARLIE *stops to speak to the* SERVANT. Is Professor Belliarti
in the hotel?

THE SERVANT. No, sir; I expect he's at the Academy of Music.

CHARLIE. Good! He's our next move.

To GUSSIE, *linking his arm in his.*

We'll go there!

They go out. CAPTAIN JINKS *looks over his shoulder and
seeing them go changes to "Shoo Fly, don't bother me"
on the piano, and just as he finishes* AURELIA *enters.*

AURELIA, *singing.* "Shoo Fly, don't bother me!"—that's a civil
greeting!
Laughing.

CAPTAIN JINKS. That was for La Martine and Van Vorkenburg.

AURELIA. Oh! Do you know—I don't want to be rude, but I
can't bear your friends.

CAPTAIN JINKS. Neither can I.

AURELIA. And by the way, before I forget it, I hope you'll
come to supper tonight—here. Will you? After the opera.

CAPTAIN JINKS. Delighted!

AURELIA. No grand powwow! Only one or two distinguished
people with the company, and Mapleson, and the Arditis.
Oh yes, and those two nice funny cretatures who wanted
to debut in oratorio. They've been most kind to Mrs. Gee
and are to be at *Traviata* tonight after all! I'll let you sit
between them!

CAPTAIN JINKS, *laughing.* There's a prize for a good boy.

AURELIA. Won't you sit down?
Sitting on the piano stool.

CAPTAIN JINKS. Won't you take the chair? Let me sit on the
piano stool?

AURELIA. No indeed, you don't wear a bustle. It's the only comfortable seat for me in the room! It was very kind of you to call this noon. I hoped you would, but—

CAPTAIN JINKS, *pulling his chair nearer her.* "But?" It was an appointment!

AURELIA. Oh yes, but I can never be certain. You remember our very first appointment you deliberately *broke!*
Teasingly.

CAPTAIN JINKS. You mean that day you landed!

AURELIA. You promised to come to the hotel at four o'clock.

CAPTAIN JINKS. Oh yes, but you forgave me for that long ago, when I told you I was *detained—in more senses than one!* And very unavoidably, not to mention unwillingly!

AURELIA. But you never told me why.

CAPTAIN JINKS. No, I couldn't, but I will *some* day. Are you nervous about tonight?

AURELIA. Frightfully.

CAPTAIN JINKS. You'll take the roof off the Academy!

AURELIA. I *hae me doots!* I'm not so sure I'm not an acquired taste, like olives and tomatoes and Russian caviar! But tell me one thing—

CAPTAIN JINKS. I'm going to before I leave this room.
He changes his seat to a chair close beside the piano.

AURELIA. Really! What?

CAPTAIN JINKS. No, let's have yours first. When I get started on mine there won't be time for anything else.

AURELIA. Well—supposing—by some heaven-sent chance—I do succeed, even like in London; then you know, after I've bowed thirty-two times with a heaving bosom, and thrown kisses like fireworks to the gallery twenty-three times, if they still keep on—and oh, goodness, how I love them when they do—then I sing something, just some little song. Now I want to sing "Home, Sweet Home." Do you know it?

CAPTAIN JINKS. Oh yes. Clara Louise Kellogg sings it on the same occasions.

AURELIA. With variations? I have trills and all sorts of monkey tricks!

CAPTAIN JINKS. So has she!

AURELIA. I was afraid so. Well, then, I think I'll sing a little song called "The Last Rose of Summer."
She sings a bar or two.
Have you heard it?
She sings the verse through.

CAPTAIN JINKS. No.

AURELIA. It's quite new and unhackneyed, isn't it? I sing it in *Martha*.

CAPTAIN JINKS. Not very lively though! Why not sing "Those Tassels on Her Boots?"

AURELIA, *laughing.* I don't know it; show me!
Getting up from the piano stool she makes him sit down and sing. CAPTAIN JINKS *sings one verse, accompanying himself with his forefinger.*
Entrancing! Only I don't think the Anti-French Literature League would approve of the sentiment!

CAPTAIN JINKS, *turning on the stool, rises, and speaks seriously.* There would be just *one* consolation to me if you didn't make a success at all!

AURELIA. You horrid brute! There would be *no* consolation for me.

CAPTAIN JINKS. That is *my* misfortune——

AURELIA. Really! How do you mean?——

CAPTAIN JINKS. It would make it so much easier for me to ask you to marry me!
A knock on the hall door.

AURELIA. Well, then, let's *pretend* I've failed!
PETER, *the newsboy, in the livery of a hotel servant, enters.*

CAPTAIN JINKS. Hello, Peter!

PETER. Hello, sir!

CAPTAIN JINKS. How do you like your new job?

PETER. Oh, it ain't bad——

Aside to CAPTAIN JINKS.

I does it for *her* sake, so as to be near *her*, but I find it very confining.

AURELIA. What is it, Peter?

PETER. Beg pardon, ma'am, the reporter from the Tribune wants to see you on a personal matter of great importance.

AURELIA. Say I'm out.

PETER. Yes, ma'am.

Exits.

AURELIA. What a horrid moment to be interrupted in. *Please* go on *just* where you left off!

CAPTAIN JINKS. You are very rich and popular and beautiful and all the rest of it——

He stops.

AURELIA, *childishly happy and delighted.* Oh, that isn't fair— to hurry through with just "all the rest of it." I wonder you didn't say I was beautiful *et cetera!* No siree! You must enumerate singly every solitary nice thing you think I am!

CAPTAIN JINKS. It would take too long!

AURELIA. How long?

CAPTAIN JINKS. The rest of my life!

Starting to embrace her. Another knock on the hall door. They start apart and sit on opposite sides of the table. Then AURELIA *speaks.*

AURELIA. Come in.

PETER *re-enters.*

PETER. Please, ma'am, the reporter from the Tribune told me to ask you, so long as you was dead-set on being out, if the news was true what has come to his office, that you was engaged to be married to *him?*

Pointing to CAPTAIN JINKS.

AURELIA, *on one side of the table.* It won't be true if he keeps on interrupting with messages all the day! You tell the gentleman, Peter, that I've gone to the Academy.

CAPTAIN JINKS, *on the other side of the table.* And if he asks you anything about me tell him you don't know who I am.

PETER. Oh, but I can't.

CAPTAIN JINKS. Why not?

PETER. 'Cause I've just told him you've been to see Madame Trentoni every day!

AURELIA. What did you do that for?

PETER. For a dollar!

CAPTAIN JINKS. That's a nice return to make to Madame Trentoni for getting you this good position in a high-toned hotel!

PETER. If you wanted me to lie about it you ought ter have told me; I thought it was something she'd be proud of.

AURELIA. That's all right, Peter; go give my message and don't answer any more questions about me at all.

PETER. Yes, ma'am.

Exits.

AURELIA. Peter wasn't so far wrong; I'm not ashamed of your visits.

CAPTAIN JINKS *rises and goes to her.* Look here, I'm not worth your little finger, but if you'll only overlook my beastly unworthiness and just let my love for you count, I'll do my best so long as I live to make my wife the happiest woman in the world.

AURELIA. But I'm *nobody.*

CAPTAIN JINKS. The woman I love—*nobody?*

AURELIA. But your family—your mother——?

CAPTAIN JINKS. *You* are the woman I love.

AURELIA. Still I mayn't be the woman your mother loves!

CAPTAIN JINKS. Oh well, say! Are you marrying mother or *me?*

AURELIA. But won't your mother be shocked at your marrying a "lady on the stage"?

CAPTAIN JINKS, *half amused.* Oh, very likely she'll carry on awful for a while! The Ladies' Anti-French Literature League is *broad-minded* compared to mother! But she's an angel all the same; and as birds of a feather flock together, she will soon chum up with *you* when she has once had a chance to know you.

AURELIA. I'm not so sure. She'll think you are going to perdition!

CAPTAIN JINKS. Oh no, to a much hotter place! But when she *knows you!*

AURELIA. You think so, because you think you are in love with me.

CAPTAIN JINKS. "Think!"

AURELIA, *rising.* It would break my heart to come between you and your mother.

CAPTAIN JINKS. Now don't be selfish; it will break mine if you refuse me, and you'd rather break your heart than mine, wouldn't you?
Coming close to her.

AURELIA, *teasing, and backing slowly away.* Oh, I don't know——

CAPTAIN JINKS, *following her.* Madame Trentoni! Oh, can't I call you something else, something more friendly, more personal?

AURELIA. Yes, you may call me—Miss Johnson; that's my real name, you know——

CAPTAIN JINKS. But you have another, a nearer one——

AURELIA. Oh well, go on with Miss Johnson for a few minutes——

CAPTAIN JINKS *makes her let him take her hand.* Listen to me seriously. This is a question for *you* and *me* to decide. Let's decide it now! Do you know that until I met you I was a lazy good-for-nothing loafer! Now I'm afraid I'm not good for much, but I'm no longer lazy, and I'm a lover instead of a loafer! Let me work for you, will you? It's no fun working only for myself! Make my dreams come true, just to prove the rule that they don't.

AURELIA. There are dreams—and *dreams!*

CAPTAIN JINKS. Yes, but mine are all alike, daydreams and all, full of one idea, one desire—your love. I can't express myself; I don't know how to say it, but what I mean is that I don't want to go anywhere, on sea, on land, in the city, in the country, anywhere, unless *you* are there beside me. Life without you doesn't seem worth the trouble! Oh! If I only dared hope you could care a little for a chap like me.

AURELIA, *softening, and with bent head, looks at him sweetly from the corner of her eye.* I give you permission to *dream* that!

CAPTAIN JINKS. Really?

AURELIA. Yes, and you can even make the *little* a *good deal!*

CAPTAIN JINKS. You——

Interrupted. He is going to say "darling."

AURELIA. Wait a minute! You know I'm not really half so nice as you think I am.

CAPTAIN JINKS. Aren't you?

AURELIA. No, but it won't make any difference, if you never find it out! Only, suppose I were to fail tonight——

CAPTAIN JINKS. Ah! That's just what I meant by having one consolation; you would know then I loved you only for your dear self, and if you loved me we could say, "Never mind, for *love* doesn't fail!"

AURELIA, *with tears in her eyes.* You *are* a darling——

A knock on the hall door. They change their places quickly. CAPTAIN JINKS *sits again on one side of the center table and* AURELIA *on the other. They exchange a smiling glance of understanding as* AURELIA *says "Come in."*

PETER *enters.*

PETER. Ice water!

He rattles the ice in a white china pitcher which he places between them on the center table. AURELIA *and* CAPTAIN JINKS *exchange hopeless glances.*

The chambermaid wants to know if she can come in and do this room now?

AURELIA. No, she can't!

She goes to the writing desk and writes in ink with the wrong end of a pen on a big sheet of fresh white blotting paper there.

CAPTAIN JINKS, *taking* PETER *to one side by the collar of his coat.* Look here, if you bring any more messages, or ice water, or reporters, or chambermaids, or any other damned thing to Madame Trentoni this afternoon, I'll break your neck! Do you understand?

PETER. No, sir!

CAPTAIN JINKS. Well, think it over as you go downstairs.

PETER. What's it worth?

CAPTAIN JINKS. Your *neck*, that's all—go on, git!

PETER. Yes, sir.

Halfway to the door, he stops.

Say! I'll bet you a quarter no one gets into this room what ain't wanted!

CAPTAIN JINKS. All right!

PETER. Thank you!

He exits, happy. AURELIA *follows him to the door with the blotting paper, which she holds in front of her, displaying it to* CAPTAIN JINKS.

AURELIA. There! How would it do if I put *this* on the door?
The paper reads in large black letters "Engaged."

CAPTAIN JINKS. It would be all right if you would add "to R. Jinks."

AURELIA, *laughing.* How dare you! Certainly *not!*

CAPTAIN JINKS. Why?

AURELIA. Because—
Closing the door she turns and faces him.
Because—
She comes slowly to him.
Because it's the truth!

CAPTAIN JINKS, *embracing her.* You *love* me!
In his arms, she doesn't answer.
Do you love me?
Still in his arms, she doesn't answer.
You don't answer?

AURELIA, *looking up at him.* Am I trying to get out of your arms?

CAPTAIN JINKS. Darling!

AURELIA. *Yours!*
She bursts into tears.

CAPTAIN JINKS, *frightened.* Dearest, what's the matter? You are crying!

AURELIA. I know it. I'm *so happy!*
PAPA BELLIARTI *comes in unannounced. He brings with him his violin in a green baize bag.*

PROFESSOR BELLIARTI. Bless my stars and ballet dancers! Ought I have knocked!
AURELIA *and* CAPTAIN JINKS *have broken quickly from each other's arms.*

CAPTAIN JINKS. Oh no, we're *accustomed* to interruptions this morning!

PROFESSOR BELLIARTI, *to* AURELIA. Having a little rehearsal with a new tenor, my dear?

Placing the bag on the piano—busy with his violin.

AURELIA, *laughing.* Yes, sort of like that.

PROFESSOR BELLIARTI. The ladies of the ballet are here to rehearse at your request, you know.

AURELIA. Oh dear, that's true. I forgot. You'll have to excuse me, Captain Jinks.

CAPTAIN JINKS *bows to* AURELIA *and turning to* PROFESSOR BELLIARTI *offers him a cigar very pleasantly.* Have a cigar?

PROFESSOR BELLIARTI. Thank you!

Takes one and puts it in his pocket.

Ahem!

Turning his back pointedly, he takes up his violin, which is in perfect tune, and tunes it, with a smile on his face but only his friendly back toward AURELIA *and* CAPTAIN JINKS.

CAPTAIN JINKS, *to* AURELIA. Shan't I tell him?

AURELIA. I think he'd rather *I* told him—he's such a dear sensitive old thing!

CAPTAIN JINKS. And then afterwards *I* will ask his consent; don't you think that would please him?

AURELIA. Oh yes, do. It will make him feel he is something to both of us! How nice of you to have the idea! Come back in quarter of an hour.

CAPTAIN JINKS. It's one o'clock; I'll be back on the minute of fifteen past! But I won't be able to stay, for I have an engagement at *two* that must not be put off.

AURELIA, *happy, and smiling.* Oh, I'll excuse you!

CAPTAIN JINKS, *stopping, and looking into her eyes a moment.* This is no dream? You're sure I'm awake?

AURELIA. Let's see!

She looks around first at PAPA BELLIARTI, *whom she sees*

still has his back turned, and then, leaning over, she kisses
CAPTAIN JINKS.

How is it? Awake?

CAPTAIN JINKS. Not sure yet—try again.

AURELIA, *laughing.* No *siree! !* Good-by——
Giving him her hand, which he presses.

CAPTAIN JINKS. Good-by.
*He starts to go. At the door he hesitates and stands look-
ing at* AURELIA. *She slowly joins him at the door, questioningly.*
Are you sure whether *you're* awake or not?

AURELIA. *Quite sure!* But I may be uncertain in fifteen minutes!

CAPTAIN JINKS. Don't ask *Papa Belliarti* then, *I'll* be back!
He goes.

AURELIA. Papa Belliarti!

PROFESSOR BELLIARTI, *with his back still turned.* Has he gone?

AURELIA. Yes, you silly old goose!
Going to him, takes him lovingly by the shoulders.
Turn around!

PROFESSOR BELLIARTI. So my singing bird is caught at last, eh!
She hides her happy, blushing face in his arms.
I'm very glad!
*He speaks this latter sentence with tears in his voice and
eyes.*
Very—glad, for her sake! But I'll miss you, little girl!

AURELIA. It isn't to make any difference to you at all! Let me
tell you——

PROFESSOR BELLIARTI. Sh! Not now. Mrs. Gee is coming; I
sent for her to accompany me on the piano for the ballet
ladies.
MRS. GREENBOROUGH *enters at this moment through the
double doors at back.*

MRS. GREENBOROUGH. Good afternoon, everybody. Papa Belliarti sent for me, Aurelia, to——

PROFESSOR BELLIARTI. I told her, madam.

MRS. GREENBOROUGH, *looking around room, under the sofa, behind the chairs, and even absent-mindedly on the piano and mantelpiece.* Aurelia, I can't find my bustle anywhere; I believe that chambermaid has stolen it!

AURELIA. Dear heart! If you had any more bustle I don't know where you'd put it!

MRS. GREENBOROUGH. Oh well, of course I had to have a makeshift, so I took all those nice newspapers that had our arrival in.

AURELIA. You both know why I've had these dancers come! I want everything tonight as near perfection as possible! No rough edges, no horrid slip-ups! And the dancing at yesterday's rehearsal was awful! How many ladies are coming, Papa?

PROFESSOR BELLIARTI. Seven—the leads!

AURELIA. Good! If *they're* all right, the others can't go wrong. I have especial reasons *besides it being my New York debut why I want everything tonight to be perfect!* Haven't I, Papa Belliarti?
Whispers to him.
Shall I tell her, Papa?

MRS. GREENBOROUGH, *curious.* Well, now, Aurelia, I consider you're real tantalizing if you have secrets——
Interrupted.

AURELIA. If you keep on talking, dear heart, I can never tell you.

MRS. GREENBOROUGH. *Talking! Me!* It's twenty years since I've spoken one complete sentence of any length, all the way through.

AURELIA. Well then, to make up, I'll tell you. Stand over there!

Placing her.

Lean against the table so as to have some support if you should feel faint! There!

Having bolstered MRS. GREENBOROUGH *against the center table, she crosses the room to* PAPA BELLIARTI *and takes his arm. They stand facing* MRS. GREENBOROUGH. PROFESSOR BELLIARTI *hums a few bars of the Mendelssohn "Wedding March," and they slowly approach* MRS. GREENBOROUGH.

MRS. GREENBOROUGH. Good gracious, I hope—

Interrupted.

AURELIA. Ssh! Papa Belliarti and I are very happy!

PROFESSOR BELLIARTI. What?

AURELIA. Well— *Aren't you?*

PROFESSOR BELLIARTI. Yes dear. Yes! Of course—only!

MRS. GREENBOROUGH, *excited.* Do go on, I'm eaten up with curiosity, I'm guessing—

Interrupted.

AURELIA. You're guessing wrong! I'm going to be married.

MRS. GREENBOROUGH. Bless my soul! To Papa Belliarti!

PROFESSOR BELLIARTI. That's a crazy idea!

AURELIA. No! No! Go on with your guessing! Who is it?

MRS. GREENBOROUGH. Dear heart, I *can't* guess!

AURELIA. Catch me and I'll tell you!

She runs, gaily laughing, around the table, then around a big armchair, and then around PAPA BELLIARTI, MRS. GREENBOROUGH *running after her and talking all the time.* AURELIA *dodges around* PAPA BELLIARTI, *turns suddenly and herself catches* MRS. GREENBOROUGH *and gives her a hug and a kiss. Then she drags her over to the piano, plumps her down on the piano stool facing the keys, and leaning over her back with her own hands on the piano plays "Captain Jinks."*

Now! Can't you guess?

MRS. GREENBOROUGH *gives a little high scream of delight.*
Eeh! It's the young man who gave me the booky the day
we landed!

AURELIA, *hugging her delightedly around the neck.* Of course!
Do you suppose there is another man in this whole world
I'd marry!

MRS. GREENBOROUGH. I *thought* he liked us that very day!

AURELIA. I'm so happy! I'm no prima donna now, I'm only a
girl, and the happiest girl that ever was! Listen! You two
dear people think I've been singing these last two years,
don't you! Wait till you hear me tonight! You'll say I never
sang before! There's only one man in this world for me,
and I'm going to marry him!

She hugs PROFESSOR BELLIARTI *impulsively.*

What do you think of that for *real* JOY!

There is a knock on the hall door.

AURELIA. Come in! Come in, *everybody!*

PETER *enters.*

PETER. Please, ma'am, there's a party of females says they has
an engagement with you. I thought they was kiddin', so
I wouldn't let 'm in till I asted you.

PROFESSOR BELLIARTI. The ballet ladies!

AURELIA. Show them up, Peter; they're *artistes!*

PETER. They're right here.

He calls into hall.

Come along in!

And goes out after they have entered.

The SEVEN BALLET LADIES *enter. Three are young and
pretty. Three are about fifty; one of these three is rather
stout and one is very thin. The seventh is inclined to
embonpoint also but bravely restricted at every curve.
She hails from the Paris Opera. The thin one is a widow
and wears a widow's weeds. Her dress is a trifle short and
shows a hair breadth escape of white stocking above her
prunella boots. She brings with her, leading by the hand,*

a small child. Her offspring is dressed in white piqué and wears pantalettes and galoshes. They all say "good day." Two of the younger ones are rather free and impertinent in their manner, the others are somewhat embarrassed; all carry little bags or parcels supposed to contain their ballet dresses. The widow's is done up in an old newspaper.

AURELIA. How do you do, ladies!

They all bow and murmur again a greeting.

PROFESSOR BELLIARTI. Madame Trentoni wants to have the performance perfection tonight, and so she thought a little quiet rehearsal of the principal ladies of the ballet here, with her, a good thing all around.

AURELIA. You did beautifully last night, but you know this new rose figure Professor Belliarti is teaching you is very difficult, and if there is the slightest mistake it is ruined.

There is a nervous movement of all the SEVEN, several clearing their throats, others slightly changing their position from one foot to the other. One or two, including the widow, look very supercilious, as if to say, "Oh dear me! think of her telling us what is and what ain't easy! Us, who are old enough to be her grandmother!" though I'm sure they wouldn't have put it in just that way. They would probably have spoken of her as a "raw amateur" and of themselves as "trained artistes."

PROFESSOR BELLIARTI, *opening the folding doors at the back, shows the big empty room.* We may use this room too if we need it to dance in.

The BALLET LADIES look in its direction.

AURELIA. We're all going to try our very best, aren't we, tonight?

THE THIRD BALLET LADY, *with a curtsy.* Si, si, signora.

THE SIXTH BALLET LADY, *the widow.* Oh, it'll be hall roight. There ain't no trouble with that polka step!

THE FOURTH BALLET LADY. Dat vas nicht ein polka shtep!

THE FIRST BALLET LADY, *Miss Pettitoes*. Yes, it was!

THE FOURTH BALLET LADY. Nein! Nein! I dell you dat vas ein——

Interrupted.

PROFESSOR BELLIARTI, *firmly*. Ladies!

THE FOURTH BALLET LADY. Dat vas nicht ein polka shtep!

THE FIRST BALLET LADY. Miss Hochspitz is always quarreling, sir; that's why she had to leave Germany and come over here!

THE FOURTH BALLET LADY. Och Himmel! Dat vas not drue, mein herr! She is von *cat*, dis Caroline Peddidoes!

PROFESSOR BELLIARTI. Come, come, fraulein, remember I always insist on my ballet being a happy family.

MISS HOCHSPITZ *pinches* MISS PETTITOES. MISS PETTITOES *slaps* MISS HOCHSPITZ's *face. All the* BALLET LADIES *join in and there is a general quarrel.*

AURELIA. Ladies! *Please* do remember we engage you to dance, not to *sing!* We'll do all the squabbling ourselves! You have some things with you to rehearse in?

THE SIXTH BALLET LADY. Oh yes, miss, we've hall got combing jackets* and hour regular re'earsing costumes the rest of the way down.

They all show their bundles.

AURELIA. Where'll they change?

PROFESSOR BELLIARTI. In here.

Motioning to the big room at back.

MRS. GREENBOROUGH. No; let them come to my room.

AURELIA. They can't go through the hall after they're dressed!

MRS. GREENBOROUGH. They don't have to; that door to the right

Pointing off in the big room.

*I.e., a jacket slipped on while combing the hair.

opens into a private passage which connects straight with my room. It's the way I always come.

AURELIA. Very well then, ladies, please, if you will kindly go with Mrs. Greenborough.

MRS. GREENBOROUGH. Follow me, etc.

She leads the way, talking, followed by the SEVEN BALLET LADIES, *the widow still leading her child.* BELLIARTI *closes the door after them. Then he comes slowly to* AURELIA, *watching her with a sweet smile. When he reaches her he takes her two hands.*

PROFESSOR BELLIARTI. I'm as happy as you, my dear. There's only one worry—is he worthy of you?

AURELIA. He's worth a dozen of me, voice and all!

PROFESSOR BELLIARTI, *sitting in the big armchair by the table.* Still, he is all the time with one gay company of young men who lead what you call *very quick lives!* So let old Papa Belliarti poke about a little and ask a few questions before you make the engagement public, will you?

AURELIA. If you want to. You will be proud, I know, of all you hear! Women, dear Papa, are perfect barometers for a good and bad man!

She sits on the floor at his feet and lays her head on his knees.

PROFESSOR BELLIARTI. And nothing gets out of order like a barometer! They're always pointing to fair weather when it's raining cats and dogs!

AURELIA, *laughing.* True; but when you hear me sing tonight, you'll acknowledge that I am in perfect condition!

PROFESSOR BELLIARTI, *leaning over and putting his arm about her neck.* I hope so. And I hope your new life, my dear, will be one long happy dance. Not the newfangled step, this polka redowa, for that is a love at first sight that will die a violent death, exhausted before the honeymoon is over! Not the waltz, for a waltz with us must need have some reverses, and I want no reverses in my little girl's life; not a Virginia reel, for that entails long separations from one's partner and a flirtatious swinging of *all* the men down the line; but I would have your life's dance the minuet, which is not so fast as to tire you out, whose music is Mozart's,—our best—a dance where you and your partner are never long separated and where you mingle with your amusement a certain graceful graciousness toward each other which will keep familiarity forever from breeding contempt.

AURELIA, *with a choke in her voice.* Our life shall be a minuet, dear father, and you must teach us *both our steps.*

A knock on the hall door.

PROFESSOR BELLIARTI, *rising.* Come in!

AURELIA *also rises.* PETER *enters.*

PETER. Two lardy-dah gents to see *you,* and an old lady for *you,* ma'am.

Giving cards to PROFESSOR BELLIARTI *and one to* AURELIA.

PROFESSOR BELLIARTI, *reading his cards.* Mr. Charles La Martine and Mr. Van Vorkenburg?

PETER. Them's the two what always finds Madame Trenton out! They've been to the theaytre after you, and they says it's important.

AURELIA, *with suppressed happiness and proudly.* See who my visitor is!

Shows PAPA BELLIARTI *her card.*

PROFESSOR BELLIARTI, *reading card.* Who is it, his mother?

AURELIA. It must be! Come already to congratulate me! He never even told me she was here, and we were both rather afraid of her.

PETER. Well, are *you* out to them gents too?

PROFESSOR BELLIARTI. No, show them to my room and say I'll be with them immediately.

PETER, *to* AURELIA. And the old party?

AURELIA, *with pointed emphasis.* Show the *distinguished lady* here at once!

PETER. Gee!

And with his tongue in his cheek, he exits.

PROFESSOR BELLIARTI. She'll be a proud mother when she sees you. I hope to be back in time to be presented to her.

AURELIA, *half teasing.* I don't know if she'll approve of you, Papa! She's against *acting!*

PROFESSOR BELLIARTI. *Dancing* is a *higher art!*

AURELIA. So it is, sometimes!

They both laugh.

PROFESSOR BELLIARTI. Margaret Fuller and Ralph Waldo Emerson were once discussing Fanny Elssler. "It isn't dancing, Margaret, it's poetry," said Emerson. "My dear Ralph," back spoke Miss Fuller, "it's not poetry, it's *religion.*"

A delicate knock is heard on the hall door.

AURELIA, *a little frightened.* There she is!

PROFESSOR BELLIARTI *opens the door, bowing low.* MRS. JINKS *enters.* PROFESSOR BELLIARTI, *bowing, goes out, closing the door after him.* MRS. JINKS *is an elderly, sweetly severe, delicate-featured little woman, dressed in rich, light brown silk but in a past fashion. She wears full spreading skirts and carries a small parasol to match her dress.*

MRS. JINKS, *inclining her head with a serious, dignified grace.* Madame Trentoni?

AURELIA, *with a low curtsy.* Yes, madam. You have heard?

MRS. JINKS *bows her head in acquiescence.*

How good of you to come so soon! Ah! I must kiss you.

MRS. JINKS. *Please don't!*

AURELIA, *kissing her.* I do so want you to love me.

MRS. JINKS, *like a stone statue when she is kissed, and showing no flurry.* Forgive me, but I extremely dislike demonstrative people!

AURELIA. I'm so sorry. Will you sit down?

MRS. JINKS, *with a quiet and firm though sweet voice, very serious and rather haughty.* Thank you, I would rather stand.

AURELIA *looks up frightened.*

I am afraid the reason for my visit is not a pleasant one. By all means, however, sit down yourself.

AURELIA, *at once on the defensive.* Oh no, I shall stand if you do!

MRS. JINKS. My son does not yet know of my arrival, but I received a letter from him the other day saying he intended asking you to marry him. I've not slept a wink since!

AURELIA. I regret that your night's rest has been disturbed.

MRS. JINKS. Hoping to reach you before he takes so fatal a step, to assure you such a thing is impossible, I took the first train.

AURELIA. I'm afraid you took a *slow* one, for you are too late!

MRS. JINKS. He's already proposed?

AURELIA. And been accepted! Not half an hour ago.

MRS. JINKS *closes her eyes as if she were going to faint and sinks into a chair.*

Don't, please, take it so to heart! Please—

MRS. JINKS. Pardon me, I don't mean to be rude. This marriage cannot take place. *You must* give him up.

AURELIA. It is quite impossible! I am no Camille, madam!
Sitting determinedly at the opposite side of the table.

MRS. JINKS. No what?

AURELIA. No Marguerite Gautier.

MRS. JINKS. I do not know the lady.

AURELIA, *bitterly.* Oh, she wouldn't move in your set! But don't you remember the scene in the play *Camille*, where she gives up the lover to satisfy her father? It ruined both their lives.

MRS. JINKS. I never go to the theatre.

AURELIA. That's a pity, because I am sure if you did you would not be giving us both this painful experience. Well, I am a good woman, Mrs. Jinks, and I love your son.

MRS. JINKS, *pointedly.* You are also an *actress*, I believe?

AURELIA. Well, there's a difference of opinions about that! But I *am* an opera singer and not ashamed of it!

MRS. JINKS. The Jinkses have never been connected with any profession, except the *Church!*

AURELIA. Every little while the Church and Stage come plump together like that, and I think it does them both good!

MRS. JINKS. The Jinkses are an old and distinguished family; and yours?

AURELIA. I'm doing my honest best to make it distinguished.

MRS. JINKS. But you must acknowledge the thing you threaten doing isn't done. Your bringing up, your lives—everything is at a variance! Happiness is *impossible!*

AURELIA. I disagree with you so long as our hearts are in accord!

MRS. JINKS. Listen. My brother has nearly arranged for a magnificent diplomatic position for my son, his nephew, in the event of Greeley's election, which is certain, of course. This marriage with you will make such a career impossible—ruin his chances—shatter all our hopes for the future!

AURELIA, *rising.* Madam, I am not much more than a girl, but really——

MRS. JINKS. You *look* very young, but they say you stage women do wonderful things with your cosmetics.

AURELIA. When I am a certain age I may resort to them.

MRS. JINKS *rises offended.*

You do not realize what sort of a woman you are speaking to. As I started to say, I am young, but I have a will of my own and a heart of my own, in which your son has told me his happiness lies. Loving him as I do and believing in him, I shall not think of insulting his *manhood* by proposing to release him from his engagement.

MRS. JINKS. You will separate me from my son?

AURELIA *goes a little nearer her.* No indeed. I will share him with you. His mother's love remains yours.

MRS. JINKS. I have not yet seen my son. I shall appeal to the mother love you speak of.
Starting to go.

AURELIA. May I give you a hint? Don't say horrid things about *me!* For if he's the man I think him, that would only steel his heart against you.

MRS. JINKS. He's cried his baby troubles out on my knees and his boy's sorrows out in my arms! He shall empty his man's heart into my arms too!

AURELIA. Dear me! If he does that, I'm afraid you'll find them rather full; for *I* was all his *man's heart* held half an hour ago!

MRS. JINKS. You are frivolous! Good-by, madam.

AURELIA. No! Don't go like that.

MRS. JINKS. Will you give my boy up?

AURELIA. No!

MRS. JINKS *makes an inclination of the head. She is about to exit but meets* PROFESSOR BELLIARTI *coming in.* PROFESSOR BELLIARTI *is very excited, which feeling he tries to control on seeing* MRS. JINKS.

AURELIA. Oh, Papa Belliarti, I'm glad you've come down. I want to present you to *Mrs. Jinks,* my *future husband's mother!* Mrs. Jinks, Professor Belliarti, my foster father and the *ballet master* of our opera company!

PROFESSOR BELLIARTI *bows low.* MRS. JINKS *closes her eyes and gasps, then, giving the merest inclination of her head, she exits.* AURELIA, *excited, slams the door after her.*

She came after my happiness, but she didn't get it! Tell Mrs. Greenborough to bring the ladies in now!

PROFESSOR BELLIARTI. Not yet—not yet! Papa Belliarti is after your happiness too, but to save it for you, to save it for you.

AURELIA. What is it? What's the matter? No accident?

PROFESSOR BELLIARTI. You mustn't marry this Captain Jinks.

AURELIA. *You* too!

PROFESSOR BELLIARTI. He's a blackguard!

AURELIA. Papa! That's not true! How dare you!

> PROFESSOR BELLIARTI *pours forth a flood of Italian, speaking rapidly and with great excitement and emotion.* AURELIA *stops him, taking hold of his arm and holding it tightly but affectionately.*

Speak English! *Speak English!* You know I can't understand Italian when you are excited! What do you mean? Does he, like his mother, want to back out?

PROFESSOR BELLIARTI, *grimly.* Oh no, not he! Not he!
> *Speaking the last "not he" very angrily.*

AURELIA. Then how dared you call him——
> *Interrupted.*

PROFESSOR BELLIARTI. He is marrying you for your money! For what *you* will *make* for him!

AURELIA. I don't believe it!

PROFESSOR BELLIARTI. He made one bet he would marry you after these young men told him they had heard from Mrs. Gee that you were rich. He made one bet with La Martine and Van Vorkenburg that he would marry you!

AURELIA. I tell you I don't believe it!

PROFESSOR BELLIARTI. A thousand dollars he bet them! Even Mapleson knows it.

AURELIA. Papa! You didn't tell *Mapleson?*

PROFESSOR BELLIARTI. He heard it from a reporter.

AURELIA. It's in the papers?

PROFESSOR BELLIARTI. No. The reporter is a nice gentleman. He was told by a newsboy on the dock the day you landed but never printed it.

AURELIA. But I don't believe the story. I tell you it isn't *true!* Captain Jinks *never* made such a bet!

PROFESSOR BELLIARTI. I have proof, and I intend to ask him to his face!

AURELIA. Yes; do that, Papa! I'm not afraid of his answer.

PROFESSOR BELLIARTI. *But* if he says he *did* bet so?

AURELIA. *Don't let* him say it!

PROFESSOR BELLIARTI. I will make him speak the *truth*, and if he confess he did make that bet you must *not* marry him. He would break your heart, darling, before the honeymoon was over.

A knock on the hall door, but neither hear it.

AURELIA. Oh no, it's too great an insult. I *know* he isn't capable!

Another knock and then PETER *enters.*

PETER. *Please*, are you all deaf? Captain Jinks is here again and says you're all expecting him, but I wouldn't let him up till I asted.

PROFESSOR BELLIARTI. Send Captain Jinks straight here.

PETER. Yes, sir. Golly!

Exits.

AURELIA. *I* couldn't ask him.

PROFESSOR BELLIARTI. You needn't. But will you give me permission to break off your engagement?

AURELIA. *If* it's true. But I *know* it isn't!

PROFESSOR BELLIARTI, *pointing to the room at the back.* Go in there. Listen to what we say, and when it is sufficient in your eyes to break off everything between us, make some signal—drop this book.

Taking a book from the table.

AURELIA. *Going to the door, she turns there.* Ask him outright
if he made the bet—and be sure he says "*No*" loud.

*She goes into the other room and closes the doors be-
hind her.*

PROFESSOR BELLIARTI. If wishing could only make him turn
out to be worthy of my girl!

A knock on the hall door. He pulls himself together.

Come in.

CAPTAIN JINKS *dashes in, very happy and expectant.*

CAPTAIN JINKS. Ah, sir! The very man I wanted to see!

PROFESSOR BELLIARTI. And *me* too.

CAPTAIN JINKS. I have a *most* important question to ask you!

PROFESSOR BELLIARTI. *Me too!*

CAPTAIN JINKS. Have a cigar?

Offering one.

PROFESSOR BELLIARTI. No, thank you! And here's the one back
you gave me a little while ago.

Giving the cigar from his pocket.

CAPTAIN JINKS, *taking the cigar, rather perplexed and not
understanding.* Have a chair?

Offering one and about to sit himself.

PROFESSOR BELLIARTI. No!

CAPTAIN JINKS, *about to sit down—doesn't.*

CAPTAIN JINKS. Ah well then, straight to the point, Signor
Belliarti.

Bowing elaborately, mocking, happy.

Will you give me your adopted daughter to be my wife?

PROFESSOR BELLIARTI. *Yes!* If you will give me your word of
honor you didn't sign that paper!

Giving him, with trembling hand, the paper CAPTAIN JINKS
signed in Act One.

CAPTAIN JINKS. *What paper?*

Taking paper from BELLIARTI—*aghast.*

By Jove! My I O U! How did you get hold of this?

PROFESSOR BELLIARTI. Good Lord! You know what it is? Then you *did* sign it? You're a blackguard, sir, to try and cheat my child!

CAPTAIN JINKS *throws the paper onto the table.* Hold on a minute! Hold on! You're an old man and I can't treat you as I would a younger, but you must take that "blackguard" back!

PROFESSOR BELLIARTI. Never! If it's true you made this wager about my little girl. Forget my age if you like, but I *won't* take "blackguard" back!

CAPTAIN JINKS. Yes, you will, if it's a lie! Where is Madame Trentoni? I want to see her herself.

PROFESSOR BELLIARTI. First answer me my question. Is that your signature? Did you make that wager?

CAPTAIN JINKS, *after a moment's pause, ashamed.* Yes——
Again a moment's pause; the book is dropped by AURELIA *in the next room and is distinctly heard as it strikes the floor. The sound rouses* CAPTAIN JINKS *and* PROFESSOR BELLIARTI.
But——
Interrupted.

PROFESSOR BELLIARTI, *beside himself. Not one other word, sir!* I am asked by Madame Trentoni to take back the troth she plighted with you and to tell you that all is forever over between you!

CAPTAIN JINKS. I won't have that! I can explain!

PROFESSOR BELLIARTI. Explain! Your signature *explains* too much already!

CAPTAIN JINKS. I don't acknowledge you or your authority! I'll see the lady herself!

PROFESSOR BELLIARTI. Not with my permission.
Stepping in front of him.

CAPTAIN JINKS. *Without* it then! I tell you I won't take your word for it! *She* herself gave me her promise, and she herself must break it.

PROFESSOR BELLIARTI. I don't believe she'll ever willingly set eyes on you again!

CAPTAIN JINKS. She *must,* I tell you! It's an outrage! It's a conspiracy!

PROFESSOR BELLIARTI. There you are right! A damnable conspiracy against a sweet woman; a contemptible insult to as lovely a girl as lives. Good-by!

CAPTAIN JINKS. I won't leave this room till I've seen her.

PROFESSOR BELLIARTI. Yes, you will.

CAPTAIN JINKS. I will not!

PROFESSOR BELLIARTI. Then the police would be called in to remove you, and you would add—to what you have already done—a public scandal for Madame Trentoni on the eve of her debut.

CAPTAIN JINKS. On the eve of her debut? No, no! I mustn't do that——

Quietly.

Listen about that bet——

Interrupted.

PROFESSOR BELLIARTI. Not one further word about it! The paper speaks for itself. Good-by.

CAPTAIN JINKS *seizes the leaf and tears it angrily.* That for your damned paper! You shall dance at our wedding yet, Papa Belliarti!

Going to the door.

PROFESSOR BELLIARTI. It will be the *danse macabre* then!

CAPTAIN JINKS, *turning at the door.* Wait and see! I'm aware who's at the bottom of this, and I'll find them both before the afternoon is over. And I'll make you glad to take that "blackguard" back! You don't know *me.*

He exits.

PROFESSOR BELLIARTI. I wish to God we didn't.

He sinks into the armchair beside the table. The double doors at the back open slowly and AURELIA *steals in. She is a tearful, tragic, woebegone looking creature.*

AURELIA. Gone?

PROFESSOR BELLIARTI. Yes.

AURELIA, *coming up behind his chair.* Didn't you hear me drop the book a second time?

PROFESSOR BELLIARTI. No; what was that for?

AURELIA. To hint perhaps I had better see him after all, just to hear what excuse he had to make.

PROFESSOR BELLIARTI. No, no, my dear, better not.

AURELIA. Why didn't he *lie* about it? Why did he own he made it?

PROFESSOR BELLIARTI. His case was desperate! Come, you must be strong now and hold up your head.

AURELIA. I can't, I can't, Papa. My head is as heavy as my heart!

Sitting on his lap and throwing her arms about his neck she sobs.

—And I shan't sing tonight! You mustn't ask me! I—I couldn't sing a note!

PROFESSOR BELLIARTI. Not make your debut tonight!

AURELIA, *her tears gone, becoming angry and a little hard.* No! You can send word to Mapleson! You can do what you please.

Leaving his knee, she paces up and down the room.

I will *not* sing tonight! Don't you know what I told you a little while ago, that I was so happy I would sing as I never sang before! Well, I was wrong.

Beginning to cry again.

What I should have said was—I will be so miserable, so utterly unhappy, that I'll never *sing another note!*

She sits on the piano stool and buries her tearful face in her arms over the keys.

PROFESSOR BELLIARTI, *really alarmed.* My dear child! My dear!

Going to her.

Where's your character? You can't give way like this.
Your whole future's at stake.

AURELIA, *sobbing.* I don't *want* any future!

PROFESSOR BELLIARTI *pulls the bell rope.*

PROFESSOR BELLIARTI. You must think of Mapleson, too! You
haven't the right to sacrifice *him.*

AURELIA. He can say I have a cold.

PROFESSOR BELLIARTI. No one will believe it.

*Moving the chairs from the center of the room back
against the wall.*

And the public will be down on you.

AURELIA. Oh, why doesn't someone invent a new kind of
cold that people will believe you when you've got it.

PETER *enters in answer to the bell.*

PETER. Yes, sir.

PROFESSOR BELLIARTI. Help me to move this table.

PETER. Yes, sir.

*They move the center table out of the way and to the
opposite side of the room from AURELIA.*

PROFESSOR BELLIARTI, *aside to PETER.* Listen! Go downstairs
to the two blackg—*gentlemen*—you will find smoking in
my room and ask them to wait a little longer. Say I may
want them to apologize to Madame Trentoni before they
leave the hotel.

PETER. All right, sir.

PROFESSOR BELLIARTI. Say nothing to anyone, but watch this
bell downstairs—you'll be *paid* for it—and if I pull *three*
hard separate *rings,* bring the two—

*The word sticks in his throat and he has to swallow before
he can speak it.*

—*gentlemen* here at once.

PETER. Yes, sir.

Goes to the hall door.

PROFESSOR BELLIARTI, *loudly.* And tell Mrs. Greenborough we are ready.

PETER. Yes, sir.

Exits.

AURELIA, *rising.* What? Do you think I can go through their dance with those women now?

PROFESSOR BELLIARTI, *putting his arm about her.* Yes; *I ask you* to do it, dear.

AURELIA. No, no! And what for? I tell you I shan't sing to-night!

PROFESSOR BELLIARTI. Dear girl, you must! Pull yourself together, if only for *my* sake!

AURELIA. Papa, Papa! I can't. My heart is really breaking!

PROFESSOR BELLIARTI *moves the rest of the furniture out of the way so as to leave the center of the room free to the dancers.* AURELIA *leans against the piano.*

PROFESSOR BELLIARTI. Don't let him see it. Don't let these three blackguard men know how hardly you take it! Let your pride save you. Be a woman!

AURELIA. I *am* one, and that's why my heart is breaking.

PROFESSOR BELLIARTI. Be a *man* then, and don't let Jinks win!

MRS. GREENBOROUGH *and the* BALLET LADIES *come volubly through the double doors. The* BALLET LADIES *are dressed in old tights, with discarded tarlatan skirts and combing jackets; several keep on their hats, and the widow has not removed her bonnet and veil.*

MRS. GREENBOROUGH. My love, I thought you'd never send for us. Whatever in the world——

Interrupted.

PROFESSOR BELLIARTI. You stop chattering, Mrs. Gee, and get to the work at the piano. What can you play?

MRS. GREENBOROUGH, *seating herself at piano.* I know the ballet out of *Robert, the Devil.*

PROFESSOR BELLIARTI, *humming a line to see if the time is right.* That will do.

He turns to the SIXTH BALLET LADY, *the widow, who still holds her child's hand.*

Did you *have* to bring that child?

THE SIXTH BALLET LADY. Yes, sir; I couldn't leave her 'ome, sir, but she's as good as gold—never stirs a 'air nor breathes a syllabub.

She takes the child to the sofa and, lifting her up in her two hands, plumps her down into the corner hard. Here the child remains without moving or speaking. MRS. MAGGITT *kisses the child and then turns to* PROFESSOR BELLIARTI.

Please, sir, I wish as you'd taike me hout of the second row and put me in the front. I don't show at hall be'ind, and I'm a poor widow and my legs is hall I've got.

PROFESSOR BELLIARTI. You forget the old adage, Mrs. Maggitt, "Distance lends enchantment." Come now, ladies!

PROFESSOR BELLIARTI *gets his violin and bow ready. The other* BALLET LADIES *stand and loll about. The* FIRST BALLET LADY *sits comfortably in a chair. The* SECOND BALLET LADY *sits on the arm of this chair and arranges the straps of her slippers. The* THIRD BALLET LADY *leans against the wall, believing that the world is hers! The* FOURTH BALLET LADY *keeps rubbing the soles of her slippers up and down on the carpet to see that it is not too slippery. The* FIFTH BALLET LADY *fidgets with her dress and her waist, etc. The* SIXTH BALLET LADY *practices her steps, and the* SEVENTH BALLET LADY *pirouettes on one toe and throws imaginary kisses.*

THE FOURTH BALLET LADY. I wish, Miss Peddidoes, you vill nicht so push me in der waist mid your elbows so sharp!

THE FIRST BALLET LADY. If you'd keep your big feet in your own place and not keep dancing on mine there wouldn't be any trouble.

THE FOURTH BALLET LADY. Och Himmel! I dance besser as you mit your Chinese does!

THE FIRST BALLET LADY. Sauerkraut!

Sticking out her tongue at her German sister artiste.

The latter devotee of Terpsichore responds with an even more unladylike grimace. This leads to an immediate general imbroglio among all the excitable coryphees, the seven dividing themselves into rival factions. PROFESSOR BELLIARTI, *after several ineffectual efforts to make himself heard, goes in amongst them, at no little personal risk, and, aided by* MRS. GREENBOROUGH, *manages to separate the two principal somewhat draggled and highly flushed contestants.*

PROFESSOR BELLIARTI, *striking his violin with his bow.* Attention, ladies, please!

There is a general movement; those sitting rise.

Let us rehearse the *pas de rose* in the first act.

He goes to AURELIA.

Make an effort, dearie. Speak to them. Tell them what you want.

AURELIA. No! You tell them. I can't, I can't!

The BALLET LADIES *go to a large bundle of artificial roses placed on a table in the corner and each takes one.* MISS PETTITOES *snatches her flower from* MISS HOCHSPITZ'S *hand. There is an awful moment, but the widow pours oil on the waters and quiet is preserved.*

PROFESSOR BELLIARTI. An elaborate ballet in this opera has not been done in America before, and we want it to be perfect.

The BALLET LADIES *take their positions.* AURELIA *starts to leave the room.* PROFESSOR BELLIARTI *stops her.*

AURELIA. Let me go to my room.

PROFESSOR BELLIARTI. No, dearie, please, *please* stay. Don't let these women see you are in trouble. Are you ready, Mrs. Gee?

MRS. GREENBOROUGH. Good gracious, I've been——

Interrupted.

PROFESSOR BELLIARTI. Very good! Ready, please!

He and MRS. GREENBOROUGH *begin playing.*

One, two, three, etc.

Ad lib. The BALLET LADIES *begin their dance,* PROFESSOR BELLIARTI *leading and directing them, dancing with them, showing them, correcting them; after a minute he speaks aside to* AURELIA.

Try to watch them, dear.

He continues with the dance, but again, a few minutes later, he stops and speaks to her, the ballet always continuing without him.

Be brave, little girl! You have your life before you, and if the fellow's worthless, why let him spoil it?

AURELIA. That's perfectly true, only——

PROFESSOR BELLIARTI. Keep only one idea now in your mind— *your appearance tonight.*

AURELIA. I'll try, I'll try!

PROFESSOR BELLIARTI. That's my brave girl. Look at that silly creature!

Directing her attention to one of the BALLET LADIES, *he tries to excite her interest in the dancers.*

They're doing very badly. What do you think?

AURELIA, *watching them.* Oh, atrocious! They aren't ballet girls, they're tenpins!

The first movement of the ballet is finished.

PROFESSOR BELLIARTI, *urging her.* Show them! That's the only way they will learn.

AURELIA. No, I can't, not now. Who dances the solo?

PROFESSOR BELLIARTI, *to the* BALLET LADIES. The *pas seul,* please!

All but the FOURTH *and* FIRST BALLET LADIES *retire and take seats. The* FOURTH BALLET LADY *comes forward.*

No, no, Miss Hochspitz, not the next figure; the *pas seul,* Miss Pettitoes!

THE FIRST BALLET LADY *laughs.* Hochspitz doing a solo! Ha, ha! A cabbage by any other name would smell as sweet! *She gracefully kicks a satirical kiss to her with her right foot.*
"Blue Danube," please.

THE THIRD BALLET LADY, *to the* FIRST BALLET LADY. Ssh! Ssh!

PROFESSOR BELLIARTI, *who has taken the* FIRST BALLET LADY *to one side.* Dance badly, *very badly!*

THE FIRST BALLET LADY, *insulted.* Badly?

PROFESSOR BELLIARTI. Yes, it will be all right. I have a reason. *The* FIRST BALLET LADY *dances not very well.* PROFESSOR BELLIARTI *watches* AURELIA, *who remains indifferent.*

PROFESSOR BELLIARTI, *to the* FIRST BALLET LADY. That isn't bad enough—dance worse!

THE FIRST BALLET LADY, *angry.* I *can't!*

PROFESSOR BELLIARTI. Try!

THE FIRST BALLET LADY, *still dancing.* I'm afraid I'll lose my job.

PROFESSOR BELLIARTI. You will if you don't do as I ask.

THE FIRST BALLET LADY, *very angry.* Oh! All right! *She dances very badly.*

PROFESSOR BELLIARTI, *to* AURELIA. Now, do watch, dear.

AURELIA, *noticing.* But that girl's awful!

PROFESSOR BELLIARTI, *to* AURELIA. Show her.

AURELIA. No. *But she rises and pins up one side of her dress.*

PROFESSOR BELLIARTI, *to the* FIRST BALLET LADY. Go on! Worse! ! *He goes to the bell rope and pulls three distinct times. The* FIRST BALLET LADY *dances a* pas seul *vilely.*

AURELIA, *excitedly.* She's wrong! She's all wrong! ! *Pinning up the other side of her dress.*

PROFESSOR BELLIARTI, *to the* FIRST BALLET LADY. You're wrong again!

The music stops.

THE FIRST BALLET LADY. Wrong!

PROFESSOR BELLIARTI. Show her, dear, show her!

AURELIA. It's simple as daylight! Give me a rose!

Seizing her rose from MISS PETTITOES.

PROFESSOR BELLIARTI. That's right!

Striking up on his violin.

Now watch Madame Trentoni.

MRS. GREENBOROUGH *begins playing again.*

AURELIA, *dancing.* One—two—three—

PROFESSOR BELLIARTI, *always playing.* Ah, do you see the difference, Miss Pettitoes?

AURELIA, *dancing.* Not as if you were made of *wood!* Ah, Papa, I wish I were!

Stopping dancing as if she couldn't do it.

PROFESSOR BELLIARTI. Careful!

PETER *enters, showing in* GUSSIE *and* CHARLIE.

PETER. Mr. La Martine, Mr. Van Vorkenburg!

The music stops again.

AURELIA, *astonished.* What?

PROFESSOR BELLIARTI, *to* AURELIA. Your pride!

CHARLIE, *coming forward.* We have come, Madame Trentoni, to apologize.

AURELIA. Apologize? I won't listen to you!

GUSSIE. We regret very much to have made you suffer.

AURELIA. Suffer! *I suffer?*

Laughing.

What for? You surely don't suppose I take this matter of Captain Jinks seriously?

Laughing a little hysterically.

I, who have the *world* at my feet! Suffer?

With increased excitement.

Excuse me, gentlemen, but I can't have my rehearsal interrupted. Continue, Mrs. Gee. Now, ladies, please watch me!

MRS. GREENBOROUGH *plays.* AURELIA *dances with abandon.*

Smile and look happy!

She does so pathetically and then dances on with ever increasing excitement.

Dance as if you *loved* it! As if it *meant* something! Put your *whole heart* into it! If you're so lucky as to have one.

Executing a difficult movement. All clap their hands, delighted at her dancing. CHARLIE *and* GUSSIE *stand by somewhat crestfallen and look questioningly at each other. They applaud, too, and then take advantage of the moment to slip out unnoticed.*

Dance!! Don't *walk! Dance*—as if you were *mad!* Dance! Never mind if you break your neck—there are worse things to break! *Dance!!* DANCE!!!

The strain of music finishes and she stops suddenly, throwing away her rose.

Papa, *I will sing*, after all! I'll sing to every woman's heart in that house, and if ever I succeed in my life, *I'll win tonight!*

PROFESSOR BELLIARTI. Bravo! Bravo!

AURELIA *turns and sees* LA MARTINE *and* VAN VORKENBURG *are gone, and in a revulsion of feeling collapses in her old foster father's arms, sobbing out pitifully, "Oh no, I can't do it, I can't do it," as the curtain falls.*

ACT THREE

Midnight of the same day. The same room as in the previous act, MADAME TRENTONI'S *parlor in the Brevoort House. The stage is lighted by chandelier with gas jets.*

PETER, *entering with his arms full of flowers.* Come on in!

> MARY *stands at the back with her arms also full of floral emblems—a large windmill, baskets, a ship, and small bouquets.*

MARY, *who speaks with a decided English cockney accent.* Oh my! Wasn't it grand!

> *Places the windmill of pink and white dried daisies on the piano.*

I could 'ear 'em shouting way hup in the dressing room!

PETER, *who is very hoarse.* I bet they heard the gallery way over to Broadway! *I* led the gallery! And gee, I guess I broke my voice.

> *Deposits his flowers about.*

MARY, *as she arranges.* Did you see General Grant?

PETER. *Did* I? Didn't you hear us give three cheers when he come in!

> *Very huskily.*

Hip! hip! hooray! And Sam Tilden—he's another big man—he got it just as good!

> *There is a knock at the hall door.*

MARY. Come in!

> *She hangs a wreath of pansies on a doorknob and meets one of the hotel* SERVANTS, *who enters laden down with more floral emblems—small baskets with huge handles, pillows with "Welcome" on them, etc.* MARY *relieves him*

of his burden and he exits. PETER *and* MARY *arrange the new pieces around the room.*

PETER. She got piles of flowers, didn't she?

MARY. Oh, this ain't harlf!

PETER, *sitting at the piano and picking out "Captain Jinks" with one hand while he talks.* When's she coming home?

MARY, *very busy.* Soon as she can shake off her the newspaper gentlemen and a 'eap of people.

PETER. She must have been tickled to death with the send-off we give her!

MARY, *loading down the mantel.* No, something's the matter with her; you'd 'ave thought they was all a 'issing instead of shouting, she looked that mournful, and heven took hon to crying once.

PETER. Aw, go West! You don't know what you're talking about! When I went behind after the show, she was grinning fit to kill, telling them newspaper gents that it was the finest gang of folks she'd ever sung afore!

MARY. Yes, she told me when she was changing hafter the third hact that they was *dears* hin front and that she just loved them and was doing her very best.

PETER. Say, who do you think was there! I seen her down in the balcony and crying fit to bust herself all through the last ack! The old lady whot was here this afternoon! *He suddenly shouts.*

Look out!

As MARY *is about to put a large horseshoe of red immortelles with a big "Pete" in white immortelles on it off at one side of the room in an inconspicuous place.*

What yer doing with my hor'shoe?

Taking it from her.

It took my first month's wages in advance to get that!

He places it proudly on the center table and stands off and looks at it.

Ain't it a dream! Don't it look just like her!

MARY. Oh, lovely! Is heverything ready for the supper?

Going towards the double doors at the back, but PETER *gets there before her and stops her.*

PETER. Here, you can't go in! The hotel folks don't want any one in there afore her. It's all done up with regular Fourth of July decorations.

MARY. Well, there's more helegant hemblems downstairs and the 'all gentleman don't seem to be bringing 'em hup. I fancy I'd better get 'em.

And she goes out.

PETER *watches that she is surely gone, and then, opening one of the big double doors, whistles softly through his fingers and waits a second.* CAPTAIN JINKS *comes in eagerly.*

CAPTAIN JINKS. Is it safe?

PETER. Yes, for a minute; she's gone after more flower pieces. Are them yourn?

Pointing to some bouquets and baskets grouped together.

CAPTAIN JINKS. Yes.

Examining them. He adds to himself in an undertone:

And not one of my notes removed! But I saw her pick up the white camellia. She must have read that!

PETER. Mary says she didn't pay no attention to none of her flowers and even piped her eyes some!

CAPTAIN JINKS. Cried! My dear Peter, that's a good sign!

Taking out a bundle of small notes from his pocket.

If only she loves me, I'm sure I can make it all right. Come along now, quick, put one of these notes on all the other flowers.

They begin quickly pinning on notes to all the bouquets, baskets, etc.

PETER. I don't know as I ought to be helping you this way. After all, I've *only got your word for* it that you didn't really mean to try and do Madame Trentoni out of her money.

CAPTAIN JINKS. Yes, but what did I tell you my word would be worth to you?

PETER. A couple o' fivers! But it's taking fearful risks, and I ain't got her *happiness* fer sale, I want yer to understand that. But say, you didn't send her all these; here's somebody else's card.

CAPTAIN JINKS. That's all right.

Crossing to the flowers on the piano.

Leave it on, but put mine too. I want one of my notes on every single thing here!

PETER, *pinning the notes about.* Gee! You're a great writer, ain't you? Have you written all them different?

CAPTAIN JINKS. No, they're all alike.

Coming to center table he starts to pin a note on PETER's *horseshoe.*

PETER. Here! No, you don't! Look out! Not on that one! That's *mine!* I ain't goin' to hev no interference with *mine!*

CAPTAIN JINKS. Oh, come on, yours might be the only one she looked at! Let me put on my note, and I'll pay for the horseshoe.

PETER. But you won't pretend *you sent it?* Honest Injun?

CAPTAIN JINKS. Honest!

PETER. All right, anything to oblige a friend; it'll be five dollars, please.

MARY's *voice is heard outside, saying:* "This way. Come straight along. Oh! I dropped a bouquet; beg pardon." PETER *and* CAPTAIN JINKS *have stopped and* CAPTAIN JINKS *goes to the double doors quickly.*

CAPTAIN JINKS. Don't forget, you're to manage somehow that I get an interview with Mrs. Greenborough. No interview —no pay.

PETER. That's all right! You just trust yourself to little brother.

CAPTAIN JINKS, *thrusting a handful of notes into* PETER's *hands.* Try and get those on the rest of the flowers.

He exits.

PETER, *calling after him.* Quick! Hide in the further room, they may go in this one.

He shuts the doors as MARY *enters loaded down with more flowers and followed by* MRS. STONINGTON *and* MISS MERRIAM *without their hats and with a flower in their hair, the waist of* MRS. STONINGTON's *dress turned in a trifle at the neck.*

MARY. Won't you sit down, please? The hother guests will suttingly be 'ere soon.

MARY *places about the flowers she has just brought up.* PETER *continues pinning on the notes.*

MRS. STONINGTON. It was very kind of Madame Trentoni to ask us to supper on such an occasion. She is the greatest singer I've ever heard.

Turns to MISS MERRIAM *and repeats with most careful enunciation.*

An elegant singer!

MISS MERRIAM *smiles and nods and makes a few rapid motions with her fingers.*

MRS. STONINGTON. Oh yes, very hot! Where we sat—we were in the back row, gallery; we found it very difficult to get seats.

MARY *is about to pass her with a small basket of flowers with a very high handle on which is perched a stuffed pigeon with outstretched wings.* MRS. STONINGTON *stops* MARY.

The dove!

She examines the card, which is tied on with a blue ribbon, and then nods to MISS MERRIAM.

Yes, *our* emblem!

MARY. I never 'eard madam sing *Traviatter* so magnificent before!

She crosses to the piano with the emblem.

MISS MERRIAM *motions again a few words to* MRS. STONINGTON.

MRS. STONINGTON. *No indeed!* I didn't see a single bad thing in it!

MISS MERRIAM *motions again.*

No, sir, not a blessed thing! I agree with you to an iota; I think it's a sweetly pretty opera!

MISS MERRIAM *makes a few more rapid passes.*

Exactly! Neither did I understand what it was about, but nobody has any need to; it's enough to hear her voice and see her clothes!

MISS MERRIAM *motions.*

My dear, you never spoke a truer word! You can find a bad meaning in most everything in this world if you want to and only try hard enough.

MRS. GREENBOROUGH *calls outside in the hall.* Mary!

MARY. Yes, madam.

Going to the hall door she opens it.

MRS. STONINGTON. Here's dear Mrs. Greenborough! And she does look sweetly pretty tonight!

MRS. GREENBOROUGH *enters, both arms full of floral trophies.*

MRS. GREENBOROUGH. What an elegant triumph, Mary! Did you *ever* in all the days you've been with Madame Trentoni—

Interrupted.

MARY. No, indeed, ma'am.

Helping MRS. GREENBOROUGH *relieve herself of the flowers.*

I *never* 'eard such a grand reception!

PETER, *who is pinning notes on bouquets in a corner.* Bet your life! you couldn't beat our gallery!

He begins to pin CAPTAIN JINKS'S *notes to the flowers* MRS. GREENBOROUGH *has just brought in.*

MRS. STONINGTON. Good evening, Mrs. Greenborough.

MRS. GREENBOROUGH, *turning*. Oh! You are *here*, my dears; excuse me, I didn't see you!

Kissing them both.

Well, what do you think? Did you ever in your life! Wasn't I right or did I——

Interrupted.

MRS. STONINGTON. No siree, you didn't exaggerate one bit! We are going to make a report to the League that her voice is superb.

MISS MERRIAM *tugs at her elbow.* MRS. STONINGTON *turns.* MISS MERRIAM *makes a few motions.*

MRS. STONINGTON, *to* MISS MERRIAM. Yes, dear.

To MRS. GREENBOROUGH.

We're going to add to our report that *anyone* can go, because no one understands what it's about unless they have an evil mind.

MRS. GREENBOROUGH. Oh, my darlings, I'm so glad you think so; you remember what I told you, what I always said was——

Interrupted.

MRS. STONINGTON. Yes indeed, we've been saying it over to ourselves! And do tell me if I've got the neck of my basque too low? I've turned in *three* buttons! I wanted to be real dressy, but I don't want to catch cold. I wouldn't let Miss Merriam turn hers in, she's so delicate! I told her she'd look very stylish in her black silk if she'd put on that pretty bib of hers.

MRS. GREENBOROUGH. You both look very fetching, but I must ask you to come into another room to wait, if you don't mind. Aurelia sent me home first to see that the guests didn't assemble here. We've taken a little parlor on the other side of the banquet room. She's all upset, poor child, unstrung! Come this way.

Leading them to the double doors. PETER *gets there first and takes* MRS. GREENBOROUGH'S *arm and whispers into her ear.*

MRS. STONINGTON *and* MISS MERRIAM *are trying to read the cards on the different bouquets, etc.*

MRS. GREENBOROUGH, *surprised at what* PETER *tells her.* What! PETER *nods his head violently.*

You little scamp! You ought to be spanked, and I'd like to do it.

PETER. Oh, would you! I guess you'd have your hands full! Let Miss Mary take them through the other way.

Motioning to the hall door.

MRS. GREENBOROUGH *gives* PETER *a speaking look and then turns.*

MRS. GREENBOROUGH. Ladies—Mary will show you into the room through the hall. I will join you presently.

MARY *goes to the door.* MISS MERRIAM *starts quickly to follow her.*

MRS. STONINGTON. Sophie! Sophie!

MISS MERRIAM *of course does not hear her and goes on.* MRS. STONINGTON *runs after her and catches her at the door. She motions to her to wait.* MRS. STONINGTON *then goes to* MRS. GREENBOROUGH *and whispers to her questioningly.*

MRS. GREENBOROUGH. I'll ask her!

MRS. STONINGTON. And do you think she *will?*

MRS. GREENBOROUGH. Yes, she's willing to do just *anything* for friends of mine, no matter *what* it is!

MRS. STONINGTON *hurries to* MISS MERRIAM *and says delightedly with very careful enunciation.* She thinks we *can* kiss her.

MISS MERRIAM *claps her hands with joy, her face wreathed in smiles, as she and* MRS. STONINGTON *follow* MARY *out into the hall.*

MRS. GREENBOROUGH, *turning upon* PETER. You naughty little boy, you! Why did you let Captain Jinks in there?

PETER. 'Cause he has my sympathies. You don't know all, but *I* do. He went to jail for her sake, and no hero ever done better'n that fur his girl, not even in The Fireside Companion!

MRS. GREENBOROUGH. You're out of your head!

PETER. No, I ain't.

Opening one of the double doors he whistles.

Wait and see!

CAPTAIN JINKS *comes in.*

MRS. GREENBOROUGH. Well, sir, I must say——

Interrupted.

CAPTAIN JINKS. Don't! Don't say it! We haven't much time! Persuade Madame Trentoni to see me.

MRS. GREENBOROUGH. Papa Belliarti has told me what you did——

Interrupted.

CAPTAIN JINKS. If I could see her I could explain.

MRS. GREENBOROUGH. I don't think explaining could do us much good!

CAPTAIN JINKS. Yes, it would, if she loves me.

MRS. GREENBOROUGH. *Loves you? Now!* After that scandalous wager?

CAPTAIN JINKS. Well, then, if she *ever* loved me, if she *ever* loved me—I'm sure I can persuade her.

MRS. GREENBOROUGH. I don't mind telling you, young man, that she *did* love you, that's the blessed truth! If you could have heard her talk in her sleep as *I* have! Why, only the other afternoon——

Interrupted.

CAPTAIN JINKS. She *did* love me?

MRS. GREENBOROUGH. Yes, she did. I don't see any harm in telling that——

Interrupted.

CAPTAIN JINKS *suddenly in outburst of joy hugs* MRS. GREEN-
BOROUGH *and kisses her.* God bless you, Mrs. Gee! God
bless you for that!

PETER *half enters hurriedly.*

PETER. Psst!

He sees them embracing.

Hully Gee!

They separate.

Say, *which one* is it you're after?

Laughing.

CAPTAIN JINKS, *laughing.* Shut up, Peter!

PETER. Well, you'd better get—— She's coming.

MRS. GREENBOROUGH. Oh, *do* go! She's in an awful hysterical
state. No, not that way!

CAPTAIN JINKS, *at the double doors.* Yes, I shall wait here till
you bring me word she *will* see me. She *must* see me!
Yes, tonight!

MRS. GREENBOROUGH. *No; tomorrow!*

CAPTAIN JINKS. No; *tonight!*

He exits.

MRS. GREENBOROUGH, *to* PETER. Take him through into the
parlor where the other guests are assembling; don't let
him stay in there.

Pushing PETER *out after* CAPTAIN JINKS.

Oh dear me, sirs, what am I to do?

PROFESSOR BELLIARTI *comes in, and* AURELIA *follows. She
is gowned in a billowy mass of white tarlatan, showered
over with pink rosebuds, and emphasized here and there
with bright green ribbon. Her bustle and train crowd the
furniture in the room. A wreath of pink rosebuds is on her
head. She carries a cloak and a white lace scarf in her
hands and a bouquet; she throws them away from her
anywhere.* MRS. GREENBOROUGH *runs after her and picks
them up.*

PROFESSOR BELLIARTI. For just five minutes, Aurelia, come, please!

AURELIA, *with determination.* No, Papa, I cannot.

PROFESSOR BELLIARTI, *to* MRS. GREENBOROUGH. I want her to be present at her supper.

AURELIA. You can make any excuse for me you like!

PROFESSOR BELLIARTI. But—my dear child——

AURELIA. I mean it, Papa. I've sung tonight for your sake more than anything else, but I can't do anything more, and it's the last time I'll do that.

MRS. GREENBOROUGH. Aurelia! When you never had so great a triumph!

AURELIA. Triumph? Triumph? Over a few people!

PROFESSOR BELLIARTI. *Few* people! Many *hundreds!*

AURELIA. *Hundreds* then! And what do I care? The only triumph I want is denied me, the *triumph of love!* Oh, Papa, you can't understand how I feel—you're only a *man!* You say the people tonight stood up and shouted themselves hoarse! Did they? I heard nothing but the beating of my poor heart. You say I have been deluged with gifts of flowers, but the only gift I want is missing—one man's honest love! *With that,* tonight *would have been* a triumph! I would have given him my success as my first gift, but without his love it all means nothing. I don't want success! I don't want anything——

MRS. GREENBOROUGH. Not even any supper?

AURELIA. No, no, ask them to excuse me.

She sinks on the piano stool and buries her face in her arms and cries. A brass band strikes up loudly outside the window, "Hail! the Conquering Hero Comes," and at the same moment PETER *rushes in.*

PETER. Hurrah! There's a big band come to serenade Madame Trentoni. You must go to the window.

He runs out.

PROFESSOR BELLIARTI *opens a window. Loud cries come from the outside—"Trentoni!" "Trentoni!"*

MRS. GREENBOROUGH, *in great excitement*. Oh! isn't it beautiful!

PROFESSOR BELLIARTI, *to* AURELIA. Come, dear. Come and bow to them.

AURELIA, *sobbing*. I can't! I can't!

PROFESSOR BELLIARTI. You must! It will anger them.

MRS. GREENBOROUGH. Oh goodness! You mustn't do that, Aurelia!

PROFESSOR BELLIARTI. Nurse your success; it will mean everything.

AURELIA. No.

Louder cries again of "Aurelia!" "Aurelia!" and "Trentoni!" and wilder shouts still outside. PETER *again runs in.*

PETER. Quick, *please!* Bow at the window! They're beginning to get mad!

Again he runs out shouting.

PROFESSOR BELLIARTI. Come! Come to the window!

A few "baas" and hisses are heard; then the shouts and the band stop.

AURELIA. No! No!

PROFESSOR BELLIARTI. Mrs. Gee! Quick, put Aurelia's scarf on your head!

She does so.

You must take her place.

MRS. GREENBOROUGH. But do you think we look anything alike?

PROFESSOR BELLIARTI. Never mind, it's dark, they can't distinguish anything! Come on!

Taking her to the window.

Bow to them and wave!

She does so.

That's it! Again!

Great shouts and hurrahs. Cries of "Trentoni forever!"
"God bless you, Aurelia!" etc. The band plays "The Star-
Spangled Banner." AURELIA *begins to listen and show*
some interest.

PROFESSOR BELLIARTI. Throw them kisses.

MRS. GREENBOROUGH *does so. Increased shouts and cries of*
"Speech!" "Speech!"

MRS. GREENBOROUGH, *laughing excitedly.* Oh good gracious!
What'll I do now?

PROFESSOR BELLIARTI. Speak! Say something!

AURELIA, *quickly.* No! Come away from the window—I'll
speak to them.

MRS. GREENBOROUGH *has come away. When she leaves the*
window the clamor outside hushes disappointedly. AU-
RELIA *takes the lace scarf and goes to the window, really*
moved, and speaks.

How good of them! This morning how I should have
loved this!

She reaches the window, and the applause and shouts
double, with louder cries of "Speech," and the band stops.

Thank you!

Hurrahs and bravos very loud outside.

Thank you all!

More shouts and greater applause.

Thank you!

She throws kisses with both hands and adds in an excited
outburst:

You're *darlings,* every one of you!

Tremendous cheers as she leaves the window, and the
brass band strikes up "Champagne Charlie." It dies away
with the shouts of the crowd outside, as they gradually
disperse. AURELIA *has gone from the window to the piano*
and takes up a note there on the flowers. She reads it.

"I must see you! There has been a terrible mistake. If you ever loved me give me an interview."

PROFESSOR BELLIARTI, *who has followed her, speaks softly over her shoulder.* Don't trust him.

AURELIA *continues reading the other notes and shows on her face her surprise at finding them all the same.*

MRS. GREENBOROUGH. Papa, you go to our guests, and I'll speak to Aurelia.

PROFESSOR BELLIARTI. No, *you* go; I have something to say to her.

AURELIA *still reads the notes.* I must see you! There is a terrible mistake! If ever you loved me——

MRS. GREENBOROUGH *goes out through the double doors.* PETER *comes in after knocking.*

PETER. Say! General Sherman's just come, and they all want to know where Madame Trentoni is.

PROFESSOR BELLIARTI. Mrs. Greenborough has gone to them.

PETER. Hurry up! They're getting mad, and one of them ballet girls—the widder—is hooking oranges from off the table. She says it's for the kid!
He exits.

AURELIA. But these notes are all the same!
Looking quickly at another.
The same!

PROFESSOR BELLIARTI, *reading one on the center table.* The same! Here, dear, don't read them.
Gathering several unread notes into his hands and crushing them.

AURELIA. No! No! Papa!
Taking them out of his hands.
Be careful! I *want* to *read* them—every one!
A knock is heard on the hall door.

PROFESSOR BELLIARTI. Come in.

AURELIA. Please! I don't want to see anyone.

The FOURTH BALLET LADY—MISS HOCHSPITZ—*enters, followed by all the other* BALLET LADIES, *who group themselves in a semicircle behind her.*

THE FOURTH BALLET LADY. Pardong! I haf com mit ein kleine message from der ballet laties.

With a curtsy.

PROFESSOR BELLIARTI. Madame Trentoni is very ill. Worn out with the excitement of her debut.

THE FOURTH BALLET LADY. Yah! Das is vat de old woman dold us, und ve vas all so traublich. I rebresend de 'ole ballet laties ven I com und says dat ve all gif to Madame Drendoni our loaf und say vat she vas vunderschone, und der pest singer vat ve has effer tanced mit!

Curtsies and kisses AURELIA's *hand.*

All the BALLET LADIES *clap their hands and cry "Hear! Hear!"*

AURELIA. Thank you very much, and all the ladies! I'm sure you all danced very well, too.

THE FOURTH BALLET LADY. Ve haf madt besser mit our feets ven you haf made so goot mit your mouth!

AURELIA. Thank you again, and I hope you will all enjoy your supper.

THE FOURTH BALLET LADY. Ve vill *eat—*

The widow here inadvertently claps.

—aber not so much ven you vas nicht mit der party. Dis wreat vas made py our own hands just now mit schnips from oud of our own bouquets—

Giving wreath.

—vat vas gif us py our *sveethearts!*

AURELIA. Thank you.

THE FOURTH BALLET LADY. Gude nacht! Ve vill all pet our toes you vas de greadest success effer vas! *Gude nacht! They all curtsy and turn to go out through the double doors at the back. As they exit,* PETTITOES *and* HOCHSPITZ *embrace, in an excess of good feeling.*

PROFESSOR BELLIARTI. Good night.

Closing the door behind them.

AURELIA. You go to the supper, too, dear Papa.

PROFESSOR BELLIARTI. No, dearie, I can't leave you.

A knock on the hall door.

AURELIA, *again bright and hopeful.* Maybe that's *he.* Come in.

PETER *enters.*

PETER. This came for you this evening from the Everett House.

Giving AURELIA *an envelope.*

AURELIA. Thank you.

PETER, *to* PROFESSOR BELLIARTI. Did you see my hor'shoe? I tell yer!

He exits haughtily.

PROFESSOR BELLIARTI. What is that?

AURELIA. Two tickets for the vessel that sails tomorrow for Liverpool.

PROFESSOR BELLIARTI. Where did you get them?

AURELIA. I sent for them between the acts—for Mary and me.

PROFESSOR BELLIARTI, *sternly.* Give me those tickets!

AURELIA. No!

PROFESSOR BELLIARTI, *determined.* I've never coerced you in your life. Have I, dear?

AURELIA, *as determined.* No, and I have never disobeyed you, have I?

PROFESSOR BELLIARTI. No, and you will not go away tomorrow.

AURELIA. This time if *you* coerce, *I* disobey.

PROFESSOR BELLIARTI. You *can't* go away! What about Mr. Mapleson?

AURELIA. He can send for Adelina Patti! She made a furor here a year or so ago.

PROFESSOR BELLIARTI. Adelina Patti isn't *you.*

AURELIA. Oh well, she's as young as I and a better singer—if the truth's told.

PROFESSOR BELLIARTI. But your contract?

AURELIA. Oh, *hang* my contract!

PROFESSOR BELLIARTI. We can't! It'll hang us! Give me those tickets.

AURELIA, *holding them up in front of his face.* In exchange for Captain Jinks—for nothing else.

PROFESSOR BELLIARTI. Won't you realize he is unworthy of you?

AURELIA. *He* said so and I wouldn't believe it, and I shan't believe it when *you* say so, either.

PROFESSOR BELLIARTI. Well, we'll go to supper now—we'll talk it over later.

AURELIA. No, I must pack with Mary; we haven't much time.

PROFESSOR BELLIARTI. No; come with me now—you *must.*

AURELIA. I *won't!* There!

Taking off one of her long curls that hang from the back of her "waterfall."

And there!

Taking off the other curl and placing both upon the piano.

Now will you believe me?

A knock on the hall door.

Oh! perhaps that's *he!* Wait a minute, Papa! Don't say "come in" yet!

And she quickly puts back both curls.

Now! Come in!

Pathetically.

The POLICEMAN, *remembered in Act One, enters with much assurance.*

THE POLICEMAN. Beg pardon, ma'am, but is Captain Jinks here?

AURELIA *echoes, surprised.* Captain Jinks!

PROFESSOR BELLIARTI. Certainly not!

THE POLICEMAN. Well, he was seen coming into the hotel not so long since, and I thought maybe as he was one of the invites at your party——

PROFESSOR BELLIARTI. I can assure you that the apartment of Madame Trentoni is the last place you would find Captain Jinks—that gentleman is no longer our friend.

THE POLICEMAN. Don't say! Well, he's skipped his bail this afternoon which your Mr. Mapleson put up for him, and he's wanted by the police.

AURELIA, *faintly, in astonishment and distress.* The police?

PROFESSOR BELLIARTI. Why did Mr. Mapleson go bail for him?

THE POLICEMAN. Give it up! Echo answers why!

PROFESSOR BELLIARTI. I mean—what's he done? Why——

AURELIA *stops* PROFESSOR BELLIARTI. Papa! That's not our affair. We have no interest in Captain Jinks's *misdeeds!* *She turns to the* POLICEMAN.
Good night, sir.

THE POLICEMAN, *going, slightly embarrassed.* Good night, ma'am.
He comes back, becoming more and more embarrassed, however.
Beg pardon, ma'am, I was in the lobby of the Academy tonight, trying to keep the aisles free, and had to give it up as a bad job! But even with the doors shut I could hear you—some of them high notes of yourn came clean through the wood! It was *grand!* They fairly put my teeth on edge! The best I ever heard!

AURELIA, *half smiling*. Thank you.

Shakes his hand, which makes him very proud.

THE POLICEMAN. Thank you. Good night, ma'am—good night, sir!

Bows, and exits.

AURELIA and PROFESSOR BELLIARTI look at each other a second in silence.

PROFESSOR BELLIARTI. Now you understand Mapleson's knowledge—and you *have* had an escape, my dear.

AURELIA. I don't believe—not even yet. I don't *want* to escape!

MRS. GREENBOROUGH *returns.*

MRS. GREENBOROUGH. Everybody's arrived, dear heart, so I thought it best for us to come into the supper room and begin. I hope I haven't gone and——

Interrupted.

PROFESSOR BELLIARTI. You haven't. You did quite right, Mrs. Gee!

MRS. GREENBOROUGH. Aurelia *won't* come?

PROFESSOR BELLIARTI. No. But I'll start things going.

They go to the double doors and MRS. GREENBOROUGH exits. PROFESSOR BELLIARTI, about to follow, changes his mind and, closing the door, goes back to AURELIA. As MRS. GREENBOROUGH exits, the guests in the back room begin to sing "Auld Lang Syne," which is heard more faintly when the door is closed. AURELIA sits on the piano stool, her head and arms on the piano.

PROFESSOR BELLIARTI *leans over her and speaks softly*. Shall I make a little speech for you, dearie, and say you thank them all and want them to have a happy evening?

AURELIA, who cannot speak because of her tears, lifts her head and nods "Yes." PROFESSOR BELLIARTI goes into the back room and the singing is louder as the door opens— till it is shut. AURELIA, when she realizes she is alone, takes from the bosom of her dress a white camellia to which is attached a note, which she reads aloud in a pathetic little voice, half crying all through and breaking down entirely at the end.

AURELIA. "I must see you—there is a terrible mistake—if you ever loved me, give me an interview——"

She cries softly, leaning her head and arms on the piano. She then rises, deliberately, and pulls the bell cord.

I'll see him myself. He hasn't had any chance to explain and I'll give it to him—but I won't make it easy!

PETER *enters in answer to the bell.*

PETER. Yes, ma'am?

AURELIA. Peter, do you want to do me a favor?

PETER. Oh! Bet your life.

AURELIA. I'll pay you well.

PETER. No, you *won't!* Not from *you.* Not *this* boy!

AURELIA. I'm afraid it'll be hard for you, but do you think you *could* find Captain Jinks *somewhere* tonight and bring him here—without telling anyone?

PETER, *secretly amused.* Well—I might *try*—if you don't mind waiting! Of course, if he's way over to Brooklyn——

AURELIA. I *won't* mind waiting if you'll only *find* him!

PETER. I guess I'll tell you the truth!

Delighted.

He's right *here!*

AURELIA. *Here?*

PETER. Yes, ma'am! He's been in this room. He and I put all them notes on!

AURELIA. You did! You brought him here? You're a dear boy!

She kisses his cheek. PETER, *overcome with joy, pride, and emotion, holds his hand to his cheek.*

PETER. *Oh! Gee!* Thank you! I'll *never wash* that spot!

AURELIA. Now listen! Don't let Captain Jinks know I sent you for him! Pretend I don't know he's here and just send him in.

PETER. It won't take much *sending*. It's been all I could do to keep him out!

He exits.

AURELIA. Of course he can explain! I knew it, and he's only been waiting for his chance.

Tears up the steamer tickets.

But he's got to work for it; he must be punished a little for—something or other! I'm sure I must look a fright, after all I've gone through.

Standing on the sofa she looks at herself in the glass over the mantel.

I'll just put a little dab of powder on——

She hurries out through the door to her bedroom as PETER *shows in* CAPTAIN JINKS.

CAPTAIN JINKS. She's not here!

PETER. Oh, I guess she has gone to her room to prink up a little!

CAPTAIN JINKS. For her guests at supper?

PETER. No, she won't join them—it's for *you*.

CAPTAIN JINKS. But she doesn't expect to see me, does she?

PETER. Look here, all's fair in love and war! Guess I'll tell you the truth—*she* sent me after you!

CAPTAIN JINKS, *not daring to believe his ears.* What!

PETER, *laughing.* She told me to try hard to find you; but don't tell—she said to keep mum!

CAPTAIN JINKS. Peter, you're an ideal boy—here's a dollar for you!

Gives him a bill.

PETER. Thank you!

Exits.

The guests are heard through the double doors singing "Champagne Charlie." AURELIA *re-enters.*

AURELIA, *stopping short in an only partially successful effort to simulate surprise.* Captain Jinks!

CAPTAIN JINKS. Madame!

AURELIA. How dared you come here? Had you sent your card I should have refused to see you!
With great but not altogether convincing hauteur.

CAPTAIN JINKS. And had you sent for me I should have refused to come!

AURELIA. *I send* for you! Impossible!

CAPTAIN JINKS. At any rate, here I am, and you won't get rid of me until I've straightened everything out. Ever since I left your room this afternoon I've been searching my brain and scouring the town for proof to show that I have done nothing dishonorable to you; to prove myself worthy at least of your—*respect.*

AURELIA. I do not ask for proofs, but I fear the *police* are not so lenient as a woman.

CAPTAIN JINKS, *surprised. The police!*

AURELIA. Yes, the police! They've been here looking for you.

CAPTAIN JINKS. By George, I forgot! At two o'clock I was due. I'll tell you why the police want me——

AURELIA, *interrupting.* Thank you, I don't care to know.

CAPTAIN JINKS. Is that honest?

AURELIA, *melting a little.* No, it's *not* honest. Of course, I'm dying to know!

CAPTAIN JINKS. The day you landed I gave the inspector a little bill to go easy with your trunks, and he gave *me* in charge—that's all! Can't you forgive me if at two o'clock I thought of nothing except that I had lost your love?

AURELIA. Yes, I think I can forgive that——
A knock on the hall door.

CAPTAIN JINKS. Please don't answer it.

AURELIA. Come in!
PETER *backs into the room.*

CAPTAIN JINKS, *to* PETER. What are you doing? Turn around!

PETER, *turning*. That's what I call having tack!

> *To* AURELIA.

> Them same two lardy-dahs—are you out as usual?

CAPTAIN JINKS. No. In!

AURELIA. Out!

CAPTAIN JINKS. In!

AURELIA, *half angry and half amused at his audacity*. How dare you? Out!

CAPTAIN JINKS. In!

PETER. Yes, sir.

CAPTAIN JINKS. Show them up.

PETER. Yes, sir.

> *He exits.*

CAPTAIN JINKS. *I sent* for La Martine and Van Vorkenburg in your name.

AURELIA. *My name?* How dared you!

CAPTAIN JINKS. Oh, it did take a little pluck, but I've so much at stake I must try everything to win.

> *A knock on the hall door.*

CAPTAIN JINKS. Come in.

> CHARLIE *and* GUSSIE *enter.*

CHARLIE. You sent for us, Madame Trentoni?

AURELIA. I did *not!* I wonder at your presumption in appearing here!

CHARLIE. No more presumption in *us* than in Jinks!

CAPTAIN JINKS. It was *I* who sent for you to come in Madame Trentoni's name.

CHARLIE. What in—what did you do that for?

CAPTAIN JINKS. Because it would be no use explaining about the cursed agreement and denying things behind your backs. I must do it before your faces and in her presence. I'm not afraid and not ashamed, because I will speak the truth!

CHARLIE. Good!

CAPTAIN JINKS. And I'm going to trust *you* to say what is *true*. I won't believe you two men would be willing to *lie* away the happiness and honor of anyone, let alone an old friend.

CHARLIE. Certainly not.

CAPTAIN JINKS. You'll tell the truth about the wager affair?

CHARLIE. Of course.

CAPTAIN JINKS. And you, Gus?

GUSSIE. Why—yes.

CAPTAIN JINKS. This bet then—did we make it *before we saw her*?

CHARLIE. I don't remember.

CAPTAIN JINKS. And didn't I repudiate it the minute I had seen this lady as an insult to her?

CHARLIE. No!

CAPTAIN JINKS. *What!*

CHARLIE. *No!*

CAPTAIN JINKS. Good evening. That's all I want out of you!

CHARLIE. What do you mean?

CAPTAIN JINKS *calls.* Peter!
    PETER *enters and stands by the door.*

PETER. Yes, sir?

CAPTAIN JINKS. Show this gentleman out!

CHARLIE. Look here!

CAPTAIN JINKS, *interrupting strongly. Out!*

    CHARLIE *sneers and snaps open his crush hat into* CAPTAIN
    JINKS'S *face and exits, bowed out by* PETER.

CAPTAIN JINKS. Now, Gussie, what do you say? Wasn't that bet made before we'd seen Madame Trentoni?

GUSSIE. No!

CAPTAIN JINKS *calls.* Peter!

PETER, *by the door.* Yes, sir?

CAPTAIN JINKS, *to* GUSSIE. Good night! Quick, Peter, this gentleman's in a hurry!

GUSSIE seizes a large bouquet which lies on the table and smashes it on the floor and then exits, followed out by PETER.

CAPTAIN JINKS. Jackasses! I sent for my friends hoping they would speak the truth and exonerate me. Now I must do without them. I did make that bet, but before I saw you.

AURELIA. But you *did make* the bet?

CAPTAIN JINKS. But before I'd seen you. *Before I'd seen you!* And then only as a joke. I've won your love honestly and I don't mean to lose it. I've waited until this evening should be over and your triumph won. The evening is over and your triumph is won! I've allowed Papa Belliarti to blackguard me, the old lady to flout me, *but now it's my turn, and you've got to believe in me!* I won't leave you till you do.

AURELIA, *reading his true nature in his face and convinced by his manly sincerity, begins to decidedly relent.* What was the old bet, anyway?

CAPTAIN JINKS. That I would get up a flirtation with you.

AURELIA. A flirtation? Is that all? But your friends said——

CAPTAIN JINKS. Oh, well, you know one's *friends* will say anything, and *such friends!*

AURELIA. And there was nothing about marriage in the bet?

CAPTAIN JINKS. No, nothing so serious as that, and I withdrew the foolish wager as soon as I had seen you.

AURELIA. Did I look so unpromising as all that?

CAPTAIN JINKS. And you meant it this morning when you told me you loved me; didn't you?

AURELIA, *softly*. Yes.

CAPTAIN JINKS. On my soul, you can trust me with your happiness. Forgive me! You *must* forgive me and *believe* in me.

AURELIA. Is that all?

CAPTAIN JINKS. No! And *love* me!

AURELIA. Oh!

CAPTAIN JINKS. Say it!

AURELIA. I forgive you, I believe in you, and——
She hesitates.

CAPTAIN JINKS. And——

AURELIA. And—I——

A knock at the door and the POLICEMAN *enters suddenly.*

THE POLICEMAN. Ah, ha! *There you are!*
He stands and looks at CAPTAIN JINKS *triumphantly.*
Great consternation on the part of AURELIA *and* CAPTAIN JINKS.

THE POLICEMAN. I thought I'd catch you near the singing bird's cage!

AURELIA. No, no!
Going to the POLICEMAN.
Mr. Policeman—Captain Jinks *isn't here!*

THE POLICEMAN. Oh, isn't he, ma'am?

AURELIA, *very persuasively. No! You* don't see him!

THE POLICEMAN, *laughing.* Oh, don't I?

AURELIA. Couldn't you be just a *little nearsighted*, just to please *me?*

THE POLICEMAN. Couldn't be stone blind, ma'am! Wouldn't be right.

CAPTAIN JINKS. I give you my word of honor I will appear in court the first thing tomorrow.

AURELIA. And I'll give you *my* word of honor, too. Now you *don't* see him here, *do you?*

THE POLICEMAN. Meaning no disrespect to you, lady, I can't take his word for it. He skipped his bail!

AURELIA. But *my* word?

THE POLICEMAN. Sorry, but we learned a passage to Europe was taken in *your name tonight.* Now you're singing here all winter and have made a P. T. Barnum success, so that there passage can't be for *you,* and we've pretty well twigged to the little game!

AURELIA. Good gracious, what an idea!

To CAPTAIN JINKS.

Look here, let's tell him the truth!

CAPTAIN JINKS, *embarrassed.* What?

AURELIA, *also embarrassed.* Why—that I—that you——

CAPTAIN JINKS, *crossing to the* POLICEMAN, *speaks desperately.* I'm head over heels in love with her, officer, and that doesn't half express it——

AURELIA, *quickly following* CAPTAIN JINKS *and taking his arm.* And we had a quarrel this noon!

CAPTAIN JINKS, *quickly.* I thought I'd lost her, and it drove everything else out of my mind!

AURELIA, *quickly.* And I felt so beastly I took that passage and was going to sail tomorrow!

CAPTAIN JINKS. Do you believe us?

THE POLICEMAN. I'm thinking——

CAPTAIN JINKS. Sh—he's thinking!

AURELIA. We've made it all up now, and we're going in there *where Mapleson* is.

Pointing to the back room.

CAPTAIN JINKS. And if I'm with *him,* surely you can trust me!

AURELIA. And you have his word of honor.

> *To* CAPTAIN JINKS.

> Give him your hand.

> CAPTAIN JINKS *does so.*

CAPTAIN JINKS. And *her* word of honor!

AURELIA. Yes, sir!

> *Putting her hand on* CAPTAIN JINKS'S *and the* POLICEMAN'S. *The* POLICEMAN *is very much embarrassed. They all separate.*

> *Do you see Captain Jinks* NOW?

THE POLICEMAN, *after a look all about the room.* Not a sign of him!

AURELIA. Oh, you darling!

> *Seizing* PETER'S *large horseshoe, she loads his arms with it, and he hurries out. She starts to go to* CAPTAIN JINKS, *but* PROFESSOR BELLIARTI *enters from the back room. She rushes to her foster father and embraces him.*

> Those two men *lied* to you! You *must* believe in him—*I do!*

> PROFESSOR BELLIARTI *comes slowly down the room.*

CAPTAIN JINKS. I made no bet about marrying Madame Trentoni, sir. I did make a foolish wager before seeing her that I would flirt with her. After meeting your foster daughter on the dock I realized the unworthiness of our wager, and I drew up that I O U to pay up as if I'd lost, so we might call it all off. *She's* forgiven me, *won't* you?

> PROFESSOR BELLIARTI *looks him searchingly straight in the eyes.*

CAPTAIN JINKS, *hesitatingly—offering his cigar case.* Have a cigar, sir?

> PROFESSOR BELLIARTI *looks from one to the other, then takes a cigar graciously and gives* CAPTAIN JINKS *his hand.*

PROFESSOR BELLIARTI. Thank you! And I do gladly take that "blackguard" back!

AURELIA *starts to embrace him; he eludes her embrace,
leaving* CAPTAIN JINKS'S *arms to enfold her.*

PROFESSOR BELLIARTI, *opening the double doors at back.*
Ladies and gentlemen, the health and happiness of Captain Jinks and his promised bride.

As PROFESSOR BELLIARTI *gives the toast, all cry "Hooray!"
and at the same moment* PETER *rushes in with his clothes
half torn off his back but with his horseshoe in his arms.*

PETER. No, he didn't! Not my hor'shoe!

*And as all the guests, having drunk the toast, begin to
sing "Captain Jinks of the Horse Marines,"* AURELIA, *happy
and proud on* CAPTAIN JINKS'S *arm, goes to join her friends,
and the curtain falls.*

THE NEW YORK IDEA

*A Comedy
in Four Acts*

by

LANGDON MITCHELL

CAST OF CHARACTERS

PHILIP PHILLIMORE

MRS. PHILLIMORE, his mother

THE REVEREND MATTHEW PHILLIMORE, his brother

GRACE PHILLIMORE, his sister

MISS HENEAGE, his aunt

WILLIAM SUDLEY, his cousin

MRS. VIDA PHILLIMORE, his divorced wife

BROOKS, her footman

BENSON, her maid

SIR WILFRID CATES-DARBY

JOHN KARSLAKE

MRS. CYNTHIA KARSLAKE, his divorced wife

NOGAM, his valet

TIM FIDDLER

THOMAS, the PHILLIMORES' family servant

Scene—New York   Time—The Present

ACT ONE

SCENE.—*Living room in the house of* PHILIP PHILLIMORE.
*Five o'clock of an afternoon of May. The general air and
appearance of the room is that of an old-fashioned,
decorous, comfortable interior. There are no electric lights
and no electric bells. Two bell ropes as in old-fashioned
houses. The room is in dark tones inclining to somber and
of old-fashioned elegance.*

The curtain rises, disclosing MISS HENEAGE, MRS. PHILLI-
MORE *and* THOMAS. MISS HENEAGE *is a solidly built, nar-
row-minded woman in her sixties. She makes no effort to
look younger than she is, and is expensively but quietly
dressed, with heavy elegance. She commands her house-
hold and her family connection, and on the strength of
a large and steady income feels that her opinion has its
value.* MRS. PHILLIMORE *is a semi-professional invalid,
refined and unintelligent. Her movements are weak and
fatigued. Her voice is habitually plaintive and she is
entirely a lady without a trace of being a woman of fashion.* THOMAS *is an easy-mannered, but entirely respectful
family servant, un-English both in style and appearance.
He has no deportment worthy of being so called, and takes
an evident interest in the affairs of the family he serves.*
MISS HENEAGE, *seated at the tea table, faces the footlights.*
MRS. PHILLIMORE *is seated at the left side of the table.*
THOMAS *stands near by. The table is set for tea. There is
a vase with flowers, a silver match box, and a large old-
fashioned tea urn on the table. The* Evening Post *is on
the table.* MISS HENEAGE *and* MRS. PHILLIMORE *both have
cups of tea.* MISS HENEAGE *sits up very straight, and pours
tea for* GRACE, *who has just entered. She is a pretty and
fashionably dressed girl of twenty. She speaks superciliously, coolly, and not too fast. She sits on the sofa, and*

does not lounge, wearing a gown suitable for spring visit-
ing, hat, parasol, and gloves.

GRACE, *as she crosses and sits down.* I never in my life walked
so far and found so few people at home.

She pauses, taking off her gloves, and somewhat queru-
lously continues.

The fact is the nineteenth of May is ridiculously late to
be in town.

MISS HENEAGE. Thomas, Mr. Phillimore's sherry?

THOMAS. The sherry, ma'am.

THOMAS *indicates a table where the decanter is set.*

MISS HENEAGE. Mr. Phillimore's *Post?*

THOMAS, *pointing to the* Evening Post *on the tea table.* The
Post, ma'am.

MISS HENEAGE *indicates the cup.* Miss Phillimore.

THOMAS *takes a cup of tea to* GRACE. *There is silence while*
they all sip tea. THOMAS *goes back, fills the sherry glass,*
remaining round and about the tea table. They all drink
tea during the following scene.

GRACE. The Dudleys were at home. They wished to know
when my brother Philip was to be married, and where
and how?

MISS HENEAGE. If the Dudleys were persons of breeding,
they'd not intrude their curiosity upon you.

GRACE. I *like* Lena Dudley.

MRS. PHILLIMORE *speaks slowly and gently.* Do I know Miss
Dudley?

GRACE. She knows Philip. She expects an announcement of
the wedding.

MRS. PHILLIMORE. I trust you told her that my son, my sister,
and myself are all of the opinion that those who have been
divorced should remarry with modesty and without parade.

GRACE. I told the Dudleys Philip's wedding was here, tomorrow.

MISS HENEAGE, *to* MRS. PHILLIMORE, *picking up a sheet of paper from the table*. I have spent the afternoon, Mary, in arranging and listing the wedding gifts and in writing out the announcements of the wedding. I think I have attained a proper form of announcement.

She takes the sheet of note paper and gives it to THOMAS.

Of course, the announcement Philip himself made was quite out of the question.

GRACE *smiles*.

However, there is mine.

She points to the paper. THOMAS *gives the list to* MRS. PHILLIMORE *and moves away*.

GRACE. I hope you'll send an announcement to the Dudleys.

MRS. PHILLIMORE, *reading plaintively, ready to make the best of things*. "Mr. Philip Phillimore and Mrs. Cynthia Dean Karslake announce their marriage, May twentieth, at three o'clock, Nineteen A, Washington Square, New York."

She replaces paper on THOMAS's *salver*.

It sounds very nice.

THOMAS *hands the paper to* MISS HENEAGE.

MISS HENEAGE. In my opinion it barely escapes sounding nasty. However, it is correct. The only remaining question is—to whom the announcement should not be sent.

Exit THOMAS.

I consider an announcement of the wedding of two divorced persons to be in the nature of an intimate communication. It not only announces the wedding—it also announces the divorce.

She returns to her teacup.

The person I shall ask counsel of is Cousin William Sudley. He promised to drop in this afternoon.

GRACE. Oh! We shall hear all about Cairo.

MRS. PHILLIMORE. William is judicious.

Re-enter THOMAS.

MISS HENEAGE, *with finality.* Cousin William will disapprove of the match unless a winter in Cairo has altered his moral tone.

THOMAS *announces.* Mr. Sudley.

> *Enter* WILLIAM SUDLEY, *a little, oldish gentleman. He is and appears thoroughly insignificant. But his opinion of the place he occupies in the world is exalted. Though he is filled with self-importance, his manners, voice, presence are all those of a man of breeding.*

MRS. PHILLIMORE *and* MISS HENEAGE. *They rise and greet* SUDLEY; *a little tremulously.* My dear William!

> *Exit* THOMAS.

SUDLEY. *He shakes hands with* MRS. PHILLIMORE, *soberly glad to see them.* How d'ye do, Mary? A very warm May you're having, Sarah.

GRACE. *She comes to him.* Dear Cousin William!

MISS HENEAGE. Wasn't it warm in Cairo when you left?

> *She will have the strict truth, or nothing; still, on account of* SUDLEY's *impeccable respectability, she treats him with more than usual leniency.*

SUDLEY, *sitting down.* We left Cairo six weeks ago, Grace, so I've had no news since you wrote in February that Philip was engaged.

> *Pause.*

I need not to say I consider Philip's engagement excessively regrettable. He is a judge upon the Supreme Court bench with a divorced wife—and such a divorced wife!

GRACE. Oh, but Philip has succeeded in keeping everything as quiet as possible.

SUDLEY, *acidly.* No, my dear! He has not succeeded in keeping his former wife as quiet as possible. We had not been in Cairo a week when who should turn up but Vida Phillimore. She went everywhere and did everything no woman should!

GRACE, *unfeignedly interested.* Oh, what did she do?

SUDLEY. She "did" Cleopatra at the tableaux at Lord Erring-
ton's! She "did" Cleopatra, and she did it robed only in
some diaphanous material of a nature so transparent that
—in fact she appeared to be draped in moonshine.

MISS HENEAGE *indicates the presence of* GRACE. *She rises.*
That was only the beginning. As soon as she heard of
Philip's engagement, she gave a dinner in honor of it!
Only divorcées were asked! And she had a dummy—yes,
my dear, a dummy—at the head of the table. He stood
for Philip—that is he sat for Philip!
He rises and goes up to table.

MISS HENEAGE, *irritated and disgusted.* Ah!

MRS. PHILLIMORE, *with dismay and pain.* Dear me!

MISS HENEAGE, *confident of the value of her opinion.* I disapprove of Mrs. Phillimore.

SUDLEY, *taking cigarette.* Of course you do, but has Philip
taken to Egyptian cigarettes in order to celebrate my
winter at Cairo?

GRACE. Those are Cynthia's.

SUDLEY, *thinking that no one is worth knowing whom he does
not know.* Who is Cynthia?

GRACE. Mrs. Karslake—— She's staying here, Cousin William.
She'll be down in a minute.

SUDLEY, *shocked.* You don't mean to tell me——?

MISS HENEAGE. Yes, William, Cynthia is Mrs. Karslake—Mrs.
Karslake has no New York house. I disliked the publicity
of a hotel in the circumstances, and accordingly when she
became engaged to Philip I invited her here.

SUDLEY, *suspicious and distrustful.* And may I ask *who* Mrs.
Karslake is?

MISS HENEAGE, *with confidence.* She was a Deane.

SUDLEY, *walking about the room, sorry to be obliged to con-
cede good birth to any but his own blood.* Oh, oh—well
the Deanes are extremely nice people.

Going to table.

Was her father J. William Deane?

MISS HENEAGE, *nodding, still more secure.* Yes.

SUDLEY, *giving in with difficulty.* The family is an old one. J. William Deane's daughter? Surely he left a very considerable——

MISS HENEAGE. Oh, fifteen or twenty millions.

SUDLEY, *determined not to be dazzled.* If I remember rightly she was brought up abroad.

MISS HENEAGE. In France and England—and I fancy brought up with a very gay set in very gay places. In fact she is what is called a "sporty" woman.

SUDLEY, *always ready to think the worst.* We might put up with that. But you don't mean to tell me Philip has the—the—the—assurance to marry a woman who has been divorced by——

MISS HENEAGE. Not at all. Cynthia Karslake divorced her husband.

SUDLEY, *gloomily, since he has less fault to find than he expected.* She divorced him! Ah!

He sips his tea.

MISS HENEAGE. The suit went by default. And, my dear William, there are many palliating circumstances. Cynthia was married to Karslake only seven months. There are no—

Glancing at GRACE.

—no hostages to fortune! Ahem!

SUDLEY, *still unwilling to be pleased.* Ah! What sort of a young woman is she?

GRACE, *with the superiority of one who is not too popular.* Men admire her.

MISS HENEAGE. She's not conventional.

MRS. PHILLIMORE, *showing a faint sense of justice.* I am bound to say she has behaved discreetly ever since she arrived in this house.

MISS HENEAGE. Yes, Mary—but I sometimes suspect that she exercises a degree of self-control——

SUDLEY, *glad to have something against someone.* She claps on the lid, eh? And you think that perhaps some day she'll boil over? Well, of course, fifteen or twenty millions—but who's Karslake?

GRACE, *very superciliously.* He owns Cynthia K. She's the famous mare.

MISS HENEAGE. He's Henry Karslake's son.

SUDLEY, *beginning to make the best of it.* Oh! Henry! Very respectable family. Although I remember his father served a term in the Senate. And so the wedding is to be tomorrow?

MRS. PHILLIMORE, *assenting.* Tomorrow.

SUDLEY, *rising, his respectability to the front when he thinks of the ceremony.* GRACE *rises.* Tomorrow. Well, my dear Sarah, a respectable family with some means. We must accept her. But on the whole, I think it will be best for me not to see the young woman. My disapprobation would make itself apparent.

GRACE, *whispering to* SUDLEY. Cynthia's coming.
He doesn't hear.
CYNTHIA *enters, absorbed in reading a newspaper. She is a young creature in her twenties, small and highbred, full of the love of excitement and sport. Her manner is wide-awake and keen, and she is evidently in no fear of the opinion of others. Her dress is exceedingly elegant, but with the elegance of a woman whose chief interests lie in life out of doors. There is nothing horsy in her style, and her expression is youthful and ingenuous.*

SUDLEY, *sententiously and determinedly epigrammatic.* The uncouth modern young woman, eight feet high, with a skin like a rhinoceros and manners like a cave dweller—an habitué of the race track and the divorce court——

GRACE, *aside to* SUDLEY. Cousin William!

SUDLEY. Eh, oh!

CYNTHIA, *coming down, reading, immersed, excited, trembling. She lowers the paper to catch the light.* "Belmont favorite—six to one—Rockaway—Rosebud, and Flying Cloud. Slow track—raw wind—hm, hm, hm—— At the half, Rockaway forged ahead, when Rosebud under the lash made a bold bid for victory—neck by neck—for a quarter —when Flying Cloud slipped by the pair and won on the post by a nose in one forty nine!"

Speaking with the enthusiasm of a sport.

Oh, I wish I'd seen the dear thing do it. Oh, it's Mr. Sudley! You must think me very rude. How do you do, Mr. Sudley?

She goes to SUDLEY.

SUDLEY, *bowing without cordiality.* Mrs. Karslake.

Pause; CYNTHIA *feels he should say something. As he says nothing, she speaks again.*

CYNTHIA. I hope Cairo was delightful? Did you have a smooth voyage?

SUDLEY, *pompously.* You must permit me, Mrs. Karslake——

CYNTHIA, *with good temper, somewhat embarrassed, and talking herself into ease.* Oh, please don't welcome me to the family. All that formal part is over, if you don't mind. I'm one of the tribe now! You're coming to our wedding tomorrow?

SUDLEY. My dear Mrs. Karslake, I think it might be wiser——

CYNTHIA, *still with cordial good temper.* Oh, but you must come! I mean to be a perfect wife to Philip and all his relations! That sounds rather miscellaneous, but you know what I mean.

SUDLEY, *very sententiously.* I am afraid——

CYNTHIA, *gay and still covering her embarrassment.* If you don't come, it'll look as if you were not standing by Philip when he's in trouble! You'll come, won't you—but of course you will.

SUDLEY, *after a self-important pause.* I will come, Mrs.
Karslake.

After a pause.

Good afternoon.

In a tone of sorrow and light compassion.

Good-by, Mary. Good afternoon, Sarah.

Sighing.

Grace, dear.

To MISS HENEAGE.

At what hour did you say the alimony commences?

MISS HENEAGE, *quickly and commandingly to cover his slip.*
The ceremony is at three P.M., William.

SUDLEY *goes toward the door.*

MRS. PHILLIMORE, *with fatigued voice and manner as she
rises.* I am going to my room to rest awhile.

MRS. PHILLIMORE *goes up.*

MISS HENEAGE, *to* SUDLEY. Oh, William, one moment—I entirely forgot! I've a most important social question to ask
you!

She goes up slowly to the door with him.

In regard to the announcements of the wedding—whom
they shall be sent to and whom not. For instance—the
Dudleys——

Exeunt SUDLEY *and* MISS HENEAGE, *talking.*

CYNTHIA. So that's Cousin William?

GRACE. Don't you like him?

CYNTHIA, *calmly sarcastic.* Like him? I love him. He's so
generous. He couldn't have received me with more warmth
if I'd been a mulatto.

THOMAS *re-enters.* PHILLIMORE *enters.* PHILIP PHILLIMORE
*is a self-centered, short-tempered, imperious member of
the respectable fashionables of New York. He is well and
solidly dressed and in manner and speech evidently a man
of family. He is accustomed to being listened to in his*

home circle and from the bench, and it is practically impossible for him to believe that he can make a mistake.

GRACE, *outraged.* Really you know—

CYNTHIA *crosses the stage and sits at the table.*

Philip!

PHILIP *nods to* GRACE *absent-mindedly. He is in his working suit and looks tired. He comes down silently, crosses to tea table, and bends over and kisses* CYNTHIA *on forehead. He goes to his chair, which* THOMAS *has moved to suit him. He sits, and sighs with satisfaction.*

PHILIP. Ah, Grace!

Exit GRACE.

Well, my dear, I thought I should never extricate myself from the courtroom. You look very debonair!

CYNTHIA. The tea's making. You'll have your glass of sherry?

PHILIP. *The strain of the day has evidently been severe.* Thanks!

Taking it from THOMAS; *sighing.*

Ah!

CYNTHIA. I can see it's been a tiring day with you.

PHILIP, *as before.* Hm!

He sips the tea.

CYNTHIA. Were the lawyers very long-winded?

PHILIP, *almost too tired for speech.* Prolix to the point of somnolence. It might be affirmed without inexactitude that the prolixity of counsel is the somnolence of the judiciary. I am fatigued, ah!

A little suddenly, awaking to the fact that his orders have not been carried out to the letter.

Thomas! My *Post* is not in its usual place!

CYNTHIA. It's here, Philip.

THOMAS *gets it.*

PHILIP. Thanks, my dear.

Opening the Post.

Ah! This hour with you—is—is really the—the—
Absently.
—the one vivid moment of the day.
Reading.
Hm—shocking attack by the president on vested interests.
Hm—too bad—but it's to be expected. The people insisted
on electing a desperado to the presidential office—they
must take the holdup that follows.
Pause; he reads.
Hm! His English is lacking in idiom, his spelling in con-
servatism, his mind in balance, and his character in repose.

CYNTHIA, *amiable but not very sympathetic.* You seem more
fatigued than usual. Another glass of sherry, Philip?

PHILIP. Oh, I ought not to——

CYNTHIA. I think you seem a little more tired than usual.

PHILIP. Perhaps I am.
She pours out sherry. PHILIP *takes the glass.*
Ah, this hour is truly a grateful form of restful excitement.
Pause.
You, too, find it—eh?
He looks at CYNTHIA.

CYNTHIA, *with veiled sarcasm.* Decidedly.

PHILIP. Decidedly what, my dear?

CYNTHIA, *as before.* Restful.

PHILIP. Hm! Perhaps I need the calm more than you do. Over
the case today I actually—eh—
Sipping.
—slumbered. I heard myself do it. That's how I know. A
dressmaker sued on seven counts.
Reading newspaper.
Really, the insanity of the United States Senate—you seem
restless, my dear. Ah—um—have you seen the evening
paper? I see there has been a lightning change in the
style or size of hats which ladies——

He sweeps a descriptive motion with his hands, giving paper to CYNTHIA, *then moves his glass, reads, and sips.*

CYNTHIA. The lamp, Thomas.

THOMAS *blows out the alcohol lamp on the tea table with difficulty. He blows twice. Each time he moves* PHILIP *starts. He blows again.*

PHILIP, *irritably.* Confound it, Thomas! What are you puffing and blowing at——?

THOMAS. It's out, ma'am—yes, sir.

PHILIP. You're excessively noisy, Thomas!

THOMAS, *in a fluster.* Yes, sir—I am.

CYNTHIA, *soothing* THOMAS's *wounded feelings.* We don't need you, Thomas.

THOMAS. Yes, ma'am.

PHILIP. Puffing and blowing and shaking and quaking like an automobile in an ecstasy!

Exit THOMAS.

CYNTHIA, *not unsympathetically.* Too bad, Philip! I hope my presence isn't too agitating?

PHILIP. Ah—it's just because I value this hour with you, Cynthia—this hour of tea and toast and tranquillity. It's quite as if we were married—happily married—already.

CYNTHIA, *admitting that married life is a blank, begins to look through paper.* Yes, I feel as if we were married already.

PHILIP, *not recognizing her tone.* Ah! It's the calm, you see.

CYNTHIA, *as before.* The calm? Yes—yes, it's—it's the calm.

PHILIP, *sighing.* Yes, the calm—the halcyon calm of—of second choice. Hm!

He reads and turns over leaves of paper. CYNTHIA *reads. Pause.*

After all, my dear—the feeling which I have for you—is—is—eh—the market is in a shocking condition of plethora! Hm—hm—and what are you reading?

CYNTHIA, *embarrassed.* Oh, eh—well—I—eh—I'm just running over the sporting news.

PHILIP. Oh!

He looks thoughtful.

CYNTHIA, *beginning to forget* PHILIP *and to remember more interesting matters.* I fancied Hermes would come in an easy winner. He came in nowhere. Nonpareil was ridden by Henslow—he's a rotten bad rider. He gets nervous.

PHILIP, *reading still.* Does he? Hm! I suppose you do retain an interest in horses and races. Hm—I trust some day the—ah—law will attract—— Oh—

Turning a page.

—here's the report of my opinion in that dressmaker's case —Haggerty *vs.* Phillimore.

CYNTHIA. Was the case brought against you?

Puzzled.

PHILIP, *a little uncomfortable.* Oh—no. The suit was brought by Haggerty, Miss Haggerty, a dressmaker, against the —in fact, my dear, against the former Mrs. Phillimore.

Pause; he reads.

CYNTHIA, *curious about the matter.* How did you decide it?

PHILIP. I was obliged to decide in Mrs. Phillimore's favor. Haggerty's plea was preposterous.

CYNTHIA. Did you—did you meet the—the—former——?

PHILIP. No.

CYNTHIA. I often see her at afternoon teas.

PHILIP. How did you recognize——

CYNTHIA. Why—

Opening paper.

—because Mrs. Vida Phillimore's picture appears in every other issue of most of the evening papers. And I must confess I was curious. But I'm sure you find it very painful to meet her again.

PHILIP, *slowly, considering.* No—would you find it so impossible to meet Mr.——

CYNTHIA, *much excited and aroused.* Philip! Don't speak of him. He's nothing. He's a thing of the past. I never think of him. I forget him!

PHILIP, *somewhat sarcastic.* That's extraordinarily original of you to forget him.

CYNTHIA, *gently, and wishing to drop the subject.* We each of us have something to forget, Philip—and John Karslake is to me—— Well, he's dead!

PHILIP. As a matter of fact, my dear, he *is* dead, or the next thing to it—for he's bankrupt.

Pause.

CYNTHIA. Bankrupt?

Excited and moved.

Let's not speak of him. I mean never to see him or think about him or even hear of him!

He assents. She reads her paper. He sips his tea and reads his paper. She turns a page, starts, and cries out.

PHILIP. God bless me!

CYNTHIA. It's a picture of—of——

PHILIP. John Karslake?

CYNTHIA. Picture of him, and one of me, and in the middle between us Cynthia K!

PHILIP. Cynthia K?

CYNTHIA, *excited.* My pet riding mare! The best horse he has! She's an angel even in a photograph! Oh!

Reading. "John Karslake drops a fortune at Saratoga."

Rises and goes up and down excitedly. PHILIP *takes paper and reads.*

PHILIP, *unconcerned, as the matter hardly touches him.* Hem —ah—advertises country place for sale—stables, famous mare, Cynthia K—favorite riding mare of former Mrs. Karslake who is once again to enter the arena of matri-

mony with the well-known and highly respected judge
of—

CYNTHIA, *sensitive and much disturbed*. Don't! Don't, Philip,
please don't!

PHILIP. My dear Cynthia—take another paper—here's my *Post!*
You'll find nothing disagreeable in the *Post*.

CYNTHIA *takes the paper*.

CYNTHIA, *after reading, sits near table*. It's much worse in
the *Post*. "John Karslake sells the former Mrs. Karslake's
jewels—the famous necklace now at Tiffany's, and the
sporty ex-husband sells his wife's portrait by Sargent"!
Philip, I can't stand this.

She puts the paper on table.

PHILIP. Really, my dear, Mr. Karslake is bound to appear
occasionally in print—or even you may have to meet him.

Enter THOMAS.

CYNTHIA, *determined and distressed*. I won't meet him! I
won't meet him. Every time I hear his name or Cynthia
K's I'm so depressed.

THOMAS, *announcing with something like reluctance*. Sir, Mr.
Fiddler. Mr. Karslake's trainer.

Enter FIDDLER.

*He is an English horse trainer, a wide-awake, stocky, well-
groomed little cockney. He knows his own mind and sees
life altogether through a stable door. Well-dressed for his
station, and not young.*

CYNTHIA, *excited and disturbed*. Fiddler? Tim Fiddler? His
coming is outrageous!

FIDDLER. A note for you, sir.

CYNTHIA, *impulsively*. Oh, Fiddler—is that you?

FIDDLER. Yes'm!

CYNTHIA, *in a half whisper, still speaking on impulse*. How is
she! Cynthia K? How's Planet II and the colt and Golden
Rod? How's the whole stable? Are they well?

FIDDLER. No'm—we're all on the bum.

Aside.

Ever since you kicked us over!

CYNTHIA, *reproving him, though pleased.* Fiddler!

FIDDLER. The horses is just simply gone to Egypt since you left, and so's the guv'nor.

CYNTHIA, *putting an end to* FIDDLER. That will do, Fiddler.

FIDDLER. I'm waiting for an answer, sir.

CYNTHIA. What is it, Philip?

PHILIP, *uncomfortable.* A mere matter of business.

Aside to FIDDLER.

The answer is, Mr. Karslake can come. The—the coast will be clear.

Exit FIDDLER.

CYNTHIA, *amazed; rising.* You're not going to see him?

PHILIP. But Karslake, my dear, is an old acquaintance of mine. He argues cases before me. I will see that you do not have to meet him.

CYNTHIA *crosses in excited dejection.*

Enter MATTHEW. *He is a High Church clergyman to a highly fashionable congregation. His success is partly due to his social position and partly to his elegance of speech, but chiefly to his inherent amiability, which leaves the sinner in happy peace and smiles on the just and unjust alike.*

MATTHEW, *most amiably.* Ah, my dear brother!

PHILIP. Matthew.

Meeting him.

MATTHEW, *nodding to* PHILIP. Good afternoon, my dear Cynthia. How charming you look!

CYNTHIA *sits at the tea table. To* CYNTHIA.

Ah—why weren't you in your pew yesterday? I preached a most original sermon.

He lays his hat and cane on the divan.

THOMAS, *aside to* PHILIP. Sir, Mrs. Vida Phillimore's maid called you up on the telephone, and you're to expect Mrs. Phillimore on a matter of business.

PHILIP, *astonished and disgusted.* Here, impossible!

To CYNTHIA.

Excuse me, my dear!

Exit PHILIP, *much embarrassed, followed by* THOMAS.

MATTHEW, *coming down to chair, happily and pleasantly self-important.* No, really, it was a wonderful sermon, my dear. My text was from Paul—"It is better to marry than to burn." It was a strictly logical sermon. I argued—that, as the grass withereth, and the flower fadeth, there is nothing final in nature; not even death! And, as there is nothing final in nature, not even death—so then if death is not final—why should marriage be final?

Gently.

And so the necessity of—eh—divorce! You see? It was an exquisite sermon! All New York was there! And all New York went away happy! Even the sinners—if there were any! I don't often meet sinners—do you?

CYNTHIA, *indulgently, in spite of his folly, because he is kind.* You're such a dear, delightful pagan! Here's your tea!

MATTHEW, *sipping his tea.* Why, my dear—you have a very sad expression!

CYNTHIA, *a little bitterly.* Why not?

MATTHEW, *with sentimental sweetness.* I feel as if I were of no use in the world when I see sadness on a young face. Only sinners should feel sad. You have committed no sin!

CYNTHIA, *impulsively.* Yes, I have!

MATTHEW. Eh?

CYNTHIA. I committed the unpardonable sin—whe—when I married for love!

MATTHEW. One must not marry for anything else, my dear!

CYNTHIA. Why am I marrying your brother?

MATTHEW. I often wonder why. I wonder why you didn't choose to remain a free woman.

CYNTHIA, *going over the ground she has often argued with herself.* I meant to; but a divorcée has no place in society. I felt horridly lonely! I wanted a friend. Philip was ideal as a friend—for months. Isn't it nice to bind a friend to you?

MATTHEW. Yes—yes!

He sets down the teacup.

CYNTHIA, *growing more and more excited and moved as she speaks.* To marry a friend—to marry on prudent, sensible grounds—a man—like Philip? That's what I should have done first, instead of rushing into marriage—because I had a wild, mad, sensitive, sympathetic—passion and pain and fury—of I don't know what—that almost strangled me with happiness!

MATTHEW, *amiable and reminiscent.* Ah—ah—in my youth—I—I too!

CYNTHIA, *coming back to her manner of every day.* And besides—the day Philip asked me I was in the dumps! And now—how about marrying only for love?

Re-enter PHILIP.

MATTHEW. Ah, my dear, love is not the only thing in the world!

PHILIP, *speaking as he enters.* I got there too late; she'd hung up.

CYNTHIA. Who, Philip?

PHILIP. Eh—a lady—eh——

Enter THOMAS, *flurried, with card on salver.*

THOMAS. A card for you, sir. Ahem—ahem—Mrs. Phillimore—that was, sir.

PHILIP. Eh?

THOMAS. She's on the stairs, sir.

He turns. Enter VIDA. THOMAS *announces her as being the best way of meeting the difficulty.*

Mrs. Vida Phillimore!

Vida comes in slowly, with the air of a spoiled beauty. She stops just inside the door and speaks in a very casual manner. Her voice is languorous and caressing. She is dressed in the excess of the French fashion and carries an outré parasol. She smiles and comes, undulating, to the middle of the stage. Exit THOMAS.

VIDA. How do you do, Philip.

Pause.

Don't tell me I'm a surprise! I had you called up on the 'phone and I sent up my card—and besides, Philip dear, when you have the—the—habit of the house, as unfortunately I have, you can't treat yourself like a stranger in a strange land. At least I can't—so here I am. My reason for coming was to ask you about that B. and O. stock we hold in common.

To MATTHEW, *condescendingly, the clergy being a class of unfortunates debarred by profession from the pleasures of the world.*

How do you do?

Pause. She then goes to the real reason of her visit.

Do be polite and present me to your wife-to-be.

PHILIP, *awkwardly.* Cynthia—

CYNTHIA, *cheerfully, with dash, putting the table between her and* VIDA. We're delighted to see you, Mrs. Phillimore. I needn't ask you to make yourself at home, but will you have a cup of tea?

MATTHEW *sits near the little table.*

VIDA, *to* PHILIP. My dear, she's not in the least what I expected. I heard she was a dove! She's a very dashing kind of a dove!

To CYNTHIA; *coming to tea table.*

My dear, I'm paying you compliments. Five lumps and quantities of cream. I find single life very thinning.

To PHILIP, *very calm and ready to be agreeable to any man.*

And how well you're looking! It must be the absence of matrimonial cares—or is it a new angel in the house?

CYNTHIA, *outraged at* VIDA's *intrusion but polite though delicately sarcastic.* It's most amusing to sit in your place. And how at home you must feel here in this house where you have made so much trouble—I mean tea.

Rising.

Do you know it would be in much better taste if you would take the place you're accustomed to?

VIDA, *as calm as before.* My dear, I'm an intruder only for a moment; I shan't give you a chance to score off me again! But I must thank you, dear Philip, for rendering that decision in my favor——

PHILIP. I assure you——

VIDA, *unable to resist a thrust at the close of this speech.* Of course, you would like to have rendered it against me. It was your wonderful sense of justice, and that's why I'm so grateful—if not to you, to your Maker!

PHILIP. *He feels that this is no place for his future wife. Rises quickly and irascibly. To* CYNTHIA. Cynthia, I would prefer that you left us.

MATTHEW *comes to the sofa and sits.*

CYNTHIA, *determined not to leave the field first, remains seated.* Certainly, Philip!

PHILIP. I expect another visitor who——

VIDA, *with flattering insistence, to* CYNTHIA. Oh, my dear— don't go! The truth is—I came to see you! I feel most cordially towards you—and really, you know, people in our position should meet on cordial terms.

CYNTHIA, *taking it with apparent calm, but pointing her remarks.* Naturally. If people in our position couldn't meet, New York society would soon come to an end.

Enter THOMAS.

VIDA, *calm, but getting her knife in too.* Precisely. Society's no bigger than a bandbox. Why, it's only a moment ago I saw Mr. Karslake walking——

CYNTHIA. Ah!

THOMAS, *announcing clearly. Everyone changes place in consternation, amusement, or surprise.* CYNTHIA *moves to leave the stage but stops for fear of attracting* KARSLAKE'S *attention.* Mr. John Karslake!

Enter KARSLAKE. *He is a powerful, generous personality, a man of affairs, breezy, gay, and careless. He gives the impression of being game for any fate in store for him. His clothes indicate sporting propensities and his taste in waistcoats and ties is brilliant.* KARSLAKE *sees first* PHILIP *and then* MATTHEW. *Exit* THOMAS.

PHILIP. How do you do?

JOHN, *very gay and no respecter of persons.* Good afternoon, Mr. Phillimore. Hello—here's the church.

Crossing to MATTHEW *and shaking hands. He slaps him on the back.*

I hadn't the least idea—how are you? By George, Your Reverence, that was a racy sermon of yours on divorce! What was your text?

Seeing VIDA *and bowing very politely.*

Galatians 4:2: "The more the merrier," or "Who next?"

Smiling.

As the whale said after Jonah!

CYNTHIA *makes a sudden movement and turns her cup over.* JOHN *faces about quickly and they face each other.* JOHN *gives a frank start. A pause.*

JOHN, *bowing; astounded, in a low voice.* Mrs. Karslake—— I was not aware of the pleasure in store for me. I understood you were in the country.

Recovering, crosses to chair.

Perhaps you'll be good enough to make me a cup of tea— that is if the teapot wasn't lost in the scrimmage.

Pause. CYNTHIA, *determined to equal him in coolness, returns to the tea tray.*

Mr. Phillimore, I came to get your signature in that matter of Cox *vs.* Keely.

PHILIP. I shall be at your service, but pray be seated.
He indicates a chair by tea table.

JOHN, *sitting beyond but not far from the tea table.*
And I also understood you to say you wanted a saddle horse.

PHILIP. You have a mare called—eh—Cynthia K?

JOHN, *promptly.* Yes—she's not for sale.

PHILIP. Oh, but she's just the mare I had set my mind on.

JOHN, *with a touch of humor.* You want her for yourself?

PHILIP, *a little flustered.* I—eh—I sometimes ride.

JOHN. *He is sure of himself now.* She's rather lively for you, Judge. Mrs. Karslake used to ride her.

PHILIP. You don't care to sell her to me?

JOHN. She's a dangerous mare, Judge, and she's as delicate and changeable as a girl. I'd hate to leave her in your charge!

CYNTHIA, *eagerly, but in a low voice.* Leave her in mine, Mr. Karslake!

JOHN, *after slight pause.* Mrs. Karslake knows all about a horse, but—
Turning to CYNTHIA.
Cynthia K's got rather tricky of late.

CYNTHIA, *haughtily.* You mean to say you think she'd chuck me?

JOHN, *with polite solicitude and still humorous. To* PHILIP.
I'd hate to have a mare of mine deprive you of a wife, Judge.
Rising.
She goes to Saratoga next week, C. W.

VIDA, *who has been sitting and talking to* MATTHEW *for lack of a better man, comes to talk to* KARSLAKE. C. W.?

JOHN, *rising as she rises.* Creditors willing.

VIDA, *crossing and sitting left of tea table.* I'm sure your creditors are willing.

JOHN. Oh, they're a breezy lot, my creditors. They're giving me a dinner this evening.

VIDA, *more than usually anxious to please.* I regret I'm not a breezy creditor, but I do think you owe it to me to let me see your Cynthia K! Can't you lead her around to my house?

JOHN. At what hour, Mrs. Phillimore?

VIDA. Say eleven? And you too might have a leading in my direction—771 Fifth Avenue.

> JOHN *bows.* CYNTHIA *hears and notes this.*

CYNTHIA. Your cup of tea, Mr. Karslake.

JOHN. Thanks.

> JOHN *gets tea and sips it.*

I beg your pardon—you have forgotten, Mrs. Karslake—very naturally it has slipped from your memory, but I don't take sugar.

> CYNTHIA, *furious with him and herself. He hands cup back. She makes a second cup.*

CYNTHIA, *cheerfully; in a rage.* Sorry!

JOHN, *also apparently cheerful.* Yes, gout. It gives me a twinge even to sit in the shadow of a sugar maple! First you riot, and then you diet!

VIDA, *calm and amused; aside to* MATTHEW. My dear Matthew, he's a darling! But I feel as if we were all taking tea on the slope of a volcano!

> MATTHEW *sits.*

PHILIP. It occurred to me, Mr. Karslake, you might be glad to find a purchaser for your portrait by Sargent?

JOHN. It's not *my* portrait. It's a portrait of Mrs. Karslake, and to tell you the truth—Sargent's a good fellow—I've made up my mind to keep it—to remember the artist by.

> CYNTHIA *is wounded by this.*

PHILIP. Hm!

CYNTHIA *hands second cup of tea to* JOHN.

CYNTHIA, *with careful politeness.* Your cup of tea, Mr. Karslake.

JOHN, *rising and taking tea with courteous indifference.* Thanks—sorry to trouble you.
He drinks the cup of tea standing by the tea table.

PHILIP, *to make conversation.* You're selling your country place?

JOHN. If I was long of hair—I'd sell that.

CYNTHIA, *excited. Taken out of herself by the news.* You're not really selling your stable?

JOHN. *Finishing his tea, he places empty cup on tea table and reseats himself.* Every gelding I've got—seven foals and a donkey! I don't mean the owner.

CYNTHIA, *still interested and forgetting the discomfort of the situation.* How did you ever manage to come such a cropper?

JOHN. Streak of blue luck!

CYNTHIA, *quickly.* I don't see how it's possible——

JOHN. You would if you'd been there. You remember the head man?
Sits.
Bloke?

CYNTHIA. Of course!

JOHN. Well, his wife divorced him for beating her over the head with a bottle of Fowler's Solution, and it seemed to prey on his mind. He sold me——

CYNTHIA, *horrified.* Sold a race?

JOHN. About ten races, I guess.

CYNTHIA, *incredulous.* Just because he'd beaten his wife?

JOHN. No. Because she divorced him.

CYNTHIA. Well, I can't see why that should prey on his mind!
Suddenly remembers.

JOHN. Well, I have known men that it stroked the wrong way.
But he cost me eighty thousand. And then Urbanity ran
third in the thousand dollar stakes for two-year-olds at
Belmont.

CYNTHIA. *She throws this remark in.* I never had faith in that
horse.

JOHN. And, of course, it never rains monkeys but it pours
gorillas! So when I was down at St. Louis on the fifth,
I laid seven to three on Fraternity—

CYNTHIA. Crazy! Crazy!

JOHN, *ready to take the opposite view.* I don't see it. With
her record she ought to have romped in an easy winner.

CYNTHIA, *pure sport.* She hasn't the stamina! Look at her
barrel!

JOHN. Well, anyhow, Geranium finished me!

CYNTHIA. You didn't lay odds on Geranium!

JOHN. Why not? She's my own mare—

CYNTHIA. Oh!

JOHN. Streak o' bad luck—

CYNTHIA, *plainly anxious to say "I told you so."* Streak of poor
judgment! Do you remember the day you rode Billy at
a six-foot stone wall, and he stopped and you didn't, and
there was a hornets' nest—

MATTHEW *rises.*

—on the other side, and I remember you were hot just because I said you showed poor judgment?
*She laughs at the memory. A general movement of dis-
approval. She remembers the situation.*

I beg your pardon.

MATTHEW, *rising to meet* VIDA. *Hastily.* It seems to me that
horses are like the fourth gospel. Any conversation about

them becomes animated almost beyond the limits of the urbane!

VIDA, *disgusted by such plainness of speech, rises and goes to* PHILIP, *who waves her to a chair.*

PHILIP, *formally.* I regret that you have endured such reverses, Mr. Karslake.

JOHN *quietly bows.*

CYNTHIA. *Concealing her interest, she speaks casually.* You haven't mentioned your new English horse—Pantomime. What did he do at St. Louis?

JOHN, *sitting.* Fell away and ran fifth.

CYNTHIA. Too bad. Was he fully acclimated? Ah, well——

JOHN. We always differed—you remember—on the time needed——

MATTHEW, *coming to* CYNTHIA, *speaking to carry off the situation as well as to get a tip.* Isn't there a—eh—a race tomorrow at Belmont Park?

JOHN. Yes. I'm going down in my auto.

CYNTHIA, *evidently wishing she might be going too.* Oh!

MATTHEW. And what animal shall you prefer?

Covering his personal interest with amiable altruism.

JOHN. I'm backing Carmencita.

CYNTHIA, *gesture of despair.* Carmencita! Carmencita!

MATTHEW *goes to* VIDA.

JOHN. You may remember we always differed on Carmencita.

CYNTHIA, *disgusted at* JOHN's *dunderheadedness.* But there's no room for difference. She's a wild, headstrong, dissatisfied, foolish little filly. The deuce couldn't ride her—she'd shy at her own shadow—Carmencita. Oh, very well, then, I'll wager you—and I'll give you odds too—Decorum will come in first, and I'll lay three to one he'll beat Carmencita by five lengths! How's that for fair?

JOHN, *never forgetting the situation.* Sorry I'm not flush enough to take you.

CYNTHIA, *impetuously.* Philip dear, you lend John enough for the wager.

MATTHEW, *as nearly horrified as so soft a soul can be.* Ahem! Really——

JOHN. It's a sporty idea, Mrs. Karslake, but perhaps in the circumstances——

CYNTHIA, *her mind on her wager.* In what circumstances?

PHILIP, *with a nervous laugh.* It does seem to me there is a certain impropriety——

CYNTHIA, *remembering the conventions which, for a moment, had actually escaped her.* Oh, I forgot. When horses are in the air——

MATTHEW, *pouring oil on troubled waters. Crossing, he speaks to* VIDA *at back of armchair, where she sits.* It's the fourth gospel, you see.
Enter THOMAS *with a letter on a salver, which he hands to* PHILIP.

CYNTHIA, *meekly.* You are quite right, Philip. The fact is, seeing Mr. Karslake again—
Laying on her indifference with a trowel.
—he seems to me as much a stranger as if I were meeting him for the first time.

MATTHEW, *aside to* VIDA. We are indeed taking tea on the slope of a volcano.

VIDA. *She is about to go, but thinks she will have a last word with* JOHN. I'm sorry your fortunes are so depressed, Mr. Karslake.

PHILIP, *looking at the card that* THOMAS *has just brought in.* Who in the world is Sir Wilfrid Cates-Darby?
General move.

JOHN. Oh—eh—Cates-Darby?
PHILIP opens letter which THOMAS has brought with card.
That's the English chap I bought Pantomime of.

PHILIP, *to* THOMAS. Show Sir Wilfrid Cates-Darby in.

Exit THOMAS. *The prospect of an Englishman with a handle to his name changes* VIDA'S *plans and instead of leaving the house, she goes to the sofa and sits there.*

JOHN. He's a good fellow, Judge. Place near Epsom. Breeder. Over here to take a shy at our races.

Enter THOMAS.

THOMAS, *announcing.* Sir Wilfrid Cates-Darby.

Enter SIR WILFRID CATES-DARBY. *He is a highbred, sporting Englishman. His manner, his dress, and his diction are the perfection of English elegance. His movements are quick and graceful. He talks lightly and with ease. He is full of life and unsmiling good temper.*

PHILIP, *to* SIR WILFRID *and referring to the letter of introduction in his hand.* I am Mr. Phillimore. I am grateful to Stanhope for giving me the opportunity of knowing you, Sir Wilfrid. I fear you find it warm?

SIR WILFRID, *delicately mopping his forehead.* Ah, well—ah— warm, no—hot, yes! Deuced extraordinary climate yours, you know, Mr. Phillimore.

PHILIP, *conventional.* Permit me to present you to——

The unconventional situation pulls him up short. It takes him a moment to decide how to meet it. He makes up his mind to pretend that everything is as usual, and presents CYNTHIA *first.*

Mrs. Karslake.

SIR WILFRID *bows, surprised and doubtful.*

CYNTHIA. How do you do?

PHILIP. And to Mrs. Phillimore.

VIDA *bows nonchalantly but with a view to catching* SIR WILFRID'S *attention.* SIR WILFRID *bows and looks from her to* PHILIP.

My brother—and Mr. Karslake you know.

SIR WILFRID. How do, my boy?

Half aside, to JOHN.

No idea you had such a charming little wife—— What?
Eh?

KARSLAKE goes up to speak to MATTHEW *and* PHILIP *in
the further room.*

CYNTHIA. You'll have a cup of tea, Sir Wilfrid?

SIR WILFRID, *at table.* Thanks awfully.

Very cheerfully.

I'd no idea old John had a wife! The rascal never told me!

CYNTHIA, *pouring tea and facing the facts.* I'm not Mr. Karslake's wife!

SIR WILFRID. Oh! Eh! I see——

Business of thinking it out.

VIDA, *who has been ready for some time to speak to him.* Sir
Wilfrid, I'm sure no one has asked you how you like our
country?

SIR WILFRID, *going to* VIDA *and speaking, standing by her at
sofa.* Oh, well, as to climate and horses I say nothing. But
I like your American humor. I'm acquiring it for home
purposes.

VIDA, *getting down to love as the basis of conversation.* Aren't
you going to acquire an American girl for home purposes?

SIR WILFRID. The more narrowly I look the agreeable project
in the face, the more I like it. Oughtn't to say that in the
presence of your husband.

He casts a look at PHILIP, *who has gone into the next
room.*

VIDA, *cheerful and unconstrained.* He's not my husband!

SIR WILFRID, *completely confused.* Oh—eh—my brain must be
boiled. You are—Mrs.—eh—ah—of course, now I see! I got
the wrong names! I thought you were Mrs. Phillimore.

He sits by her.

And that nice girl, Mrs. Karslake! You're deucedly lucky
to be Mrs. Karslake. John's a prime sort. I say, have you
and he got any kids? How many?

VIDA, *horrified at being suspected of maternity but speaking very sweetly.* He's not my husband.

SIR WILFRID, *his good spirits all gone, but determined to clear things up.* Phew! Awfully hot in here! Who the deuce is John's wife?

VIDA. He hasn't any.

SIR WILFRID. Who's Phillimore's wife?

VIDA. He hasn't any.

SIR WILFRID. Thanks fearfully!

To MATTHEW, *whom he approaches; suspecting himself of having lost his wits.*

Would you excuse me, my dear and reverend sir—you're a churchman and all that—would you mind straightening me out?

MATTHEW, *most gracious.* Certainly, Sir Wilfrid. Is it a matter of doctrine?

SIR WILFRID. Oh damme—beg your pardon—no, it's not words, it's women.

MATTHEW, *ready to be outraged.* Women!

SIR WILFRID. It's divorce. Now, the lady on the sofa——

MATTHEW. *Was* my brother's wife; he divorced her—incompatibility—Rhode Island. The lady at the tea table *was* Mr. Karslake's wife; she divorced him—desertion—Sioux Falls. One moment—she is about to marry my brother.

SIR WILFRID, *cheerful again.* I'm out! Thought I never would be! Thanks!

VIDA *laughs.*

VIDA, *not a whit discountenanced and ready to please.* Have you got me straightened out yet?

SIR WILFRID. Straight as a die! I say, you had lots of fun, didn't you?

Going back to sofa.

And so *she's* Mrs. John Karslake?

VIDA, *calm, but secretly disappointed.* Do you like her?

SIR WILFRID. My word!

VIDA, *fully expecting personal flattery.* Eh?

SIR WILFRID. She's a box o' ginger!

VIDA. You haven't seen many American women!

SIR WILFRID. Oh, haven't I?

VIDA. If you'll pay me a visit tomorrow—at twelve, you shall meet a most charming young woman who has seen you once, and who admires you—ah!

SIR WILFRID. I'm there—what!

VIDA. Seven hundred and seventy-one Fifth Avenue.

SIR WILFRID. Seven seventy-one Fifth Avenue—at twelve.

VIDA. At twelve.

SIR WILFRID. Thanks!
Indicating CYNTHIA.
She's a thoroughbred—you can see that with one eye shut. Twelve.
Shaking hands.
Awfully good of you to ask me.
He joins JOHN.
I say, my boy, your former's an absolute certainty.
To CYNTHIA.
I hear you're about to marry Mr. Phillimore, Mrs. Karslake?
KARSLAKE *crosses to* VIDA; *they both go to sofa, where they sit.*

CYNTHIA. Tomorrow, 3 P.M., Sir Wilfrid.

SIR WILFRID. *Much taken with* CYNTHIA, *he addresses her.*
Afraid I've run into a sort of family party, eh?
Indicating VIDA.
The past and the future—awfully chic way you Americans

have of asking your divorced husbands and wives to drop in, you know—celebrate a christenin', or the new bride, or——

CYNTHIA. Do you like your tea strong?

SIR WILFRID. Middlin'.

CYNTHIA. Sugar?

SIR WILFRID. One!

CYNTHIA. Lemon?

SIR WILFRID. Just torture a lemon over it.

He makes a gesture as of twisting a lemon peel. She gives tea.

Thanks! So you do it tomorrow at three?

CYNTHIA. At three, Sir Wilfrid.

SIR WILFRID. Sorry!

CYNTHIA. Why are you sorry?

SIR WILFRID. Hate to see a pretty woman married. Might marry her myself.

CYNTHIA. Oh, but I'm sure you don't admire American women.

SIR WILFRID. Admire you, Mrs. Karslake——

CYNTHIA. Not enough to marry me, I hope.

SIR WILFRID. Marry you in a minute! Say the word. Marry you now—here.

CYNTHIA. You don't think you ought to know me a little before——

SIR WILFRID. Know you? Do know you.

CYNTHIA *covers her hair with her handkerchief.*

CYNTHIA. What color is my hair?

SIR WILFRID. Pshaw!

CYNTHIA. You see! You don't know whether I'm a chestnut or a strawberry roan! In the States we think a few months of friendship is quite necessary.

SIR WILFRID. Few months of moonshine! Never was a friend to a woman—thank God, in all my life.

CYNTHIA. Oh—oh, oh!

SIR WILFRID. Might as well talk about being a friend to a whisky and soda.

CYNTHIA. A woman has a soul, Sir Wilfrid.

SIR WILFRID. Well, good whisky is spirits—dozens o' souls!

CYNTHIA. You are so gross!

SIR WILFRID, *changing seat to above table*. Gross? Not a bit! Friendship between the sexes is all fudge! I'm no friend to a rose in my garden. I don't call it friendship—eh—eh—a warm, starry night, moonbeams and ilex trees, "and a spirit who knows how" and all that—eh——

Getting closer to her.

You make me feel awfully poetical, you know——

PHILIP *comes down, glances nervously at* CYNTHIA *and* SIR WILFRID, *and walks up again.*

What's the matter? But, I say—poetry aside—do you, eh——

Looking around to place PHILIP.

Does he—y'know—is he—does he go to the head?

CYNTHIA. Sir Wilfrid, Mr. Phillimore is my sober second choice.

SIR WILFRID. Did you ever kiss him? I'll bet he fined you for contempt of court. Look here, Mrs. Karslake, if you're marryin' a man you don't care about——

CYNTHIA, *amused and excusing his audacity as a foreigner's eccentricity.* Really!

SIR WILFRID. Well, I don't offer myself——

CYNTHIA. Oh!

SIR WILFRID. Not this instant——

CYNTHIA. Ah!

SIR WILFRID. But let me drop in tomorrow at ten.

CYNTHIA. What country and state of affairs do you think you have landed in?

SIR WILFRID. New York, by Jove! Been to school, too. New York is bounded on the north, south, east, and west by the state of Divorce! Come, come, Mrs. Karslake, I like your country. You've no fear and no respect—no can't and lots of can. Here you all are, you see—your former husband, and your new husband's former wife—sounds like Ollendoff! Eh? So there you are, you see! But, jokin' apart —why do you marry him? Oh well, marry him if you must! You can run around the corner and get a divorce afterwards——

CYNTHIA. I believe you think they throw one in with an ice-cream soda!

SIR WILFRID, *rising.* Damme, my dear lady, a marriage in your country is no more than a—eh—eh—what do you call 'em? A "thank you, ma'am." That's what an American marriage is—a "thank you, ma'am." Bump—bump—you're over it and on to the next.

CYNTHIA. You're an odd fish! What? I believe I like you!

SIR WILFRID. 'Course you do! You'll see me when I call tomorrow—at ten? We'll run down to Belmont Park, eh?

CYNTHIA. Don't be absurd!

VIDA. *She has finished her talk with* JOHN, *and breaks in on* SIR WILFRID, *who has hung about* CYNTHIA *too long to suit her.*
Tomorrow at twelve, Sir Wilfrid!

SIR WILFRID. Twelve!

VIDA, *shaking hands with* JOHN. Don't forget, Mr. Karslake—eleven o'clock tomorrow.

JOHN, *bowing assent.* I won't!

VIDA, *coming to the middle of the stage and speaking to* CYNTHIA. Oh, Mrs. Karslake, I've ordered Tiffany to send you something. It's a sugar bowl to sweeten the matrimonial lot! I suppose nothing would induce you to call?

CYNTHIA, *distantly and careless of offending.* Thanks, no—that
is, is Cynthia K really to be there at eleven? I'd give a
gold mine to see her again.

VIDA. Do come!

CYNTHIA. If Mr. Karslake will accommodate me by his absence.

VIDA. Dear Mr. Karslake, you'll have to change your hour.

JOHN. Sorry, I'm not able to.

CYNTHIA. I can't come later, for I'm to be married.

JOHN. It's not as bad as that with me, but I am to be sold
up—sheriff, you know. Can't come later than eleven.

VIDA, *to* CYNTHIA. Any hour but eleven, dear.

CYNTHIA, *perfectly regardless of* VIDA, *and ready to vex* JOHN
if possible. Mrs. Phillimore, I shall call on you at eleven—
to see Cynthia K. I thank you for the invitation. Good
afternoon.

VIDA, *aside to* JOHN, *crossing to speak quietly to him.* It's mere
bravado; she won't come.

JOHN. You don't know her.

Pause. There is general embarrassment. SIR WILFRID *plays
with his eyeglass.* JOHN *is angry;* CYNTHIA *is triumphant;*
MATTHEW *is embarrassed;* VIDA *is irritated;* PHILIP *is
puzzled; everybody is at odds.*

SIR WILFRID. *For the first time being a witness to the pretty
complications of divorce, he speaks to* MATTHEW. Do you
have it as warm as this ordinarily?

MATTHEW, *for whom these moments are more than usually
painful, and wiping his brow.* It's not so much the heat
as the humidity.

JOHN, *looking at watch; he is glad to be off.* I shall be late
for my creditors' dinner.

SIR WILFRID, *coming down.* Creditors' dinner.

JOHN, *reading note.* Fifteen of my sporting creditors have arranged to give me a blowout at Sherry's, and I'm expected

right away or sooner. And by the way, I was to bring my friends—if I had any. So now's the time to stand by me! Mrs. Phillimore?

VIDA. Of course!

JOHN, *ready to embarrass* CYNTHIA, *if possible, and speaking as if he had quite forgotten their former relations.*

Mrs. Karslake—I beg your pardon. Judge?

PHILIP *declines.*

No? Sir Wilfrid?

SIR WILFRID. I'm with you!

JOHN, *to* MATTHEW. Your Reverence?

MATTHEW. I regret——

SIR WILFRID. Is it the custom for creditors——

JOHN. Come on, Sir Wilfrid!

THOMAS *opens the door.*

Good night, Judge—Your Reverence——

SIR WILFRID. Is it the custom——

JOHN. Hang the custom! Come on—I'll show you a gang of creditors worth having!

Exit SIR WILFRID *with* JOHN, *preceded by* VIDA. MATTHEW *crosses the stage, smiling, as if pleased, in a Christian way, with this display of generous gaiety. He looks at his watch.*

MATTHEW. Good gracious! I had no idea the hour was so late. I've been asked to a meeting with Maryland and Iowa, to talk over the divorce situation.

Exit. His voice is heard off the stage.

Good afternoon! Good afternoon!

CYNTHIA *is evidently much excited. The outer door slams.* PHILIP *comes down the stage slowly.* CYNTHIA *stands, her eyes wide, her breathing rapid, until* PHILIP *speaks, when she seems suddenly to realize her position. There is a long pause.*

PHILIP, *with a superior air.* I have seldom witnessed a more amazing cataclysm of jocundity! Of course, my dear, this has all been most disagreeable for you.

CYNTHIA, *excitedly*. Yes, yes, yes!

PHILIP. I saw how much it shocked your delicacy.

CYNTHIA, *distressed and moved*. Outrageous.

PHILIP sits.

PHILIP. Do be seated, Cynthia.

Taking up paper. Quietly.

Very odd sort of an Englishman—that Cates-Darby!

CYNTHIA. Sir Wilfrid? Oh, yes!

PHILIP settles down to paper. To herself.

Outrageous! I've a great mind to go at eleven—just as I said I would!

PHILIP. Do sit down, Cynthia!

CYNTHIA. What? What?

PHILIP. You make me so nervous——

CYNTHIA. Sorry—sorry.

She sits down and, seeing the paper, she takes it, looking at the picture of JOHN KARSLAKE.

PHILIP, *sighing with content*. Ah! now that I see him, I don't wonder you couldn't stand him. There's a kind of—ah—spontaneous inebriety about him. He is incomprehensible! If I might with reverence cross-question the Creator, I would say to him: "Sir, to what end or purpose did you create Mr. John Karslake?" I believe I should obtain no adequate answer! However—

Sighing.

—at last we have peace—and the *Post!*

PHILIP, *settling himself, reads paper;* CYNTHIA *looks at her paper, occasionally looking across at* PHILIP.

Forget the dust of the arena—the prolixity of counsel—the involuntary fatuity of things in general.

Pause. He reads.

Compose yourself!

MISS HENEAGE, MRS. PHILLIMORE *and* GRACE *enter.*

CYNTHIA *sighs without letting her sigh be heard. She tries to compose herself. She glances at paper and then hearing* MISS HENEAGE, *starts slightly.* MISS HENEAGE *and* MRS. PHILLIMORE *stop at table.*

MISS HENEAGE. *She carries a sheet of paper.* There, my dear Mary, is the announcement as I have now reworded it. I took William's suggestion.

MRS. PHILLIMORE *takes and casually reads it.*

I also put the case to him, and he was of the opinion that the announcement should be sent *only* to those people who are really *in* society.

She sits near table. CYNTHIA *braces herself to bear the Phillimore conversation.*

GRACE. I wish you'd make an exception of the Dudleys.

CYNTHIA *rises and crosses to chair by the table.*

MISS HENEAGE. And of course that excludes the Oppenheims —the Vance-Browns.

MRS. PHILLIMORE. It's just as well to be exclusive.

GRACE. I do wish you'd make an exception of Lena Dudley.

MISS HENEAGE. We might, of course, include those new Girardos and possibly—possibly the Paddingtons.

GRACE. I do wish you would take in Lena Dudley.

They are now sitting.

MRS. PHILLIMORE. The mother Dudley is as common as a charwoman and not nearly as clean.

PHILIP, *sighing, his own feelings as usual to the fore.* Ah! I certainly am fatigued!

CYNTHIA *begins to slowly crush the newspaper she has been reading with both hands, as if the effort of self-repression were too much for her.*

MISS HENEAGE, *making the best of a gloomy future.* We shall have to ask the Dudleys sooner or later to dine, Mary— because of the elder girl's marriage to that dissolute French marquis.

MRS. PHILLIMORE, *plaintively.* I don't like common people any more than I like common cats and, of course, in my time—

MISS HENEAGE. I think I shall include the Dudleys.

MRS. PHILLIMORE. You think you'll include the Dudleys?

MISS HENEAGE. Yes, I think I will include the Dudleys!

Here CYNTHIA *gives up. Driven desperate by their chatter, she has slowly rolled her newspaper into a ball and at this point tosses it violently to the floor and bursts into hysterical laughter.*

MRS. PHILLIMORE. Why, my dear Cynthia—compose yourself.

PHILIP, *hastily.* What is the matter, Cynthia?

They speak together.

MISS HENEAGE. Why, Mrs. Karslake, what is the matter?

GRACE. *She comes quickly forward, saying,* Mrs. Karslake!

ACT TWO

SCENE.—MRS. VIDA PHILLIMORE's *boudoir. The room is furnished to please an empty-headed, pleasure-loving, and fashionable woman. The furniture, the ornaments, what pictures there are, are all witness to taste up-to-date. Two french windows open on to a balcony, from which the trees of Central Park can be seen. There is a table between them; a mirror and a scent bottle upon it. A lady's writing table stands between two doors, nearer center of stage. There is another door near an open fireplace, which is filled with potted plants and andirons not in use. Over it is a tall mirror. On the mantelpiece are French clock, candelabra, and vases. On a line with the fireplace, a lounge, gay with silk pillows. A florist's box, large and long, filled with American Beauty roses is on a low table near the head of the lounge. Small tables and light chairs are here and there. At rise of the curtain* BENSON *is seen looking about her. She is a neat and pretty little English lady's maid in black silk and a thin apron. She comes down the stage still looking about her and inspects the flower box, then goes to the door of* VIDA's *room and speaks to her.*

BENSON. Yes, ma'am, the flowers have come.
She holds the door open.

VIDA, *in a morning gown, enters slowly. She is smoking a cigarette in as aesthetic a manner as she can and is evidently turned out in her best style for conquest.*

VIDA, *speaking with her back to the audience, always calm and, though civil, a little disdainful of her servant.* Terribly garish light, Benson. Pull down the——

BENSON *obeys.*

Lower still—that will do.

As she speaks, she goes about the room, giving the furniture a push here and there, arranging vases, etc.

Men hate a clutter of chairs and tables.

Stopping and taking up hand mirror, standing with back to audience.

I really think I'm too pale for this light.

BENSON, *quickly, understanding what is implied.* Yes, ma'am.

Exit BENSON.

VIDA *sits at the table. Knock at the door.* Come!

Enter BROOKS.

BROOKS, *an ultra-English footman in plush and calves.* Any horders, m'lady?

VIDA, *incapable of remembering the last man or of considering the new one.*

Oh—of course! You're the new——

BROOKS. Footman, m'lady.

VIDA, *as a matter of form.* Your name?

BROOKS. Brooks, m'lady.

Re-enter BENSON *with rouge.*

VIDA, *carefully giving instructions while she keeps her eyes on the glass and is rouged by* BENSON. Brooks, I am at home to Mr. Karslake at eleven, not to anyone else till twelve, when I expect Sir Wilfrid Cates-Darby.

BROOKS *is inattentive, watching* BENSON.

BROOKS. Yes, m'lady.

VIDA, *calm, but wearied by the ignorance of the lower classes.*

And I regret to inform you, Brooks, that in America there are no ladies, except salesladies!

BROOKS, *without a trace of comprehension.* Yes, m'lady.

VIDA. I am at home to no one but the two names I have mentioned.

BROOKS *bows and goes out. She dabs on rouge while* BENSON *holds glass.*

Is the men's club room in order?

BENSON. Perfectly, ma'am.

VIDA. Whisky and soda?

BENSON. Yes, ma'am, and the ticker's been mended. The British sporting papers arrived this morning.

VIDA, *looking at her watch, which lies on the dressing table.* My watch has stopped.

BENSON, *glancing at the French clock on the chimney piece.* Five to eleven, ma'am.

VIDA, *getting promptly to work.* Hm, hm, I shall be caught. *Rises.*

The box of roses, Benson!

BENSON *brings the box of roses, uncovers the flowers, and places them at* VIDA's *side.*

My gloves—the clippers, and the vase!

Each of these things BENSON *places in turn within* VIDA's *range where she sits on the sofa. She has the long box of roses at her side on a small table, a vase of water on the floor by her side. She cuts the stems and places the roses in the vase. When she feels that she has reached a picturesque position, in which any onlooker would see in her a creature filled with the love of flowers and of her fellow man, she says:*

There!

The door opens and BROOKS *enters;* VIDA *nods to* BENSON.

BROOKS, *announcing stolidly.* Sir John Karslake.

Enter JOHN, *dressed in very nobby riding togs.*

He comes in gaily and forcibly. BENSON *gives way as he comes down. Exeunt* BROOKS *and* BENSON. JOHN *stops near the table.* VIDA, *from this point on, is busied with her roses.*

VIDA, *languorously, but with a faint suggestion of humor.* Is that really you, Sir John?

JOHN, *lively and far from being impressed by* VIDA. I see now where we Americans are going to get our titles. Good morning! You look as fresh as paint.

He takes chair.

VIDA, *facing the insinuation with gentle pain.* I hope you don't mean that? I never flattered myself for a moment you'd come. You're riding Cynthia K?

JOHN, *who has laid his gloves and riding crop on the table.* Fiddler's going to lead her round here in ten minutes!

VIDA. Cigars and cigarettes! Scotch?
She indicates that he will find them on a small table up stage.

JOHN. Scotch!
Going up quickly to the table and helping himself to scotch and seltzer.

VIDA. And now *do* tell me all about *her!*
Putting in her last roses; she keeps one rosebud in her hand, of a size suitable for a man's buttonhole.

JOHN, *as he drinks.* Oh, she's an adorable creature—delicate, highbred, sweet-tempered——

VIDA, *showing her claws for a moment.* Sweet-tempered? Oh, you're describing the horse! By "her," I meant——

JOHN, *irritated by the remembrance of his wife.* Cynthia Karslake? I'd rather talk about the last tornado.
Sits.

VIDA, *soothing the savage beast.* There is only one thing I want to talk about, and that is, *you!* Why were you unhappy?

JOHN, *still cross.* Why does a dollar last such a short time?

VIDA, *with curiosity.* Why did you part?

JOHN. Did you ever see a schooner towed by a tug? Well, I parted from Cynthia for the same reason that the hawser parts from the tug—I couldn't stand the tug.

VIDA, *sympathizing.* Ah!
Pause.

JOHN, *still cross.* Awful cheerful morning chat.

VIDA, *excusing her curiosity and coming back to love as the only subject for serious conversation.* I must hear the story, for I'm anxious to know why I've taken such a fancy to you!

JOHN, *very nonchalantly*. Why do *I* like you?

VIDA, *doing her best to charm*. I won't tell you—it would flatter you too much.

JOHN, *not a bit impressed by* VIDA *but as ready to flirt as another*. Tell me!

VIDA. There's a rose for you.

Giving him the one she has in her hand.

JOHN, *saying what is plainly expected of him*. I want more than a rose——

VIDA, *putting this insinuation by*. You refuse to tell me——?

JOHN, *once more reminded of* CYNTHIA, *speaks with sudden feeling*. There's nothing to tell. We met, we loved, we married, we parted; or at least we wrangled and jangled.

Sighing.

Ha! Why weren't we happy? Don't ask me why! It may have been *partly* my fault!

VIDA, *with tenderness*. Never!

JOHN, *his mind on* CYNTHIA. But I believe it's all in the way a girl's brought up. Our girls are brought up to be ignorant of life—they're ignorant of life. Life is a joke, and marriage is a picnic, and a man is a shawl-strap—— 'Pon my soul, Cynthia Deane—no, I can't tell you!

During the following, he walks about in his irritation.

VIDA, *gently*. Please tell me!

JOHN. Well, she was an heiress, an American heiress—and she'd been taught to think marriage meant burnt almonds and moonshine and a yacht and three automobiles, and she thought—I don't know what she thought, but I tell you, Mrs. Phillimore, marriage is three parts love and seven parts forgiveness of sins.

VIDA, *flattering him as a matter of course*. She never loved you.

JOHN, *on whom she has made no impression at all.* Yes, she
did. For six or seven months there was not a shadow between us. It was perfect, and then one day she went off
like a pistol shot! I had a piece of law work and couldn't
take her to see Flashlight race the Maryland mare. The
case meant a big fee, big kudos, and in sails Cynthia,
Flashlight mad! And will I put on my hat and take her?
No—and bang she goes off like a stick o' dynamite—what
did I marry her for—and words—pretty high words, until
she got mad, when she threw over a chair and said, oh,
well—marriage was a failure, or it was with me, so I said
she'd better try somebody else. She said she would and
marched out of the room.

VIDA, *gently sarcastic.* But she came back!

JOHN. She came back, but not as you mean. She stood at the
door and said, "Jack, I shall divorce you." Then she came
over to my study table, dropped her wedding ring on my
law papers, and went out. The door shut, I laughed; the
front door slammed, I damned.

Pause. He crosses to the window.

She never came back.

He comes back to where VIDA *sits. She catches his hands.*

VIDA, *hoping for a contradiction.* She's broken your heart.

JOHN. Oh no!

He crosses to the chair by the lounge.

VIDA, *encouraged, begins to play the game again.* You'll never
love again!

JOHN, *speaking to her from the foot of her sofa.* Try me! Try
me! Ah, no, Mrs. Phillimore, I shall laugh, live, love, and
make money again! And let me tell you one thing—I'm
going to rap her one over the knuckles. She had a stick
of a Connecticut lawyer, and he—well, to cut a legal story
short, since Mrs. Karslake's been in Europe, I have been
quietly testing the validity of the decree of divorce. Perhaps you don't understand?

VIDA, *letting her innate shrewdness appear.* Oh, about a
divorce, everything!

JOHN. I shall hear by this evening whether the divorce will stand or not.

VIDA. But it's today at three she marries—you won't let her commit bigamy?

JOHN, *shaking his head.* I don't suppose I'd go as far as that. It may be the divorce will hold, but, anyway, I hope never to see her again.

He sits beside her, facing up the stage as she faces down.

VIDA. Ah, my poor boy, she has broken your heart.

Believing that this is her psychological moment, she lays her hand on his arm but draws it back as soon as he attempts to take it.

Now don't make love to me.

JOHN, *bold and amused but never taken in.* Why not?

VIDA, *with immense gentleness.* Because I like you too much!
More gaily.

I might give in and take a notion to like you still more!

JOHN. Please do!

VIDA, *with gush, and determined to be womanly at all hazards.*
Jack, I believe you'd be a lovely lover!

JOHN, *as before.* Try me!

VIDA, *not hoping much from his tone.* You charming, tempting, delightful fellow, I could love you without the least effort in the world—but no!

JOHN, *playing the game.* Ah, well, now *seriously!* Between two people who have *suffered* and made their own mistakes——

VIDA, *playing the game too, but not playing it well.* But you see, you don't really love me!

JOHN, *still ready to say what is expected.* Cynthia—Vida, no man can sit beside you and look into your eyes without feeling——

VIDA, *speaking the truth as she sees it, seeing that her methods don't succeed.* Oh! That's not love! That's simply—well, my dear Jack, it's beginning at the wrong end. And the truth is you hate Cynthia Karslake with such a whole-hearted hate that you haven't a moment to think of any other woman.

JOHN, *with sudden anger.* I hate her!

VIDA, *very softly and most sweetly.* Jack—Jack, I could be as foolish about you as—oh, as foolish as anything, my dear! And perhaps some day—perhaps some day you'll come to me and say, Vida, I am totally indifferent to Cynthia—and then——

JOHN. And then?

VIDA, *the ideal woman in mind.* Then, perhaps, you and I may join hands and stroll together into the Garden of Eden. It takes two to find the Garden of Eden, you know—and once we're on the inside, we'll lock the gate.

JOHN, *gaily, and seeing straight through her veneer.* And lose the key under a rosebush!

VIDA, *agreeing very softly.* Under a rosebush!
Very soft knock.
Come!
JOHN *rises quickly.*
Enter BENSON *and* BROOKS.

BROOKS, *stolid and announcing.* My lady—Sir Wilf——
BENSON *stops him with a sharp movement and turns toward* VIDA.

BENSON, *with intention.* Your dressmaker, ma'am.
BENSON *waves* BROOKS *to go. Exit* BROOKS, *very haughtily.*

VIDA, *wonderingly.* My dressmaker, Benson?
With quick intelligence.
Oh, of course, show her up. Mr. Karslake, you won't mind for a few minutes using my men's club room? Benson will show you! You'll find cigars and the ticker, sporting papers, whisky; and, if you want anything special, just phone down to my chef.

JOHN, *looking at his watch.* How long?

VIDA, *very anxious to please.* Half a cigar! Benson will call you.

JOHN, *practical.* Don't make it too long. You see, there's my sheriff's sale on at twelve and those races this afternoon. Fiddler will be here in ten minutes, remember!
Door opens.

VIDA, *to* JOHN. Run along!
Exit JOHN. VIDA *suddenly practical, and with a broad gesture to* BENSON.

Everything just as it was, Benson!
BENSON *whisks the roses out of the vase and replaces them in the box. She gives* VIDA *scissors and empty vases, and when* VIDA *finds herself in precisely the same position which preceded* JOHN's *entrance, she says,*
There!
Enter BROOKS, *as* VIDA *takes a rose from the basket.*

BROOKS, *stolidly.* Your ladyship's dressmaker! M'lady!
Enter SIR WILFRID *in morning suit with boutonniere.*

VIDA, *with tender surprise and busy with the roses.* Is that really you, Sir Wilfrid! I never flattered myself for an instant that you'd remember to come.

SIR WILFRID, *coming to her above end of sofa.* Come? 'Course I come! Keen to come see you. By Jove, you know, you look as pink and white as a huntin' mornin'.

VIDA, *ready to make any man as happy as possible.* You'll smoke?

SIR WILFRID. Thanks!
He watches her as she trims and arranges the flowers.
Awfully long fingers you have! Wish I was a rose, or a ring, or a pair of shears! I say, d'you ever notice what a devil of a fellow I am for originality, what?
Unlike JOHN, *he is evidently impressed by her.*
You've got a delicate little den up here! Not so much low

livin' and high thinkin', as low lights and no thinkin' at all,
I hope—eh?

By this time VIDA *has filled a vase with roses and rises
to sweep by him and if possible make another charming
picture to his eyes.*

VIDA. You don't mind my moving about?

SIR WILFRID, *impressed.* Not if you don't mind my watchin'.
He sits on the sofa.
And sayin' how well you do it.

VIDA. It's most original of you to come here this morning. I
don't quite see why you did.

*She places the roses here and there, as if to see their
effect, and leaves them on a small table near the door
through which her visitors entered.*

SIR WILFRID. Admiration.

VIDA, *sauntering slowly toward the mirror as she speaks.* Oh,
I saw that you admired her! And of course she did say
she was coming here at eleven! But that was only bravado!
She won't come, and besides, I've given orders to admit
no one!

SIR WILFRID. May I ask you——
*He throws this in in the middle of her speech, which flows
gently and steadily on.*

VIDA. And indeed, if she came now, Mr. Karslake has gone,
and her sole object in coming was to make him uncomfortable.

*She goes toward the table, stopping a half minute at the
mirror to see that she looks as she wishes to look.*

Very dangerous symptom, too, that passionate desire to
make one's former husband unhappy! But I can't believe
that your admiration for Cynthia Karslake is so warm
that it led you to pay me this visit a half hour too early
in the hope of seeing——

SIR WILFRID, *rising; most civil, but speaking his mind like a
Briton.*

I say, would you mind stopping a moment!

She smiles.

I'm not an American, you know; I was brought up not to interrupt. But you Americans, it's different with you! If somebody didn't interrupt you, you'd go on forever.

VIDA. *She passes him to tantalize.* My point is you come to see Cynthia——

SIR WILFRID. *He believes she means it.* I came hopin' to see——

VIDA, *as before.* Cynthia!

SIR WILFRID, *perfectly single-minded and entirely taken in.* But I would have come even if I'd known——

VIDA, *evading him while he follows.* I don't believe it!

SIR WILFRID, *as before.* Give you my word I——

VIDA, *the same.* You're here to see *her!* And of course——

SIR WILFRID, *determined to be heard because, after all, he's a man.* May I have the—eh—the floor?

VIDA *sits in a chair.*

I was jolly well bowled over with Mrs. Karslake, I admit that, and I hoped to see her here, but——

VIDA, *talking nonsense and knowing it.* You had another object in coming. In fact, you came to see Cynthia, and you came to see me! What I really long to know is why you wanted to see *me!* For, of course, Cynthia's to be married at three! And, if she wasn't she wouldn't have you!

SIR WILFRID, *not intending to wound; merely speaking the flat truth.* Well, I mean to jolly well ask her.

VIDA, *indignant.* To be your wife?

SIR WILFRID. Why not?

VIDA, *as before.* And you came here, to my house—in order to ask her——

SIR WILFRID, *truthful even on a subtle point.* Oh, but that's only my first reason for coming, you know.

VIDA, *concealing her hopes.* Well, now I *am* curious—what is the second?

SIR WILFRID, *simply.* Are you feelin' pretty robust?

VIDA. I don't know!

SIR WILFRID, *crossing to buffet.* Will you have something, and then I'll tell you!

VIDA, *gaily.* Can't I support the news without——

SIR WILFRID, *trying to explain his state of mind, a thing he has never been able to do.* Mrs. Phillimore, you see it's this way. Whenever you're lucky, you're too lucky. Now, Mrs. Karslake is a nipper and no mistake, but as I told you, the very same evenin' and house where I saw her—
He attempts to take her hand.

VIDA, *gently rising and affecting a tender surprise.* What!

SIR WILFRID, *rising with her.* That's it! You're over!
He suggests with his right hand the movement of a horse taking a hurdle.

VIDA, *very sweetly.* You don't really mean——

SIR WILFRID, *carried away for the moment by so much true womanliness.* I mean I stayed awake for an hour last night, thinkin' about you.

VIDA, *speaking to be contradicted.* But you've just told me—that Cynthia——

SIR WILFRID, *admitting the fact.* Well, she did—she did bowl my wicket, but so did you——

VIDA, *taking him very gently to task.* Don't you think there's a limit to——
She sits.

SIR WILFRID, *roused by so much loveliness of soul.* Now, see here, Mrs. Phillimore! You and I are not bottle babies, eh, are we? You've been married and—I—I've knocked about, and we both know there's a lot of stuff talked about—eh, eh, well, you know—the one and only—that a fellow can't

be awfully well smashed by two at the same time, don't
you know! All rubbish! You know it, and the proof of the
puddin's in the eatin', I am!

VIDA, *as before.* May I ask where I come in?

SIR WILFRID. Well, now, Mrs. Phillimore, I'll be frank with
you. Cynthia's my favorite, but you're runnin' her a close
second in the popular esteem!

VIDA, *laughing, determined not to take offense.* What a delightful, original, fantastic person you are!

SIR WILFRID, *frankly happy that he has explained everything
so neatly.* I knew you'd take it that way!

VIDA. And what next, pray?

SIR WILFRID. Oh, just the usual—eh—thing—the—eh—the same
old question, don't you know. Will you have me if she
don't?

VIDA, *a shade piqued but determined not to risk showing it.*
And you call that the same old usual question?

SIR WILFRID. Yes, I know, but—but will you? I sail in a week;
we can take the same boat. And—eh—eh—my dear Mrs.—
mayn't I say Vida, I'd like to see you at the head of my
table.

VIDA, *with velvet irony.* With Cynthia at the foot?

SIR WILFRID, *practical, as before.* Never mind Mrs. Karslake.
I admire her—she's—but you have your own points! And
you're here, and so'm I! Damme, I offer myself and my
affections, and I'm no icicle, my dear, tell you that for a
fact, and, and in fact what's your answer!
VIDA *sighs and shakes her head.*
Make it yes! I say, you know, my dear Vida——
He catches her hands.

VIDA. *She slips them from him.* Unhand me, dear villain! And
sit further away from your second choice! What can I say?
I'd rather have *you* for a lover than any man I know!
You must be a lovely lover!

SIR WILFRID. I am!

He makes a second effort to catch her fingers.

VIDA. Will you kindly go further away and be good!

SIR WILFRID, *quite forgetting* CYNTHIA. Look here, if you say yes, we'll be married——

VIDA. In a month!

SIR WILFRID. Oh no—this evening!

VIDA, *incapable of leaving a situation unadorned.* This evening! And sail in the same boat with *you?* And shall we sail to the Garden of Eden and stroll into it and lock the gate on the inside and then lose the key—under a rose-bush?

SIR WILFRID, *pausing and, after consideration, saying.* Yes; yes, I say—that's too clever for me!

He draws nearer to her to bring the understanding to a crisis.

VIDA. *A soft knock at the door.* My maid—come!

SIR WILFRID, *swinging out of his chair and going to sofa.* Eh?
Enter BENSON.

BENSON, *to* VIDA. The new footman, ma'am—he's made a mistake. He's told the lady you're at home.

VIDA. What lady?

BENSON. Mrs. Karslake; and she's on the stairs, ma'am.

VIDA. Show her in.

SIR WILFRID *has been turning over the roses. On hearing this, he faces about with a long-stemmed one in his hand. He uses it in the following scene to point his remarks.*

SIR WILFRID, *to* BENSON, *who stops.* One moment!
To VIDA.

I say, eh—I'd rather not see her!

VIDA, *very innocently.* But you came here to see her.

SIR WILFRID, *a little flustered.* I'd rather not. Eh—I fancied I'd find you and her together—but her—

Coming a step nearer.

—findin' me with you looks so dooced intimate—no one else, d'ye see, I believe she'd—draw conclusions——

BENSON. Pardon me, ma'am—but I hear Brooks coming!

SIR WILFRID, *to* BENSON. Hold the door!

VIDA. So you don't want her to know——?

SIR WILFRID, *to* VIDA. Be a good girl now—run me off somewhere!

VIDA, *to* BENSON. Show Sir Wilfrid the men's room.
Enter BROOKS.

SIR WILFRID. The men's room! Ah! Oh! Eh!

VIDA, *beckoning him to go at once.* Sir Wil——
He hesitates, then as BROOKS *comes on, he flings off with*
BENSON.

BROOKS. Lady Karslake, milady!

VIDA. Anything more inopportune! I never dreamed she'd come——
Enter CYNTHIA, *veiled. She comes down quickly.*
My dear Cynthia, you don't mean to say——
Languorously.

CYNTHIA, *rather short, and visibly agitated.* Yes, I've come.

VIDA, *polite but not urgent.* Do take off your veil.

CYNTHIA, *doing as* VIDA *asks.* Is no one here?

VIDA, *as before.* Won't you sit down?

CYNTHIA, *agitated and suspicious.* Thanks, no—— That is, yes, thanks. Yes! You haven't answered my question?
CYNTHIA waves her hand through the smoke, looks at the smoke suspiciously, looks for the cigarette.

VIDA, *playing innocence in the first degree.* My dear, what makes you imagine that anyone's here!

CYNTHIA. You've been smoking.

VIDA. Oh, puffing away!

CYNTHIA *sees the glasses on the table.*

CYNTHIA. And drinking—a pair of drinks?

She sees JOHN's *gloves on the table at her elbow.*

Do they fit you, dear?

VIDA *smiles;* CYNTHIA *picks up crop and looks at it and reads her own name.*

"Jack, from Cynthia."

VIDA, *without taking the trouble to double for a mere woman.* Yes, dear; it's Mr. Karslake's crop, but I'm happy to say he left me a few minutes ago.

CYNTHIA. He left the house?

VIDA *smiles.*

I wanted to see him.

VIDA, *with a shade of insolence.* To quarrel?

CYNTHIA, *frank and curt.* I wanted to see him.

VIDA, *determined to put* CYNTHIA *in the wrong.* And I sent him away because I didn't want you to repeat the scene of last night in my house.

CYNTHIA *looks at* JOHN's *riding crop and is silent.* Well, I can't stay. I'm to be married at three, and I had to play truant to get here!

Enter BENSON.

BENSON, *to* VIDA. There's a person, ma'am, on the sidewalk.

VIDA. What person, Benson?

BENSON. A person, ma'am, with a horse.

CYNTHIA, *happily agitated.* It's Fiddler with Cynthia K.

She goes up rapidly and looks out back through the window.

VIDA, *to* BENSON. Tell the man I'll be down in five minutes.

CYNTHIA, *looking down from the balcony with delight.* Oh, there she is!

VIDA, *aside to* BENSON. Go to the club room, Benson, and say to the two gentlemen I can't see them at present—I'll send for them when——

BENSON, *listening*. I hear someone coming.

VIDA. Quick!

> BENSON *leaves the door which opens, and* JOHN *enters.* JOHN *comes in slowly, carelessly.* VIDA *whispers to* BENSON.

BENSON *crosses, goes close to* JOHN, *and whispers.* Beg par——

VIDA, *under her breath*. Go back!

JOHN, *not understanding*. I beg pardon!

VIDA, *as before*. Go back!

JOHN, *the same*. Can't! I've a date! With the sheriff!

VIDA, *a little cross*. Please use your eyes.

JOHN, *laughing and flattering* VIDA. I am using my eyes.

VIDA, *fretted*. Don't you see there's a lovely creature in the room?

JOHN, *again taking the loud upper hand*. Of course there is.

VIDA. Hush!

JOHN, *teasingly*. But what I want to know is——

VIDA. Hush!

JOHN, *delighted at getting a rise*. —is when we're to stroll in the Garden of Eden——

VIDA. Hush!

JOHN. —and lose the key.

> *To put a stop to this, she lightly tosses her handkerchief into his face.*

> By George, talk about attar of roses!

CYNTHIA, *up at window, excited and moved at seeing her mare once more*. Oh, she's a darling!
> *She turns.*

A perfect darling!

JOHN starts; he sees CYNTHIA *at the same instant that she sees him.*

Oh! I didn't know you were here.

Pause; then with take-it-or-leave-it frankness.

I came to see *you!*

JOHN looks extremely dark and angry; VIDA *rises.*

VIDA, *to* CYNTHIA, *most gently, and seeing there's nothing to to be made of* JOHN. Oh, pray feel at home, Cynthia, dear!

Stands by door; to JOHN.

When I've a nice street frock on, I'll ask you to present me to Cynthia K.

Exit VIDA.

CYNTHIA, *agitated and frank.* Of course, I told you yesterday I was coming here.

JOHN, *irritated.* And I was to deny myself the privilege of being here?

CYNTHIA, *curt and agitated.* Yes.

JOHN, *ready to fight.* And you guessed I would do that?

CYNTHIA. No.

JOHN. What?

CYNTHIA, *above table. She speaks with agitation, frankness, and good will.* Jack—I mean, Mr. Karslake—no, I mean, Jack! I came because—well, you see, it's my wedding day— and—and—I—I—was rude to you last evening. I'd like to apologize and make peace with you before I go——

JOHN, *determined to be disagreeable.* Before you go to your last, long home!

CYNTHIA. I came to apologize.

JOHN. But you'll remain to quarrel!

CYNTHIA, *still frank and kind.* I will not quarrel. No! And I'm only here for a moment. I'm to be married at three, and just look at the clock! Besides, I told Philip I was going to Louise's shop, and I did—on the way here; but, you see, if I stay too long he'll telephone Louise and find I'm not there, and he might guess I was here. So you see I'm risking a scandal. And now, Jack, see here, I lay my hand on the table, I'm here on the square, and—what I want to say is, why—Jack, even if we have made a mess of our married life, let's put by anger and pride. It's all over now and can't be helped. So let's be human, let's be reasonable, and let's be kind to each other! Won't you give me your hand?

JOHN *refuses.*

I wish you every happiness!

JOHN, *turning away, the past rankling.* I had a client once, a murderer; he told me he murdered the man, and he told me, too, that he never felt so kindly to anybody as he did to that man after he'd killed him!

CYNTHIA. Jack!

JOHN, *unforgiving.* You murdered my happiness!

CYNTHIA. I won't recriminate!

JOHN. And now I must put by anger and pride! I do! But not self-respect, not a just indignation—not the facts and my clear memory of them!

CYNTHIA. Jack!

JOHN. No!

CYNTHIA, *with growing emotion, and holding out her hand.* I give you one more chance! Yes, I'm determined to be generous. I forgive everything you ever did to me. I'm ready to be friends. I wish you every happiness and every —every—horse in the world! I can't do more than that! *She offers her hand again.* You refuse?

JOHN, *moved but surly.* I like wildcats and I like Christians, but I don't like Christian wildcats! Now I'm close-hauled, trot out your tornado. Let the tiger loose! It's the tamer, the man in the cage that has to look lively and use the

red-hot crowbar! But by Jove, I'm out of the cage! I'm
a mere spectator of the married circus!

He puffs vigorously.

CYNTHIA. Be a game sport then! Our marriage was a wager;
you wagered you could live with me. You lost; you paid
with a divorce; and now is the time to show your sporting
blood. Come on, shake hands and part friends.

JOHN. Not in this world! Friends with you, no! I have a proper
pride. I don't propose to put my pride in my pocket.

CYNTHIA, *jealous and plain-spoken.* Oh, I wouldn't ask you to
put your pride in your pocket while Vida's handkerchief
is there.

JOHN *looks angered.*

Pretty little bijou of a handkerchief!

CYNTHIA *takes handkerchief out.* And she is charming,
and divorced, and reasonably well made-up.

JOHN. Oh well, Vida is a woman.

Toying with handkerchief.

I'm a man, a handkerchief is a handkerchief, and as some
old Aristotle or other said, whatever concerns a woman
concerns me!

CYNTHIA, *not oblivious of him, but in a low voice.* Insufferable! Well, yes.

*She sits. She is too much wounded to make any further
appeal.*

You're perfectly right. There's no possible harmony between divorced people! I withdraw my hand and all good
feeling. No wonder I couldn't stand you. Eh? However,
that's pleasantly past! But at least, my dear Karslake, let
us have some sort of beauty of behavior! If we cannot be
decent, let us endeavor to be graceful. If we can't be
moral, at least we can avoid being vulgar.

JOHN. Well——

CYNTHIA. If there's to be no more marriage in the world——

JOHN, *cynical.* Oh, but that's not it; there's to be more and more and more!

CYNTHIA, *with a touch of bitterness.* Very well! I repeat then, if there's to be nothing but marriage and divorce, and remarriage and redivorce, at least, at least, those who *are* divorced can avoid the vulgarity of meeting each other here, there, and everywhere!

JOHN. Oh, that's where you come out!

CYNTHIA. I thought so yesterday, and today I know it. It's an insufferable thing to a woman of any delicacy of feeling to find her husband——

JOHN. Ahem—former!

CYNTHIA. *Once* a husband always——

JOHN, *still cynical.* Oh no! Oh dear, no.

CYNTHIA. To find her—to find the man she has once lived with —in the house of—making love to—to find you here!
JOHN *smiles and rises.*
You smile—but I say it should be a social axiom, no woman should have to meet her former husband.

JOHN, *cynical and cutting.* Oh, I don't know; after I've served my term I don't mind meeting my jailer.

CYNTHIA. JOHN *takes a chair near* CYNTHIA. It's indecent—at the horse show, the opera, at races and balls, to meet the man who once—— It's not civilized! It's fantastic! It's half-baked! Oh, I never should have come here!
He sympathizes, and she grows irrational and furious.
But it's entirely your fault!

JOHN. My fault?

CYNTHIA, *working herself into a rage.* Of course. What business have you to be about—to be at large. To be at all!

JOHN. Gosh!

CYNTHIA, *as before.* To be where I am! Yes, it's just as horrible for you to turn up in my life as it would be for a dead person to insist on coming back to life and dinner and bridge!

JOHN. Horrid idea!

CYNTHIA. Yes, but it's *you* who behave just as if you were not dead, just as if I'd not spent a fortune on your funeral. You do; you prepare to bob up at afternoon teas—and dinners—and embarrass me to death with your extinct personality!

JOHN. Well, of course we *were* married, but it didn't quite kill me.

CYNTHIA, *angry and plain-spoken*. You killed yourself for me— I divorced you. I buried you out of my life. If any human soul was ever dead, you are! And there's nothing I so hate as a gibbering ghost.

JOHN. Oh, I say!

CYNTHIA, *with hot anger*. Go gibber and squeak where gibbering and squeaking are the fashion!

JOHN, *laughing and pretending to a coldness he does not feel*. And so, my dear child, I'm to abate myself as a nuisance! Well, as far as seeing you is concerned, for my part it's just like seeing a horse who's chucked you once. The bruises are O.K., and you see him with a sort of easy curiosity. Of course, you know, he'll jolly well chuck the next man! Permit me!

JOHN picks up gloves, handkerchief, and parasol and gives her these as she drops them one by one in her agitation.

There's pleasure in the thought.

CYNTHIA. Oh!

JOHN. And now may I ask you a very simple question? Mere curiosity on my part, but why did you come here this morning?

CYNTHIA. I have already explained that to you.

JOHN. Not your real motive. Permit me!

CYNTHIA. Oh!

JOHN. But I believe I have guessed your real—permit me— your real motive!

CYNTHIA. Oh!

JOHN, *with mock sympathy.* Cynthia, I am sorry for you.

CYNTHIA. H'm?

JOHN. Of course we had a pretty lively case of the fever—the mutual attraction fever, and we *were* married a very short time. And I conclude that's what's the matter with *you!* You see, my dear, seven months of married life is too short a time to cure a bad case of the fancies.

CYNTHIA, *in angry surprise.* What?

JOHN, *calm and triumphant.* That's my diagnosis.

CYNTHIA, *slowly and gathering herself together.* I don't think I understand.

JOHN. Oh yes, you do; yes, you do.

CYNTHIA, *with blazing eyes.* What do you mean?

JOHN. Would you mind not breaking my crop! Thank you! I mean—

With polite impertinence.

—that ours was a case of premature divorce, and, ahem, you're in love with me still.

He pauses. CYNTHIA *has one moment of fury, then she realizes at what a disadvantage this places her. She makes an immense effort, recovers her calm, thinks hard for a moment more, and then has suddenly an inspiration.*

CYNTHIA. Jack, some day you'll get the blind staggers from conceit. No, I'm not in love with you, Mr. Karslake, but I shouldn't be at all surprised if she were. She's just your sort, you know. She's a man-eating shark, and you'll be a toothsome mouthful. Oh come now, Jack, what a silly you are! Oh yes, you are, to get off a joke like that; me— in love with——

She looks at him.

JOHN. Why are you here?

She laughs and begins to play her game.

Why are you here?

CYNTHIA. Guess!

She laughs.

JOHN. Why are you——

CYNTHIA, *quickly.* Why am I here! I'll tell you. I'm going to be married. I had a longing, an irresistible longing to see you make an ass of yourself just once more! It happened!

JOHN, *uncertain and discomfited.* I know better!

CYNTHIA. But I came for a more serious purpose, too. I came, my dear fellow, to make an experiment on myself. I've been with you thirty minutes; and——

She sighs with content.

It's all right!

JOHN. What's all right?

CYNTHIA, *calm and apparently at peace with the world.* I'm immune.

JOHN. Immune?

CYNTHIA. You're not catching any more! Yes, you see, I said to myself, if I fly into a temper——

JOHN. You did!

CYNTHIA. If I fly into a temper when I see him, well, that shows I'm not yet so entirely convalescent that I can afford to have Jack Karslake at my house. If I remain calm I shall ask him to dinner.

JOHN, *routed.* Ask me if you dare!

He rises.

CYNTHIA, *getting the whip hand for good.* Ask you to dinner? Oh, my dear fellow.

JOHN rises.

I'm going to do much more than that.

She rises.

We must be friends, old man! We must meet, we must meet often, we must show New York the way the thing should be done, and, to show you I mean it—I want you to be my best man and give me away when I'm married this afternoon.

JOHN, *incredulous and impatient.* You don't mean that!
He puts back chair.

CYNTHIA. There you are! Always suspicious!

JOHN. You don't mean that!

CYNTHIA, *hiding her emotion under a sportswoman's manner.* Don't I? I ask you, come! And come as you are! And I'll lay my wedding gown to Cynthia K that you won't be there! If you're there, you get the gown, and if you're not, I get Cynthia K!

JOHN, *determined not be worsted.* I take it!

CYNTHIA. Done! Now, then, we'll see which of us two is the real sporting goods! Shake!
They shake hands on it.
Would you mind letting me have a plain soda?
JOHN goes to the table, and, as he is rattled and does not regard what he is about, he fills the glass three-fourths full with whisky. He comes to CYNTHIA and gives her this. She looks him in the eye with an air of triumph.
Thanks.
Maliciously, as VIDA enters.
Your hand is a bit shaky. I think *you* need a little King William.
JOHN shrugs his shoulders, and as VIDA immediately speaks, CYNTHIA defers drinking.

VIDA, *to* CYNTHIA. My dear, I'm sorry to tell you your husband —I mean my husband—I mean Philip—he's asking for you over the phone. You must have said you were coming here. Of course I told him you were not here and hung up.
Enter BENSON.

BENSON, *to* VIDA. Ma'am, the new footman's been talking with Mr. Phillimore on the wire.
VIDA makes a gesture of regret.

He told Mr. Phillimore that his lady was here, and if I can believe my ears, ma'am, he's got Sir Wilfrid on the phone now!

Enter SIR WILFRID.

SIR WILFRID *comes from room, perplexed and annoyed.* I say y'know—extraordinary country; that old chap, Phillimore, he's been damned impertinent over the wire! Says I've run off with Mrs. Karslake—talks about "Louise"! Now who the dooce is Louise? He's comin' round here, too—I said Mrs. Karslake wasn't here——

Seeing CYNTHIA.

Hello! Good job! What a liar I am!

BENSON, *to* VIDA. Mr. Fiddler, ma'am, says the mare is gettin' very restive.

JOHN *hears this and moves at once. Exit* BENSON.

JOHN, *to* VIDA. If that mare's restive, she'll break out in a rash.

VIDA, *to* JOHN. Will you take me?

JOHN. Of course.

They go to the door.

CYNTHIA, *to* JOHN. Tata, old man! Meet you at the altar! If I don't, the mare's mine!

SIR WILFRID *looks at her amazed.*

VIDA, *to* CYNTHIA. Do the honors, dear, in my absence!

JOHN. Come along, come along, never mind them! A horse is a horse!

Exeunt JOHN *and* VIDA, *gaily and in haste. At the same moment* CYNTHIA *drinks what she supposes to be her glass of plain soda. As it is whisky straight, she is seized with astonishment and a fit of coughing.* SIR WILFRID *relieves her of the glass.*

SIR WILFRID, *indicating contents of glass.* I say, do you ordinarily take it as high up—as seven fingers and two thumbs?

CYNTHIA *coughs.* Jack poured it out. Just shows how groggy he was! And now, Sir Wilfrid——

She gets her things to go.

SIR WILFRID. Oh, you can't go!

Enter BROOKS.

CYNTHIA. I am to be married at three.

SIR WILFRID. Let him wait.

Aside to BROOKS, *whom he meets near the door.*

If Mr. Phillimore comes, bring his card up.

BROOKS, *going.* Yes, Sir Wilfrid.

SIR WILFRID, *to* BROOKS, *as before.* To me!

He tips him.

BROOKS, *bowing.* To you, Sir Wilfrid.

Exit BROOKS.

SIR WILFRID, *returning to* CYNTHIA. I've got to have my innings, y'know!

He looks at her more closely.

I say, you've been crying!

CYNTHIA. King William!

SIR WILFRID. You *are* crying! Poor little gal!

CYNTHIA, *tears in her eyes.* I feel all shaken and cold.

Enter BROOKS, *with card.*

SIR WILFRID, *astonished and sympathetic.* Poor little gal.

CYNTHIA, *as before.* I didn't sleep a wink last night.

With disgust.

Oh, what is the matter with me?

SIR WILFRID. Why, it's as plain as a pikestaff! You——

BROOKS *has brought salver to* SIR WILFRID. *A card lies upon it.* SIR WILFRID *takes it and says aside to* BROOKS.

Phillimore?

BROOKS *assents. Aloud to* CYNTHIA, *calmly deceitful.*

Who's Waldorf Smith?

CYNTHIA *shakes her head. To* BROOKS, *returning card to salver.*

Tell the gentleman Mrs. Karslake is not here!

Exit BROOKS.

CYNTHIA, *aware that she has no business where she is.* I
thought it was Philip!

SIR WILFRID, *telling the truth as if it were a lie.* So did I!
With cheerful confidence.
And now, Mrs. Karslake, I'll tell you why you're cryin'.
He sits beside her.
You're marryin' the wrong man! I'm sorry for you, but
you're such a goose. Here you are, marryin' this legal
luminary. What for? You don't know! He don't know!
But I do! You pretend you're marryin' him because it's
the sensible thing; not a bit of it. You're marryin' Mr. Phillimore because of all the other men you ever saw he's the
least like Jack Karslake.

CYNTHIA. That's a very good reason.

SIR WILFRID. There's only one good reason for marrying and
that is because you'll die if you don't!

CYNTHIA. Oh, I've tried that!

SIR WILFRID. The Scripture says: "Try, try again!" I tell you,
there's nothing like a w'im!

CYNTHIA. What's that? W'im? Oh, you mean a *whim!* Do
please try and say w*h*im!

SIR WILFRID, *for the first time emphasizing his h in the word.*
W*h*im. You must have a w'im—w'im for the chappie you
marry.

CYNTHIA. I had—for Jack.

SIR WILFRID. Your w'im wasn't w'immy enough, my dear! If
you'd had more of it, and tougher, it would ha' stood, y'
know! Now, I'm not proposin'!

CYNTHIA, *diverted at last from her own distress.* I hope not!

SIR WILFRID. Oh, I will later! It's not time yet! As I was saying——

CYNTHIA. And pray, Sir Wilfrid, when will it be time?

SIR WILFRID. As soon as I see you have a w'im for me!
Rising, he looks at his watch.

And now, I'll tell you what we'll do! We've got just an hour to get there in; my motor's on the corner, and in fifty minutes we'll be at Belmont Park.

CYNTHIA, *her sporting blood fired.* Belmont Park!

SIR WILFRID. We'll do the races, and dine at Martin's——

CYNTHIA, *tempted.* Oh, if I only could! I can't! I've got to be married! You're awfully nice; I've almost got a "w'im" for you already.

SIR WILFRID, *delighted.* There you are! I'll send a telegram! *She shakes her head. He sits and writes at the table.*

CYNTHIA. No, no, no!

SIR WILFRID *reads what he writes.* "Off with Cates-Darby to races. Please postpone ceremony till seven-thirty."

CYNTHIA. Oh, no, it's impossible!

SIR WILFRID, *accustomed to have things go his way.* No more than breathin'! You can't get a w'im for me, you know, unless we're together, so together we'll be!
Enter JOHN KARSLAKE.
And tomorrow you'll wake up with a jolly little w'im—— *Reads.*
"Postpone ceremony till seven-thirty." There.
He puts on her cloak. Sees JOHN.
Hello!

JOHN, *surly.* Hello! Sorry to disturb you.

SIR WILFRID, *cheerful as possible.* Just the man!
Giving him the telegraph form.
Just step round and send it, my boy. Thanks!
JOHN *reads it.*

CYNTHIA. No, no, I can't go!

SIR WILFRID. Cockety-coo-coo-can't. I say, you must!

CYNTHIA, *positively.* NO!

JOHN, *astounded.* Do you mean you're going——

SIR WILFRID, *very gay.* Off to the races, my boy!

JOHN, *angry and outraged.* Mrs. Karslake can't go with you there!

CYNTHIA *starts, amazed at his assumption of marital authority and delighted that she will have an opportunity of outraging his sensibilities.*

SIR WILFRID. Oho!

JOHN. An hour before her wedding!

SIR WILFRID, *gay and not angry.* May I know if it's the custom——

JOHN, *jealous and disgusted.* It's worse than eloping——

SIR WILFRID. —custom, y'know, for the husband-that-was to dictate——

JOHN, *thoroughly vexed.* By George, there's a limit!

CYNTHIA. What? What? What?

Gathers up her things.

What did I hear you say?

SIR WILFRID. Ah!

JOHN, *angry.* I say there's a limit——

CYNTHIA, *more and more determined to arouse and excite* JOHN. Oh, there's a limit, is there?

JOHN. There is! I bar the way! It means reputation—it means——

CYNTHIA, *enjoying her opportunity.* We shall see what it means!

SIR WILFRID. Aha!

JOHN, *to* CYNTHIA. I'm here to protect your reputation——

SIR WILFRID, *to* CYNTHIA. We've got to make haste, you know.

CYNTHIA. Now, I'm ready——

JOHN, *to* CYNTHIA. Be sensible. You're breaking off the match——

CYNTHIA, *excitedly.* What's that to you?

SIR WILFRID. It's boots and saddles!

JOHN. *He takes his stand between them and the door.* No thoroughfare!

SIR WILFRID. Look here, my boy——!

CYNTHIA, *catching at the opportunity of putting* JOHN *in an impossible position.* Wait a moment, Sir Wilfrid! Give me the wire!

Facing him.

Thanks!

She takes the telegraph form from him and tears it up. There! Too rude to chuck him by wire! But you, Jack, you've taken on yourself to look after my interests, so I'll just ask you, old man, to run down to the Supreme Court and tell Philip—nicely, you know—I'm off with Sir Wilfrid and where! Say I'll be back by seven, if I'm not later! And make it clear, Jack, I'll marry him by eight-thirty or nine at the latest! And mind *you're* there, dear! And now, Sir Wilfrid, we're off.

JOHN, *staggered and furious, giving way as they pass him.* I'm not the man to—to carry——

CYNTHIA, *quick and dashing.* Oh yes, you are.

JOHN. —a message from you.

CYNTHIA, *triumphant.* Oh, yes, you are; you're just exactly the man!

Exeunt CYNTHIA *and* SIR WILFRID.

JOHN. Great miracles of Moses!

ACT THREE

SCENE.—*The same as that of Act One, but the room has been cleared of too much furniture and arranged for a wedding ceremony. The curtain rises on* MRS. PHILLIMORE *reclining on the sofa,* MISS HENEAGE *is seated left of table,* SUDLEY *is seated at its right, while* GRACE *is on the sofa. There are cushions of flowers, alcove of flowers, flowers in vase, pink and white hangings, wedding bell of roses, calla lilies, orange blossoms, a ribbon of white stretched in front of an altar of flowers; two cushions for the couple to kneel in; two candelabra at each side of back of arch on pedestals. The curtain rises. There is a momentary silence, that the audience may take in these symbols of marriage. Every member of the Phillimore family is irritable, with suppressed irritation.*

SUDLEY, *impatiently.* All very well, my dear Sarah. But you see the hour. Twenty to ten! We have been here since half past two.

MISS HENEAGE. You had dinner?

SUDLEY. I did not come here at two to have dinner at eight and be kept waiting until ten! And, my dear Sarah, when I ask where the bride is——

MISS HENEAGE, *with forced composure.* I have told you all I know. Mr. John Karslake came to the house at lunch time, spoke to Philip, and they left the house together.

GRACE. Where is Philip?

MRS. PHILLIMORE, *feebly irritated.* I don't wish to be censorious or to express an actual opinion, but I must say it's a bold bride who keeps her future mother-in-law waiting for eight hours. However, I will not venture to——

MRS. PHILLIMORE *reclines again and fades away into silence.*

GRACE, *sharply and decisively.* I do! I'm sorry I went to the expense of a silver ice pitcher.

MRS. PHILLIMORE *sighs.* MISS HENEAGE *keeps her temper with an effort which is obvious.*

Enter THOMAS.

SUDLEY, *to* MRS. PHILLIMORE. For my part, I don't believe Mrs. Karslake means to return here or to marry Philip at all!

THOMAS, *to* MISS HENEAGE. Two telegrams for you, ma'am! The choir boys have had their supper.

Slight movement from everyone; THOMAS *steps back.*

SUDLEY *rises.* At last we shall know!

MISS HENEAGE. From the lady! Probably!

MISS HENEAGE *opens telegram. She reads first one at a glance, laying it on salver again with a glance at* SUDLEY. THOMAS *passes salver to* SUDLEY, *who takes telegram.*

GRACE. There's a toot now.

MRS. PHILLIMORE, *feebly confused.* I don't wish to intrude, but really I can't imagine Philip marrying at midnight.

As SUDLEY *reads,* MISS HENEAGE *opens the second telegram but does not read it.*

SUDLEY *reads.* "Accident, auto struck"—something! "Gasoline" —did something—illegible, ah!

Reads.

"Home by nine forty-five! Hold the church!"

General movement from all.

MISS HENEAGE, *profoundly shocked.* "Hold the church!" William, she still means to marry Philip—and tonight, too!

SUDLEY. It's from Belmont Park.

GRACE, *making a great discovery.* She went to the races!

MISS HENEAGE. This is from Philip!

MISS HENEAGE *reads second telegram.*

"I arrive at ten o'clock. Have dinner ready."

MISS HENEAGE *motions to* THOMAS *to withdraw. Exit*
THOMAS. MISS HENEAGE *looks at her watch.*

They are both due now.

Movement.

What's to be done?

She rises. SUDLEY *shrugs shoulders.*

SUDLEY, *rising.* After a young woman has spent her wedding
day at the races? Why, I consider that she has broken the
engagement—and when she comes, tell her so.

MISS HENEAGE. I'll telephone Matthew. The choir boys can
go home—her maid can pack her belongings—and when
the lady arrives——

*Very distant toot of an auto horn is heard coming nearer
and nearer.* GRACE *flies up stage and looks out of door.*
MRS. PHILLIMORE *does not know what to do or where to
go.* SUDLEY *moves about excitedly.* MISS HENEAGE *stands
ready to make herself disagreeable.*

GRACE, *speaking rapidly and with excitement.* I hear a man's
voice. Cates-Darby and brother Matthew.

Loud toot. Laughter and voices off back heard faintly.
GRACE *looks out of the door and leaves it rapidly.*

MISS HENEAGE. Outrageous!

SUDLEY. Disgraceful!

MRS. PHILLIMORE, *partly rising as voices and horn are heard.*
Shocking! I shall not take any part at all, in the—eh——
She fades away.

MISS HENEAGE, *interrupting her.* Don't trouble yourself.

Voices and laughter grow louder. CYNTHIA's *voice is heard.*
SIR WILFRID *appears at the back. He turns and waits for*
CYNTHIA *and* MATTHEW. *He carries wraps. He speaks to*
CYNTHIA, *who is still off of stage.* MATTHEW's *voice is
heard and* CYNTHIA's. CYNTHIA *appears at back, followed
by* MATTHEW. *As they appear,* CYNTHIA *speaks to* MAT-
THEW. SIR WILFRID *carries a newspaper and a parasol.
The hat is the one she wore in Act Two. She is in getup*

for auto. Goggles, veil, an exquisite duster in latest Paris style. All three come down rapidly. As she appears, SUD-LEY *and* MISS HENEAGE *exclaim, and there is a general movement.*

SUDLEY. 'Pon my word!

GRACE. Hah!

MISS HENEAGE, *rising with shocked propriety.* Shocking!

> GRACE *remains standing above sofa.* SUDLEY *moves toward her.* MISS HENEAGE *sits down again.* MRS. PHILLIMORE *reclines on sofa.* CYNTHIA *begins to speak as soon as she appears and speaks fluently to the end.*

CYNTHIA. No! I never was so surprised in my life as when I strolled into the paddock and they gave me a rousing reception—old Jimmy Withers, Debt Gollup, Jack Deal, Monty Spiffles, the Governor, and Buckeye. All of my old admirers! They simply fell on my neck, and, dear Matthew, what do you think I did? I turned on the water main!

> *Movements and murmurs of disapprobation from the family.* MATTHEW *indicates a desire to go.*

Oh, but you can't go!

MATTHEW. I'll return in no time!

CYNTHIA. I'm all ready to be married. Are they ready?

> MATTHEW *waves a pious, polite gesture of recognition to the family.*

I beg everybody's pardon!

> *She takes off her wrap and puts it on the back of a chair.*

My goggles are so dusty, I can't see who's who!

> *To* SIR WILFRID.

Thanks! You *have* carried it well!

> *Takes parasol from* SIR WILFRID.

SIR WILFRID, *aside to* CYNTHIA. When may I——?

CYNTHIA. See you next Goodwood!

SIR WILFRID, *imperturbably.* Oh, I'm coming back!

> CYNTHIA *comes down.*

CYNTHIA. Not a bit of use in coming back! I shall be married before you get here! Ta! Ta! Goodwood!

SIR WILFRID, *as before.* I'm coming back.

He goes out quickly. More murmurs of disapprobation from family. Slight pause.

CYNTHIA, *beginning to take off her goggles and coming down slowly.* I do awfully apologize for being so late!

MISS HENEAGE, *importantly.* Mrs. Karslake——

SUDLEY, *importantly.* Ahem!

CYNTHIA lays down her goggles and sees their severity.

CYNTHIA. Dear me!

She surveys the flowers and for a moment pauses.
Oh good heavens! Why, it looks like a smart funeral!

MISS HENEAGE moves, then speaks in a perfectly ordinary natural tone, but her expression is severe. CYNTHIA *immediately realizes the state of affairs in its fullness.*

MISS HENEAGE, *to* CYNTHIA. After what has occurred, Mrs. Karslake——

CYNTHIA glances at table.

CYNTHIA *sits at table, composed and good-tempered.* I see you got my wire—so you know where I have been.

MISS HENEAGE. To the racecourse.

SUDLEY. With a rowdy Englishman.

CYNTHIA glances at SUDLEY, *uncertain whether he means to be disagreeable or whether he is only naturally so.*

MISS HENEAGE. We concluded you desired to break the engagement!

CYNTHIA, *indifferently.* No! No! Oh! No!

MISS HENEAGE. Do you intend, despite of our opinion of you——

CYNTHIA. The only opinion that would have any weight with me would be Mrs. Phillimore's.

She turns expectantly to MRS. PHILLIMORE.

MRS. PHILLIMORE. I am generally asleep at this hour, and accordingly I will not venture to express any—eh—any—actual opinion.

She fades away. CYNTHIA *smiles.*

MISS HENEAGE, *coldly.* You smile. We simply inform you that as regards *us,* the alliance is not grateful.

CYNTHIA, *affecting gaiety and unconcern.* And all this because the gasoline gave out.

SUDLEY. My patience has given out!

GRACE. So has mine. I'm going.

Exit GRACE.

SUDLEY, *vexed beyond civility. To* CYNTHIA. My dear young lady. You come here, to this sacred—eh—eh—spot—altar—odoriferous of the paddock—speaking of Spiffles and Buckeye, having practically eloped, having created a scandal and disgraced our family!

CYNTHIA, *as before.* How does it disgrace you? Because I like to see a highbred, clean, nervy, sweet little four-legged gee play the antelope over a hurdle!

MISS HENEAGE. Sister, it is high time that you——

Turns to CYNTHIA.

CYNTHIA, *with quiet irony.* Mrs. Phillimore is generally asleep at this hour, and accordingly she will not venture to express——

SUDLEY, *spluttering with irritation.* Enough, madam—I *venture* to—to—to—to say you are leading a fast life.

CYNTHIA, *with powerful intention.* Not in this house! For six heavy weeks have I been laid away in the grave, and I've found it very slow indeed trying to keep pace with the dead!

SUDLEY, *despairingly.* This comes of horses!

CYNTHIA, *indignant.* Of what?

SUDLEY. C-c-caring for horses!

MISS HENEAGE, *with sublime morality.* What Mrs. Karslake cares for is—men.

CYNTHIA, *angry and gay.* What would you have me care for? The *Ornithorhynchus paradoxus?* Or *Pithacanthropus erectus?* Oh, I refuse to take you seriously.

SUDLEY *begins to prepare to leave; he buttons himself into respectability and his coat.*

SUDLEY. My dear madam, I take myself seriously—and madam, I—I retract what I have brought with me—

He feels in his waistcoat pocket.

—as a graceful gift, an Egyptian scarab—a—a—sacred beetle, which once ornamented the person of a—eh— mummy.

CYNTHIA, *getting even with him.* It should never be absent from your pocket, Mr. Sudley.

SUDLEY *walks away in a rage.*

MISS HENEAGE, *rising. To* SUDLEY. I've a vast mind to with-draw my——

CYNTHIA *moves.*

CYNTHIA *interrupts, maliciously.* Your wedding present? The little bronze cat!

MISS HENEAGE *moves, angrily.* Oh!

Even MRS. PHILLIMORE *comes momentarily to life and expresses silent indignation.*

SUDLEY, *loftily.* Sarah, I'm going.

Enter PHILIP *at back with* GRACE. PHILIP *looks dusty and grim.* GRACE, *as they come in, speaks to him.* PHILIP *shakes his head. They pause up stage.*

CYNTHIA, *emotionally.* I shall go to my room! However, all I ask is that you repeat to Philip——

She comes suddenly on PHILIP *and speaks to him in a low tone.*

SUDLEY, *to* MISS HENEAGE, *determined to win.* As I go out, I shall do myself the pleasure of calling a hansom for Mrs. Karslake——

PHILIP *comes down two or three steps.*

PHILIP. As you go out, Sudley, have a hansom called, and when it comes, get into it.

SUDLEY, *furious and speaking to* PHILIP. Eh—eh—my dear sir, I leave you to your fate.

PHILIP *angrily points him the door.* SUDLEY *goes out.*

MISS HENEAGE, *with weight.* Philip, you've not heard——

PHILIP *interrupts.* Everything—from Grace!

CYNTHIA *goes to the table.*

My sister has repeated your words to me—and her own! I've told her what I think of *her.*

PHILIP *looks witheringly at* GRACE.

GRACE. I shan't wait to hear any more.

Exit GRACE, *indignantly.*

PHILIP. Don't make it necessary for me to tell you what I think of you.

PHILIP *gives his arm to his mother.* MISS HENEAGE *goes towards the door.*

Mother, with your permission, I desire to be alone. I expect you and Grace, Sarah, to be dressed and ready for the ceremony a half hour from now.

As PHILIP *and* MRS. PHILLIMORE *are about to cross,* MISS HENEAGE *speaks.*

MISS HENEAGE. I shall come or not as I see fit. And let me add, my dear nephew, that a fool at forty is a fool indeed.

Exit MISS HENEAGE, *high and mighty, and much pleased with her quotation.*

MRS. PHILLIMORE, *stupid and weary as usual, to* PHILIP, *as he leads her to the door.*

My dear son—I won't venture to express——

CYNTHIA *goes to the table.*

PHILIP, *soothing a silly mother.* No, mother, don't! But I shall expect you, of course, at the ceremony.

Exit MRS. PHILLIMORE. PHILIP *takes the tone and assumes the attitude of the injured husband.*

It is proper for me to tell you that I followed you to
Belmont. I am aware—I know with whom—in fact, *I know
all!*

Pauses. He indicates the whole censorious universe.

And now let me assure you—I am the last man in the world
to be jilted on the very eve of—of—everything with you.
I won't be jilted.

CYNTHIA *is silent.*

You understand? I propose to marry you. I won't be made
ridiculous.

CYNTHIA, *glancing at* PHILIP. Philip, I didn't mean to make
you——

PHILIP. Why, then, did you run off to Belmont Park with
that fellow?

CYNTHIA. Philip, I—eh——

PHILIP, *sitting at the table.* What motive? What reason? On
our wedding day? Why did you do it?

CYNTHIA. I'll tell you the truth. I was bored.

PHILIP. Bored? In my company?

PHILIP, *in a gesture, gives up.*

CYNTHIA. I was bored, and then—and besides, Sir Wilfrid
asked me to go.

PHILIP. Exactly, and that was why you went. Cynthia, when
you promised to marry me, you told me you had forever
done with love. You agreed that marriage was the rational
coming together of two people.

CYNTHIA. I know, I know!

PHILIP. Do you believe that now?

CYNTHIA. I don't know what I believe. My brain is in a whirl!
But, Philip, I am beginning to be—I'm afraid—yes, I am
afraid that one can't just select a great and good man—
She indicates him.

—and say: I will be happy with him.

PHILIP, *with dignity.* I don't see why not. You must assuredly
do one or the other: You must either let your heart choose
or your head select.

CYNTHIA, *gravely.* No, there's a third scheme; Sir Wilfrid
explained the theory to me. A woman should marry whenever she has a whim for the man, and then leave the rest
to the man. Do you see?

PHILIP, *furious.* Do I see? Have I ever seen anything else?
Marry for whim! That's the New York idea of marriage.

CYNTHIA, *giving a cynical opinion.* New York ought to know.

PHILIP. Marry for whim and leave the rest to the divorce
court! Marry for whim and leave the rest to the man. That
was the former Mrs. Phillimore's idea. Only she spelled
"whim" differently; she omitted the *w.*

He rises in his anger.

And now you—*you* take up with this preposterous—

CYNTHIA *moves uneasily.*

But, nonsense! It's impossible! A woman of your mental
caliber—— No. Some obscure, primitive, female *feeling* is
at work corrupting your better judgment! What is it you
feel?

CYNTHIA. Philip, you never felt like a fool, did you?

PHILIP. No, never.

CYNTHIA, *politely.* I thought not.

PHILIP. No, but whatever your feelings, I conclude you are
ready to marry me.

CYNTHIA, *uneasy.* Of course, I came back. I am here, am I not?

PHILIP. You are ready to marry me?

CYNTHIA, *twisting in the coils.* But you haven't had your
dinner.

PHILIP. Do I understand you refuse?

CYNTHIA. Couldn't we defer——?

PHILIP. You refuse?

CYNTHIA, *a slight pause, trapped and seeing no way out*. No,
I said I'd marry you. I'm a woman of my word. I will.

PHILIP, *triumphant*. Ah! Very good, then. Run to your room.

CYNTHIA *turns to* PHILIP.

Throw something over you. In a half hour I'll expect you
here! And, Cynthia, my dear, remember! I cannot cuculate
like a wood pigeon, but—I esteem you!

CYNTHIA, *hopelessly*. I think I'll go, Philip.

PHILIP. I may not be fitted to play the lovebird, but——

CYNTHIA, *as before*. I think I'll go, Philip.

PHILIP. I'll expect you—in half an hour.

CYNTHIA, *with leaden despair*. Yes.

PHILIP. And, Cynthia, don't think any more about that fellow,
Cates-Darby.

CYNTHIA, *amazed and disgusted by his misapprehension*. No.

Exit CYNTHIA.

THOMAS *enters from the opposite door*.

PHILIP, *not seeing* THOMAS *and clumsily defiant*. And if I had
that fellow, Cates-Darby, in the dock——!

THOMAS. Sir Wilfrid Cates-Darby.

PHILIP. Sir what—what—wh-who?

Enter SIR WILFRID *in evening dress*. PHILIP *looks* SIR WIL-
FRID *in the face and speaks to* THOMAS.

Tell Sir Wilfrid Cates-Darby I am not at home to him.

THOMAS *embarrassed*.

SIR WILFRID, *undaunted*. My dear Lord Eldon——

PHILIP *speaks to* THOMAS, *as before*.

Show the gentleman the door.

Pause. SIR WILFRID *glances at door with a significant
gesture*.

SIR WILFRID *goes to the door, examines it, and returns to*
PHILIP. Eh—I admire the door, my boy! Fine, old, carved

mahogany panel; but don't ask me to leave by it, for Mrs. Karslake made me promise I'd come, and that's why I'm here.

THOMAS *exits.*

PHILIP. Sir, you are—impudent!

SIR WILFRID, *interrupting.* Ah, you put it all in a nutshell, don't you?

PHILIP. To show your face here, after practically eloping with my wife!

SIR WILFRID, *pretending ignorance.* When were you married?

PHILIP. We're as good as married.

SIR WILFRID. Oh, pooh, pooh! You can't tell me that grace before soup is as good as a dinner!

He takes cigar case out.

PHILIP. Sir—I—demand——

SIR WILFRID, *calmly carrying the situation.* Mrs. Karslake is *not* married. *That's* why I'm here. I am here for the same purpose *you* are: to ask Mrs. Karslake to be my wife.

PHILIP. Are you in your senses?

SIR WILFRID, *touching up his American cousin in his pet vanity.* Come, come, Judge—you Americans have no sense of humor.

He takes a small jewel case from his pocket.

There's my regards for the lady—and—

Reasonably.

—if I must go, I will. Of course, I would like to see her, but—if it isn't your American custom——

Enter THOMAS.

THOMAS. Mr. Karslake.

SIR WILFRID. Oh well, I say, if he can come, I can!

Enter JOHN KARSLAKE *in evening dress, carrying a large and very smart bride's bouquet which he hands to* PHILIP. PHILIP *takes it because he isn't up to dropping it but gets*

it out of his hands as soon as he can. PHILIP *is transfixed;*
JOHN *comes to the front of the stage. Deep down he is
feeling wounded and unhappy. But, as he knows his
coming to the ceremony on whatever pretext is a social
outrage, he carries it off by assuming an air of its being
the most natural thing in the world. He controls the expression of his deeper emotion, but the pressure of this
keeps his face grave, and he speaks with force.*

JOHN. My compliments to the bride, Judge.

PHILIP, *angry.* And you, too, have the effrontery?

SIR WILFRID. There you are!

JOHN, *pretending ease.* Oh, call it friendship——

THOMAS *goes out.*

PHILIP *puts bouquet on table. Ironically.* I suppose Mrs.
Karslake——

JOHN. She wagered me I wouldn't give her away, and of
course——

Throughout this scene JOHN *hides the emotions he will
not show behind a daring irony. He has* PHILIP *on his left,
walking about in a fury;* SIR WILFRID *sits on the edge of
the table, gay and undisturbed.*

PHILIP, *taking a step toward* JOHN. You will oblige me—both
of you—by immediately leaving——

JOHN, *smiling and going to* PHILIP. Oh, come, come, Judge—
suppose I *am* here? Who has a better right to attend his
wife's obsequies! Certainly I come as a mourner—for *you!*

SIR WILFRID. I say, is it the custom?

JOHN. No, no—of course it's not the custom, no. But we'll
make it the custom. After all, what's a divorced wife
among friends?

PHILIP. Sir, your humor is strained!

JOHN. Humor, Judge?

PHILIP. It is, sir, and I'll not be bantered! Your both being
here is—it is—gentlemen, there is a decorum which the
stars in their courses do not violate.

JOHN. Now, Judge, never you mind what the stars do in their divorces! Get down to earth of the present day. Rufus Choate and Daniel Webster are dead. You must be modern. You must let peroration and poetry alone! Come along now. Why shouldn't I give the lady away?

SIR WILFRID. Hear! Hear! Oh, I beg your pardon!

JOHN. And why shouldn't we both be here? American marriage is a new thing. We've got to strike the pace, and the only trouble is, Judge, that the judiciary have so messed the thing up that a man can't be sure he *is* married until he's divorced. It's a sort of marry-go-round, to be sure! But let it go at that! Here we all are, and we're ready to marry my wife to you and start her on her way to him!

PHILIP, *brought to a standstill.* Good Lord! Sir, you cannot trifle with monogamy!

JOHN. Now, now, Judge, monogamy is just as extinct as knee breeches. The new woman has a new idea, and the new idea is—well, it's just the opposite of the old Mormon one. Their idea is one man, ten wives, and a hundred children. Our idea is one woman, a hundred husbands, and one child.

PHILIP. Sir, this is polyandry.

JOHN. Polyandry? A hundred to one it's polyandry; and that's it, Judge! Uncle Sam has established consecutive polyandry, but there's got to be an interval between husbands! The fact is, Judge, the modern American marriage is like a wire fence. The woman's the wire—the posts are the husbands.

He indicates himself and then SIR WILFRID *and* PHILIP. One—two—three! And if you cast your eye over the future you can count them, post after post, up hill, down dale, all the way to Dakota!

PHILIP. All very amusing, sir, but the fact remains——

JOHN, *going to* PHILIP. PHILIP *moves away.* Now, now, Judge, I like you. But you're asleep; you're living in the Dark

Ages. You want to call up Central. "Hello, Central! Give
me the present time, 1906, New York!"

SIR WILFRID. Of course you do, and—there you are!

PHILIP, *heavily*. There I am not, sir! And—

To JOHN.

—as for Mr. Karslake's ill-timed jocosity, sir, in the
future——

SIR WILFRID. Oh, hang the future!

PHILIP. I begin to hope, Sir Wilfrid, that in the future I shall
have the pleasure of hanging you!

To JOHN.

And as to you, sir, your insensate idea of giving away your
own—your former—my—your—oh! Good Lord! This is a
nightmare!

He turns to go in despair.

Enter MATTHEW, *who, seeing* PHILIP, *speaks as he comes
in from door.*

MATTHEW, *to* PHILIP. My dear brother, Aunt Sarah Heneage
refuses to give Mrs. Karslake away, unless you yourself—
eh——

PHILIP, *as he exits*. No more! I'll attend to the matter!

Exit. The choir boys are heard practicing in the next room.

MATTHEW, *mopping his brow*. How do you both do? My aunt
has made me very warm.

He rings the bell.

You hear our choir practicing—sweet angel boys! Hm! Hm!
Some of the family will not be present. I am very fond of
you, Mr. Karslake, and I think it admirably Christian of
you to have waived your—eh—your—eh—that is, now that
I look at it more narrowly, let me say that in the excitement of pleasurable anticipation, I forgot, Karslake, that
your presence might occasion remark——

Enter THOMAS.

Thomas! I left, in the hall, a small handbag or satchel
containing my surplice.

THOMAS. Yes, sir. Ahem!

MATTHEW. You must really find the handbag at once.

THOMAS turns to go, when he stops startled.

THOMAS. Yes, sir.

Announcing in consternation.

Mrs. Vida Phillimore.

Enter VIDA PHILLIMORE *in full evening dress. She steps gently to* MATTHEW.

MATTHEW, *always piously serene.* Ah, my dear child! Now this is just as it should be! That is, eh——

He comes to the front of the stage with her; she pointedly looks away from SIR WILFRID.

That is, when I come to think of it—your presence might be deemed inauspicious.

VIDA. But, my dear Matthew, I had to come.

Aside to him.

I have a reason for being here.

THOMAS *enters.*

MATTHEW. But, my dear child——

THOMAS, *with sympathetic intention.* Sir, Mr. Phillimore wishes to have your assistance, sir—with Miss Heneage *immediately!*

MATTHEW. Ah!

To VIDA.

One moment! I'll return.

To THOMAS.

Have you found the bag with my surplice?

He goes out with THOMAS, *speaking.* SIR WILFRID *comes to* VIDA. JOHN *watches the door.*

SIR WILFRID, *to* VIDA. You're just the person I most want to see!

VIDA, *with affected iciness.* Oh no, Sir Wilfrid, Cynthia isn't here yet!

Crossing to table. JOHN *comes toward her and she speaks to him with obvious sweetness.*

Jack, dear, I never was so ravished to see anyone.

SIR WILFRID, *taken aback.* By Jove!

VIDA, *very sweet.* I knew I should find you here!

JOHN, *annoyed but civil.* Now don't do that!

VIDA, *as before.* Jack!

They sit down.

JOHN, *civil but plain-spoken.* Don't do it!

VIDA, *in a voice dripping with honey.* Do what, Jack?

JOHN. Touch me with your voice! I have troubles enough of my own.

He sits not far from her; the table is between them.

VIDA. And I know *who* your troubles are! Cynthia!

From this moment VIDA *gives up* JOHN *as an object of the chase and lets him into her other game.*

JOHN. I hate her. I don't know why I came.

VIDA. You came, dear, because you couldn't stay away—you're in love with her.

JOHN. All right, Vida, what I feel may be *love*—but all I can say is, if I could get even with Cynthia Karslake——

VIDA. You can, dear—it's as easy as powdering one's face; all you have to do is to be too nice to me!

JOHN *looks inquiringly at* VIDA. Eh!

VIDA. Don't you realize she's jealous of you? Why did she come to my house this morning? She's jealous—and all you have to do——

JOHN. If I can make her wince, I'll make love to you till the heavenly cows come home!

VIDA. Well, you see, my dear, if you make love to me it will—

She delicately indicates SIR WILFRID.

—cut both ways at once!

JOHN. Eh—what! Not Cates-Darby?

Starting.

Is that Cynthia?

VIDA. Now don't get rattled and forget to make love to me.

JOHN. I've got the jumps.

Trying to accept her instructions.

Vida, I adore you.

VIDA. Oh, you must be more convincing; that won't do at all.

JOHN, *listening.* Is that she now?

Enter MATTHEW, *who goes to the inner room.*

VIDA. It's Matthew. And, Jack dear, you'd best get the hang of it before Cynthia comes. You might tell me all about your divorce. That's a sympathetic subject. Were you able to undermine it?

JOHN. No. I've got a wire from my lawyer this morning. The divorce holds. She's a free woman. She can marry whom she likes.

The organ is heard, very softly played.

Is that Cynthia?

He rises quickly.

VIDA. It's the organ!

JOHN, *overwhelmingly excited.* By George! I should never have come! I think I'll go.

He crosses to go to the door.

VIDA. *She rises and follows him remonstratingly.* When I need you?

JOHN. I can't stand it.

VIDA. Oh, but, Jack——

JOHN. Good night!

VIDA. I feel quite ill.

Seeing that she must play her last card to keep him, pretends to faintness, sways and falls into his arms.

Oh!

JOHN, *in a rage, but beaten.* I believe you're putting up a fake.

The organ swells as CYNTHIA *enters sweepingly, dressed in full evening dress for the wedding ceremony.* JOHN, *not knowing what to do, holds* VIDA *up as a horrid necessity.*

CYNTHIA, *speaking as she comes on, to* MATTHEW. Here I am. Ridiculous to make it a conventional thing, you know. Come in on the swell of the music and all that, just as if I'd never been married before. Where's Philip?

She looks for PHILIP *and sees* JOHN *with* VIDA *in his arms. She stops short.*

JOHN, *uneasy and embarrassed.* A glass of water! I beg your pardon, Mrs. Karslake——

The organ plays on.

CYNTHIA, *ironical and calm.* Vida!

JOHN. She has fainted.

CYNTHIA, *as before.* Fainted?

Without pause. Dear, dear, dear, terrible! So she has.

SIR WILFRID *takes flowers from a vase and prepares to sprinkle* VIDA's *forehead with the water it contains.*

No, no, not her forehead, Sir Wilfrid, her frock! Sprinkle her best Paquin! If it's a real faint, she will not come to!

VIDA, *as her Paris importation is about to suffer, comes to her senses.* I almost fainted.

CYNTHIA. Almost!

VIDA, *using the stock phrase as a matter of course and reviving rapidly.* Where am I?

JOHN *glances at* CYNTHIA *sharply.*

Oh, the bride! I beg everyone's pardon. Cynthia, at a crisis like this, I simply couldn't stay away from Philip!

CYNTHIA. Stay away from Philip?

JOHN *and* CYNTHIA *exchange glances.*

VIDA. Your arm, Jack; and lead me where there is air.

JOHN *and* VIDA *go into the further room;* JOHN *stands left of her. The organ stops.* SIR WILFRID *comes down. He and*

CYNTHIA *are practically alone on the stage.* JOHN *and* VIDA *are barely within sight. You first see him take her fan and give her air; then he picks up a book and reads from it to her.*

SIR WILFRID. I've come back.

CYNTHIA, *to* SIR WILFRID. Asks for air and goes to the green house.

CYNTHIA *crosses stage.* SIR WILFRID *offers her a seat.*

I know why you are here. It's that intoxicating little whim you suppose me to have for you. My regrets! But the whim's gone flat. Yes, yes, my gasoline days are over. I'm going to be garaged for good. However, I'm glad you're here; you take the edge off——

SIR WILFRID. Mr. Phillimore?

CYNTHIA, *sharply.* No, Karslake. I'm just waiting to say the words—

Enter THOMAS.

—"love, honor and obey" to Phillimore—

Looks up back.

—and *at* Karslake!

CYNTHIA *sees* THOMAS.

What is it? Mr. Phillimore?

THOMAS. Mr. Phillimore will be down in a few minutes, ma'am. He's very sorry, ma'am—

Lowers his voice and comes nearer CYNTHIA, *mindful of the respectabilities.*

—but there's a button off his waistcoat.

CYNTHIA, *excited, with irony. Rising.* Button off his waistcoat!

Exit THOMAS.

SIR WILFRID, *delightedly.* Ah! So much the better for me.

CYNTHIA *looks up back.*

Now then, never mind those two!

CYNTHIA *moves restlessly.*

Sit down.

CYNTHIA. I can't.

SIR WILFRID. You're as nervous as——

CYNTHIA. Nervous! Of course I'm nervous! So would you be nervous if you'd had a runaway and smashup and you were going to try it again.

Looking up back. SIR WILFRID *is uneasy.*

And if someone doesn't do away with those calla lilies—the odor makes me faint!

SIR WILFRID *moves.* No, it's not the lilies! It's the orange blossoms!

SIR WILFRID. Orange blossoms.

CYNTHIA. The flowers that grow on the tree that hangs over the abyss.

SIR WILFRID gets the vase of orange blossoms.

They smell of six o'clock in the evening. When Philip's fallen asleep, and the little boys are crying the winners outside, and I'm crying inside, and dying inside and outside and everywhere.

SIR WILFRID *comes down.*

SIR WILFRID. Sorry to disappoint you. They're artificial.

CYNTHIA *shrugs her shoulders.*

That's it! They're emblematic of artificial domesticity! And I'm here to help you balk it.

He sits; CYNTHIA *half rises and looks toward* JOHN *and* VIDA.

Keep still now, I've a lot to say to you. Stop looking——

CYNTHIA. Do you think I can listen to you make love to me when the man who—who—whom I most despise in all the world is reading poetry to the woman who—who got me into the fix I'm in!

SIR WILFRID, *leaning over the chair in which she sits.* What do you want to look at 'em for?

CYNTHIA *moves.*

Let 'em be and listen to me! Sit down; for damme, I'm determined.

CYNTHIA *at the table.*

CYNTHIA, *half to herself.* I won't look at them! I won't think of them. Beasts!

SIR WILFRID *interposes between her and her view of* JOHN.
Enter THOMAS.

SIR WILFRID. Now then——

He sits.

CYNTHIA. Those two *here!* It's just as if Adam and Eve should invite the snake to their golden wedding.

She sees THOMAS.

What is it, what's the matter?

THOMAS. Mr. Phillimore's excuses, ma'am. In a very short time——

THOMAS *exits.*

SIR WILFRID. I'm on to you! You hoped for more buttons!

CYNTHIA. I'm dying of the heat; fan me.

SIR WILFRID *fans* CYNTHIA.

SIR WILFRID. Heat! No! You're dying because you're ignorin' nature. Certainly you are! You're marryin' Phillimore!

CYNTHIA *appears faint.*

Can't ignore nature, Mrs. Karslake. Yes, you are; you're forcin' your feelin's.

CYNTHIA *glances at him.*

And what you want to do is to let yourself go a bit—up anchor and sit tight! I'm no seaman, but that's the idea!

CYNTHIA *moves and shakes her head.*

So just throw the reins on nature's neck, jump this fellow Phillimore, and marry me!

He leans over to CYNTHIA.

CYNTHIA, *naturally, but with irritation.* You propose to me here, at a moment like this? When I'm on the last lap—

just in sight of the goal—the gallows—the halter—the altar,
I don't know what its name is! No, I won't have you!

Looking toward KARSLAKE *and* VIDA.

And I won't have you stand near me! I won't have you
talking to me in a low tone!

As before.

Stand over there—stand where you are.

SIR WILFRID. I say——

CYNTHIA. I can hear you—I'm listening!

SIR WILFRID. Well, don't look so hurried and worried. You've
got buttons and buttons of time. And now my offer. You
haven't yet said you would——

CYNTHIA. Marry you? I don't even know you!

SIR WILFRID, *feeling sure of being accepted.* Oh—tell you all
about myself. I'm no duke in a pickle o' debts, d'ye see?
I can marry where I like. Some o' my countrymen are
rotters, ye know. They'd marry a monkey, if poppa-up-
the-tree had a corner in coconuts! And they do marry some
queer ones, y'know.

CYNTHIA *looks up, exclaims and turns.* SIR WILFRID *turns.*

CYNTHIA. Do they?

SIR WILFRID. Oh, rather. That's what's giving your heiresses
such a bad name lately. If a fellah's in debt he can't pick
and choose, and then he swears that American gals are
awfully fine lookers but they're no good when it comes to
continuin' the race! Fair dolls in the drawin' room but no
good in the nursery.

CYNTHIA, *thinking of* JOHN *and* VIDA *and nothing else.* I can
see Vida in the nursery.

SIR WILFRID. You understand when you want a brood mare
you don't choose a Kentucky mule.

CYNTHIA. I think I see one.

SIR WILFRID. Well, that's what they're saying over there. They
say your gals run to talk—

He plainly remembers VIDA's *volubility.*

—and I have seen gals here that would chat life into a wooden Indian! That's what you Americans call being clever—all brains and no stuffin'! In fact, some of your American gals are the nicest boys I ever met.

CYNTHIA. So that's what you think?

SIR WILFRID. Not a bit what *I* think—what my countrymen think!

CYNTHIA. Why are you telling me?

SIR WILFRID. Oh, just explaining my character. I'm the sort that can pick and choose—and what I want is heart.

CYNTHIA, *always having* VIDA *and* JOHN *in mind.* No more heart than a dragonfly!

The organ begins to play softly.

SIR WILFRID. That's it, dragonfly. Cold as stone and never stops buzzing about and showin' off her colors. It's that American dragonfly girl that I'm afraid of, because, d'ye see, I don't know what an American expects when he marries; yes, but you're not listening!

CYNTHIA. I am listening. I am!

SIR WILFRID, *speaking directly to her.* An Englishman, ye see, when he marries, expects three things: love, obedience, and five children.

CYNTHIA. Three things! I make it seven!

SIR WILFRID. Yes, my dear, but the point is, will you be mistress of Traynham?

CYNTHIA, *who has only half listened to him.* No, Sir Wilfrid, thank you, I won't.

She turns to see JOHN *crossing the drawing room at back with* VIDA, *apparently absorbed in what she says.*

It's outrageous!

SIR WILFRID. Eh? Why, you're cryin'!

CYNTHIA, *almost sobbing.* I am not.

SIR WILFRID. You're not crying because you're in love with me?

CYNTHIA. I'm not crying—or if I am, I'm crying because I love my country. It's a disgrace to America—castoff husbands and wives getting together in a parlor and playing tag under a palm tree.

JOHN, *with intention and determined to stab* CYNTHIA, *kisses* VIDA's *hand.*

SIR WILFRID. Eh! Oh! I'm damned!

To CYNTHIA. What do you think that means?

CYNTHIA. I don't doubt it means a wedding here at once—after mine!

VIDA *and* JOHN *come down.*

VIDA, *affecting an impossible intimacy to wound* CYNTHIA *and tantalize* SIR WILFRID. Hush, Jack—I'd much rather no one should know anything about it until it's all over!

CYNTHIA *starts and looks at* SIR WILFRID. What did I tell you?

VIDA, *to* CYNTHIA. Oh, my dear, he's asked me to champagne and lobster at *your* house—his house! Matthew is coming!

CYNTHIA *starts but controls herself.*

And you're to come, Sir Wilfrid.

VIDA *speaks, intending to convey the idea of a sudden marriage ceremony.*

Of course, my dear, I would like to wait for your wedding, but something rather—rather important to me is to take place, and I know you'll excuse me.

Organ stops.

SIR WILFRID, *piqued at being forgotten.* All very neat, but you haven't given me a chance even.

VIDA. Chance? You're not serious?

SIR WILFRID. I am!

VIDA, *striking while the iron is hot.* I'll give you a minute to offer yourself.

SIR WILFRID. Eh?

VIDA. Sixty seconds from now.

SIR WILFRID, *uncertain.* There's such a thing as bein' silly.

VIDA, *calm and determined.* Fifty seconds left.

SIR WILFRID. I take you—count fair.

He hands her his watch and goes to where CYNTHIA *stands.*

I say, Mrs. Karslake——

CYNTHIA, *overwhelmed with grief and emotion.* They're engaged; they's going to be married tonight over champagne and lobster at my house!

SIR WILFRID. Will you consider your——

CYNTHIA, *hastily, to get rid of him.* No, no, no, no! Thank you, Sir Wilfrid, I will not.

SIR WILFRID, *calm and not to be laid low.* Thanks awfully.

Crosses to VIDA. CYNTHIA *walks away.*

Mrs. Phillimore——

VIDA. *She gives him back his watch.* Too late!

To KARSLAKE.

Jack dear, we must be off.

SIR WILFRID, *standing and making a general appeal for information.* I say, is it the custom for American girls—that sixty seconds or too late? Look here! Not a bit too late. I'll take you around to Jack Karslake's, and I'm going to ask you the same old question again, you know.

To VIDA.

By Jove, you know in your country it's the pace that kills.

Exeunt SIR WILFRID *and* VIDA.

JOHN, *gravely to* CYNTHIA, *who comes to the front of the stage.*

Good night, Mrs. Karslake, I'm going; I'm sorry I came.

CYNTHIA. Sorry? Why are you sorry?

JOHN *looks at her; she winces a little.*

You've got what you wanted.

Pause.

I wouldn't mind your marrying Vida——

JOHN, *gravely.* Oh, wouldn't you?

CYNTHIA. —but I don't think you showed good taste in engaging yourselves *here.*

JOHN. Of course, I should have preferred a garden of roses and plenty of twilight.

CYNTHIA, *rushing into speech.* I'll tell you what you *have* done —you've thrown yourself away! A woman like that! No head, no heart! All languor and loose—loose frocks—she's the typical, worst thing America can do! She's the regular American marriage worm!

JOHN. I have known others——

CYNTHIA, *quickly.* Not me. I'm not a patch on that woman. Do you know anything about her life? Do you know the things she did to Philip? Kept him up every night of his life—forty days out of every thirty—and then, without his knowing it, put brandy in his coffee to make him lively at breakfast.

JOHN, *banteringly.* I begin to think she is just the woman——

CYNTHIA, *unable to quiet her jealousy.* She is *not* the woman for *you!* A man with your bad temper—your airs of authority—your assumption of—of—everything. What you need is a good, old-fashioned, bread poultice woman!

CYNTHIA *comes to a full stop and faces* JOHN.

JOHN, *sharply.* Can't say I've had any experience of the good, old-fashioned, bread poultice.

CYNTHIA. I don't care what you say! If you marry Vida Phillimore—— You shan't do it.

Tears of rage choking her.

No, I liked your father and for *his* sake, I'll see that his son doesn't make a donkey of himself a second time.

JOHN, *too angry to be amused.* Oh, I thought I was divorced. I begin to feel as if I had you on my hands still.

CYNTHIA. You have! You shall have! If you attempt to marry her, I'll follow you—and I'll find her—I'll tell Vida——

He turns to her.

I will. I'll tell Vida just what sort of a dance you led me.

JOHN, *quickly on her last word but speaking gravely.* Indeed! Will you? And *why* do you care what happens to me?

CYNTHIA, *startled by his tone.* I—I—ah—

JOHN, *insistently and with a faint hope.* Why do you *care?*

CYNTHIA. I don't. Not in your sense——

JOHN. How dare you then pretend——

CYNTHIA. I don't pretend.

JOHN, *interrupting her, proud, serious, and strong.* How dare you look me in the face with the eyes that I once kissed and pretend the least regard for me?

CYNTHIA *recoils and looks away. Her own feelings are revealed to her clearly for the first time.*

I begin to understand our American women now. Fireflies —and the fire they gleam with is so cold that a midge couldn't warm his heart at it, let alone a man. You're not of the same race as a man! You married me for nothing, divorced me for nothing, because you *are* nothing!

CYNTHIA, *wounded to the heart.* Jack! What are you saying?

JOHN, *with unrestrained emotion.* What—you feigning an interest in me, feigning a lie—and in five minutes——

Gesture indicating altar.

Oh, you've taught me the trick of your sex—you're the woman who's not a woman!

CYNTHIA, *weakly.* You're saying terrible things to me.

JOHN, *low and with intensity.* You haven't been divorced from me long enough to forget—what you should be ashamed to remember.

CYNTHIA, *unable to face him and pretending not to understand him.* I don't know what you mean.

JOHN, *more forcibly and with manly emotion.* You're not able to forget me! You know you're not able to forget me; ask yourself if you are able to forget me, and when your heart, such as it is, answers "no," then—

The organ is plainly heard.

—well, then, prance gaily up to the altar and marry that, if you can!

He exits quickly. CYNTHIA *crosses to armchair and sinks into it. She trembles as if she were overdone. Voices are heard speaking in the next room. Enter* MATTHEW *and* MISS HENEAGE. *Enter* PHILIP. CYNTHIA *is so sunk in the chair they do not see her.* MISS HENEAGE *goes up to sofa back and waits. They all are dressed for an evening reception and* PHILIP *in the traditional bridegroom's rig.*

MATTHEW, *as he enters.* I am sure you will do your part, Sarah—in a spirit of Christian decorum.

To PHILIP.

It was impossible to find my surplice, Philip, but the more informal the better.

PHILIP, *with pompous responsibility.* Where's Cynthia?

MATTHEW *gives glance around room.*

MATTHEW. Ah, here's the choir!

He goes to meet it. Choir boys come in very orderly; divide and take their places, an even number on each side of the altar of flowers. MATTHEW *vaguely superintends.* PHILIP *gets in the way of the bell. Moves out of the way. Enter* THOMAS.

Thomas, I directed you—— One moment, if you please.

He indicates table and chairs. THOMAS *hastens to move the chairs and the table against the wall.* PHILIP *comes down.*

PHILIP, *looking for her.* Where's Cynthia?

CYNTHIA *rises.* PHILIP *sees her when she moves and crosses toward her, but stops. The organ stops.*

CYNTHIA, *faintly.* Here I am.

MATTHEW *comes down. The organ plays softly.*

MATTHEW, *coming to* CYNTHIA. Ah, my very dear Cynthia, I knew there was something. Let me tell you the words of the hymn I have chosen:

> *Enduring love, sweet end of strife*
> *Oh, bless this happy man and wife!*

I'm afraid you feel—eh—eh!

CYNTHIA, *desperately calm.* I feel awfully queer—I think I need a scotch.

The organ stops. PHILIP *remains uneasily at a little distance.* MRS. PHILLIMORE *and* GRACE *enter back slowly, as cheerfully as if they were going to hear the funeral service read. They remain near the doorway.*

MATTHEW. Really, my dear, in the pomp and vanity—I mean —ceremony of this—this unique occasion, there should be sufficient exhilaration.

CYNTHIA, *as before.* But there isn't!

She sits.

MATTHEW. I don't think my bishop would approve of—eh— anything *before!*

CYNTHIA, *too agitated to know how much she is moved.* I feel very queer.

MATTHEW, *piously sure that everything is for the best.* My dear child——

CYNTHIA. However, I suppose there's nothing for it—now—but —to—to——

MATTHEW. Courage!

CYNTHIA, *desperate and with sudden explosion.* Oh, don't speak to me. I feel as if I'd been eating gunpowder and the very first word of the wedding service would set it off!

MATTHEW. My dear, your indisposition is the voice of nature.

CYNTHIA *speaks more rapidly and with growing excitement,* MATTHEW *going toward the choir boys.*

CYNTHIA. Ah—that's it—nature!

MATTHEW *shakes his head.*

I've a great mind to throw the reins on nature's neck.

PHILIP. Matthew!

He moves to take his stand for the ceremony.

MATTHEW, *looking at* PHILIP. *To* CYNTHIA. Philip is ready.

PHILIP *comes down. The organ plays "The Wedding March."*

CYNTHIA, *to herself, as if at bay.* Ready? Ready? Ready?

MATTHEW. Cynthia, you will take Miss Heneage's arm.

MISS HENEAGE *comes down near table.*

Sarah!

MATTHEW *indicates to* MISS HENEAGE *where* CYNTHIA *is.* MISS HENEAGE *advances a step or two.* MATTHEW *goes up and speaks in a low voice to choir.*

Now please don't forget, my boys. When I raise my hands so, you begin, "Enduring love; sweet end of strife."

CYNTHIA *has risen. On the table is her long lace cloak. She stands by this table.* MATTHEW *assumes sacerdotal importance and takes his position inside the altar of flowers.*

Ahem! Philip!

He indicates to PHILIP *that he take his position.*

Sarah!

CYNTHIA *breathes fast and supports herself on table.* MISS HENEAGE *goes toward her and stands for a moment looking at* CYNTHIA.

The ceremony will now begin.

The organ plays Mendelssohn's "Wedding March." CYNTHIA *turns and faces* MISS HENEAGE. MISS HENEAGE *comes to* CYNTHIA *slowly and extends her hand in her readiness to lead the bride to the altar.*

MISS HENEAGE. Mrs. Karslake!

PHILIP. Ahem!

MATTHEW *steps forward two or three steps.* CYNTHIA *stands turned to stone.*

MATTHEW. My dear Cynthia. I request you—to take your place.

CYNTHIA *moves one or two steps across as if to go up to the altar. She takes* MISS HENEAGE's *hand, and slowly they walk toward* MATTHEW.

Your husband-to-be—is ready, the ring is in my pocket. I have only to ask you the—eh—necessary questions—and—eh—all will be blissfully over in a moment.

The organ is louder.

CYNTHIA. *At this moment, just as she reaches* PHILIP, *she stops, faces round, looks him,* MATTHEW, *and the rest in the face and cries out in despair.* Thomas! Call a hansom!

THOMAS *exits and leaves door open.* MISS HENEAGE *crosses the stage.* MRS. PHILLIMORE *rises.* CYNTHIA *grasps her cloak on table.* PHILIP *turns and* CYNTHIA *comes forward and stops.*

I can't, Philip—I can't.

Whistle of hansom is heard off; the organ stops.

It is simply a case of throwing the reins on nature's neck—up anchor—and sit tight!

MATTHEW *crosses to* CYNTHIA.

Matthew, don't come near me! Yes, yes, I distrust you. It's your business, and you'd marry me if you could.

PHILIP, *watching her in dismay as she throws on her cloak.* Where are you going?

CYNTHIA. I'm going to Jack.

PHILIP. What for?

CYNTHIA. To stop his marrying Vida. I'm blowing a hurricane inside, a horrible, happy hurricane! I know myself—I know what's the matter with me. If I married you and Miss Heneage—what's the use of talking about it—he mustn't marry that woman. He shan't.

CYNTHIA *has now all her wraps on; goes up rapidly. To* PHILIP. Sorry! So long! Good night and see you later.

CYNTHIA *goes to door rapidly;* MATTHEW, *in absolute amazement, throws up his arms.* PHILIP *is rigid.* MRS. PHILLIMORE *sinks into a chair.* MISS HENEAGE *is super-*

cilious and unmoved. GRACE *is the same. The choir, at* MATTHEW'S *gesture, mistakes it for the concerted signal and bursts lustily into the Epithalamium.*

Enduring love, sweet end of strife
Oh, bless this happy man and wife!

ACT FOUR

The scene is laid in JOHN KARSLAKE'S *study and smoking room. There is a bay window on the right. A door on the right leads to stairs and the front door of house, while a door at the back leads to the dining room. A fireplace is on the left and a mantel. A bookcase contains law books and sporting books. A full-length portrait of* CYNTHIA *is on the wall. Nothing of this portrait is seen by the audience except the gilt frame and a space of canvas. A large table with writing materials is littered over with law books, sporting books, papers, pipes, crops, and a pair of spurs. A wedding ring lies on it. There are three very low easy chairs. The general appearance of the room is extremely gay and garish in color. It has the easy confusion of a man's room. There is a small table on which is a woman's sewing basket. The sewing basket is open. A piece of rich fancywork lies on the table, as if a lady had just risen from sewing. On the corner are a lady's gloves. On a chair back is a lady's hat. It is a half hour later than the close of Act Three. Curtains are drawn over the window. A lamp on the table is lighted. Electric lights about the room are also lighted. One chair is conspicuously standing on its head.*

Curtain rises on NOGAM, *who busies himself at a table at the back. The door at the back is half open.*

SIR WILFRID, *coming in door.* Eh—what did you say your name was?

NOGAM. Nogam, sir.

SIR WILFRID. Nogam? I've been here thirty minutes. Where are the cigars?

NOGAM *motions to a small table near the entrance door where the cigars are.*

Thank you. Nogam, Mr. Karslake was to have followed us here immediately.

He lights a cigar.

NOGAM. Mr. Karslake just now phoned from his club—

SIR WILFRID *comes down the stage.*

—and he's on his way home, sir.

SIR WILFRID. Nogam, why is that chair upside down?

NOGAM. Our orders, sir.

VIDA, *speaking as she comes on.* Oh, Wilfrid!

SIR WILFRID *turns.* VIDA *comes slowly down the stage.*

I can't be left longer alone with the lobster! He reminds me too much of Phillimore!

SIR WILFRID. Karslake's coming; stopped at his club on the way!

To NOGAM.

You haven't heard anything of Mrs. Karslake——?

NOGAM, *surprised.* No, sir!

SIR WILFRID, *in an aside to* VIDA, *as they move to appear to be out of* NOGAM's *hearing.* Deucedly odd, ye know—for the Reverend Matthew declared she left Phillimore's house before *he* did—and she told him she was coming here!

NOGAM *evidently takes this in.*

VIDA. Oh, she'll turn up.

SIR WILFRID. Yes, but I don't see how the Reverend Phillimore had the time to get here and make us man and wife, don't y'know——

VIDA. Oh, Matthew had a fast horse and Cynthia a slow one —or she's a woman and changed her mind! Perhaps she's gone back and married Phillimore. And besides, dear, Matthew wasn't in the house four minutes and a half; only just long enough to hoop the hoop.

She twirls her new wedding ring gently about her finger.

Wasn't it lucky he had a ring in his pocket?

SIR WILFRID. Rather.

VIDA. And are you aware, dear, that Phillimore bought and intended it for Cynthia? Do come,

She goes up to the door through which she entered.

I'm desperately hungry! Whenever I'm married that's the effect it has!

VIDA *goes out.* SIR WILFRID *sees her through door but stops to speak to* NOGAM.

SIR WILFRID. We'll give Mr. Karslake ten minutes, Nogam. If he does not come then, you might serve supper.

He follows VIDA.

NOGAM, *to* SIR WILFRID. Yes, sir.

Door opens.

Enter FIDDLER.

FIDDLER, *easy and businesslike.* Hello, Nogam, where's the guv'nor? That mare's off her oats, and I've got to see him.

NOGAM. He'll soon be here.

FIDDLER. Who was the parson I met leaving the house?

NOGAM, *whispering.* Sir Wilfrid and Mrs. Phillimore have a date with the guv'nor in the dining room, and the reverend gentleman——

He makes a gesture as of giving an ecclesiastical blessing.

FIDDLER, *amazed.* He hasn't spliced them?

NOGAM *assents.*

He has? They're married? Never saw a parson could resist it!

NOGAM. Yes, but I've got another piece of news for you. Who do you think the Reverend Phillimore expected to find here?

FIDDLER, *proud of having the knowledge.* Mrs. Karslake? I saw her headed this way in a hansom with a balky horse only a minute ago. If she hoped to be in at the finish——

FIDDLER *is about to set chair on its legs.*

NOGAM, *quickly.* Mr. Fiddler, sir, please to let it alone.

FIDDLER, *putting chair down in surprise.* Does it live on its blooming head?

NOGAM. Don't you remember? *She* threw it on its head when she left here, and he won't have it up. Ah, that's it—hat, sewing basket, and all—the whole rig is to remain as it was when she handed him his knockout.

A bell rings outside.

FIDDLER. There's the guv'nor—I hear him!

NOGAM. I'll serve the supper.

Taking letter from pocket and putting it on mantel.

Mr. Fiddler, would you mind giving this to the guv'nor? It's from his lawyer—his lawyer couldn't find him and left it with me. He said it was very important.

Bell rings again. Speaking off to SIR WILFRID.

I'm coming, sir!

NOGAM *goes out and shuts door. Enter* JOHN KARSLAKE. *He looks downhearted, his hat is pushed over his eyes. His hands are in his pockets. He enters slowly and heavily. He sees* FIDDLER, *who salutes, forgetting the letter.* JOHN *slowly sits in armchair at the study table.*

JOHN, *speaking as he walks to his chair.* Hello, Fiddler!

Pause. JOHN *throws himself into chair, keeping his hat on. Throws down his gloves, sighing.*

FIDDLER. Came in to see you, sir, about Cynthia K.

JOHN, *drearily.* Damn Cynthia K!

FIDDLER. Couldn't have a word with you?

JOHN, *grumpy.* No!

FIDDLER. Yes, sir.

JOHN. Fiddler.

FIDDLER. Yes, sir.

JOHN. Mrs. Karslake——

FIDDLER *nods.*

You used to say she was our mascot?

FIDDLER. Yes, sir.

JOHN. Well, she's just married herself to a—a sort of a man!

FIDDLER. Sorry to hear it, sir.

JOHN. Well, Fiddler, between you and me, we're a pair of idiots.

FIDDLER. Yes, sir.

JOHN. And now it's too late!

FIDDLER. Yes, sir—oh, beg your pardon, sir—your lawyer left a letter.

JOHN *takes the letter, opens it, and reads it, indifferently at first.*

JOHN, *as he opens letter.* What's he got to say, more than what his wire said? Eh—

As he reads, he is dumfounded.

—what? Will explain. Error in wording of telegram. Call me up.

Turning to telephone quickly.

The man can't mean that she's still—— Hello! Hello!

JOHN *listens.*

FIDDLER. Would like to have a word with you, sir——

JOHN. Hello, Central!

FIDDLER. That mare——

JOHN *looks at letter, speaks into phone.* 33246a–38! Did you get it?

FIDDLER. That mare, sir, she's got a touch of malaria——

JOHN, *at the phone.* Hello, Central—33246a–38—Clayton Osgood—yes, yes, and say, Central, get a move on you!

FIDDLER. If you think well of it, sir, I'll give her a tonic——

JOHN, *still at the phone.* Hello! Yes—yes—Jack Karslake. Is that you, Clayton? Yes—yes—well——

FIDDLER. Or if you like, sir, I'll give her——

JOHN, *turning on* FIDDLER. Shut up!

To phone.

What was that? Not you—not you—a technical error? You mean to say that Mrs. Karslake is still—my— Hold the wire, Central—get off the wire! Get off the wire! Is that you, Clayton? Yes, yes—she and I are still— I got it! Good-by!

He hangs up the receiver and falls back in the chair. For a moment he is overcome. He takes up the telephone book.

FIDDLER. All very well, Mr. Karslake, but I must know if I'm to give her a—

JOHN, *turning over the leaves of the telephone book in hot haste.* What's Phillimore's number?

FIDDLER. If you've no objections, I think I'll give her a—

JOHN, *as before.* L—M—N—O—P— It's too late! She's married by this! Married—and—my God—I—I am the cause. Phillimore—

FIDDLER. I'll give her—

JOHN. Give her Wheatena—give her Grape-Nuts—give her away!

FIDDLER *moves away.*

Only be quiet! Phillimore!

Enter SIR WILFRID.

SIR WILFRID. Hello! We'd almost given you up!

JOHN, *still in his agitation unable to find* PHILLIMORE'S *number.* Just a moment! I'm trying to get Phillimore on the phone to—to tell Mrs. Karslake—

SIR WILFRID. No good, my boy—she's on her way here!

JOHN *drops book and looks up dumfounded.*

The Reverend Matthew was here, y'see—and he said—

JOHN, *rising, he turns.* Mrs. Karslake is coming here?

SIR WILFRID *nods.*

To this house? Here?

SIR WILFRID. That's right.

JOHN. Coming here? You're sure?

SIR WILFRID *nods assent.*

Fiddler, I want you to stay here, and if Mrs. Karslake comes, don't fail to let me know! Now then, for heaven's sake, what did Matthew say to you?

SIR WILFRID. Come along in and I'll tell you.

JOHN. On your life now, Fiddler, don't fail to let me——

Exeunt JOHN *and* SIR WILFRID.

VIDA, *voice off.* Ah, here you are!

FIDDLER. Phew!

There is a moment's pause, and CYNTHIA *enters. She comes in very quietly, almost shyly, and as if she were uncertain of her welcome.*

CYNTHIA. Fiddler! Where is he? Has he come? Is he here? Has he gone?

FIDDLER, *rattled.* Nobody's gone, ma'am, except the Reverend Matthew Phillimore.

CYNTHIA. Matthew? He's been here and gone?

FIDDLER *nods assent.*

You don't mean I'm too late? He's married them already?

FIDDLER. Nogam says he married them!

CYNTHIA. He's married them! Married! Married before I could get here!

Sitting in armchair.

Married in less time than it takes to pray for rain! Oh, well, the church—the church is a regular quick marriage counter.

Voices of VIDA *and* JOHN *heard in lighthearted laughter.* Oh!

FIDDLER. I'll tell Mr. Karslake——

CYNTHIA, *rising and going to the door through which* JOHN *left the stage; she turns the key in the lock and takes it out.* No—I wouldn't see him for the world!

She comes down with key to the worktable.

If I'm too late, I'm too late, and that's the end of it!

She lays key on table and remains standing near it.

I've come and now I'll go!

Long pause. CYNTHIA *looks about the room and changes her tone.*

Well, Fiddler, it's all a good deal as it used to be in my day.

FIDDLER. No, ma'am—everything changed, even the horses.

CYNTHIA, *absent-mindedly.* Horses—how are the horses?

Throughout this scene she gives the idea that she is saying good-by to her life with JOHN.

FIDDLER. Ah, when husband and wife splits, ma'am, it's the horses that suffer. Oh yes, ma'am, we're all changed since you give us the go-by—even the guv'nor.

CYNTHIA. How's he changed?

FIDDLER. Lost his sharp for horses, and ladies, ma'am—gives 'em both the boiled eye.

CYNTHIA. I can't say I see any change; there's my portrait—I suppose he sits and pulls faces at me.

FIDDLER. Yes, ma'am, I think I'd better tell him of your bein' here.

CYNTHIA, *gently but decidedly.* No, Fiddler, no!

She again looks about her.

The room's in a terrible state of disorder. However, your new mistress will attend to that.

Pause.

Why, that's not her hat!

FIDDLER. Yours, ma'am.

CYNTHIA. Mine!

She goes to the table to look at it.

Is that my workbasket?

Pause.

My gloves?

FIDDLER *assents.*

And I suppose——

She hurriedly goes to the writing table.

My—yes, there it is: my wedding ring—just where I dropped it! Oh, oh, oh, he keeps it like this—hat, gloves, basket, and ring, everything just as it was that crazy, mad day when I——

Glances at FIDDLER *and breaks off.*

But for heaven's sake, Fiddler, set that chair on its feet!

FIDDLER. Against orders, ma'am.

CYNTHIA. Against orders?

FIDDLER. You kicked it over, ma'am, the day you left us.

CYNTHIA. No wonder he hates me with the chair in that state! He nurses his wrath to keep it warm. So, after all, Fiddler, everything *is* changed, and that chair is the proof of it. I suppose Cynthia K is the only thing in the world that cares a whinny whether I'm alive or dead.

She breaks down and sobs.

How is she, Fiddler?

FIDDLER. Off her oats, ma'am, this evening.

CYNTHIA. Off her oats! Well, she loves me, so I suppose she will die, or change, or—or something. Oh, she'll die, there's no doubt about that—she'll die.

FIDDLER, *who has been watching his chance, takes the key off the table while she is sobbing, tiptoes up the stage, unlocks the door, and goes out. After he has done so,* CYNTHIA *rises and dries her eyes.*

There—I'm a fool—I must go—before—before—he——

As she speaks her last word JOHN *comes on.*

JOHN. Mrs. Karslake!

CYNTHIA, *confused.* I—I—I just heard Cynthia K was ill——

JOHN *assents.* CYNTHIA *tries to put on a cheerful and indifferent manner.*

I—I ran round—I—and—and——
Pausing, she turns and comes down.
Well, I understand it's all over.

JOHN, *cheerfully.* Yes, it's all over.

CYNTHIA. How is the bride?

JOHN. Oh, she's a wonder.

CYNTHIA. Indeed! Did she paw the ground like the war horse
in the Bible? I'm sure when Vida sees a wedding ring
she smells the battle afar off. As for you, my dear Karslake, I should have thought once bitten, twice shy! But,
you know best.
Enter VIDA.

VIDA. Oh, Cynthia, I've just been through it again, and I feel
as if I were eighteen. There's no use talking about it, my
dear, with a woman it's never the second time! And how
nice you were, Jack, he never even laughed at us!
Enter SIR WILFRID *with hat and cane.* VIDA *kisses* JOHN.
That's the wages of virtue!

SIR WILFRID, *in time to see her kiss* JOHN. I say, is it the cus-
tom? Every time she does that, my boy, you owe me a
thousand pounds.
Seeing CYNTHIA, *who approaches them, he looks at her
and* JOHN *in turn.*
Mrs. Karslake.
To JOHN.
And then you say it's not an extraordinary country!
CYNTHIA *is more and more puzzled.*

VIDA, *to* JOHN. See you next Derby, Jack.
Crossing to door. To SIR WILFRID.
Come along, Wilfrid! We really ought to be going.
To CYNTHIA.
I hope, dear, you haven't married him! Phillimore's a
tomb! Good-by, Cynthia—I'm so happy!
As she goes.

Just think of the silly people, dear, that only have this sensation once in a lifetime!

Exit VIDA. JOHN *follows* VIDA *off.*

SIR WILFRID, *to* CYNTHIA. Good-by, Mrs. Karslake. And I say, ye know, if you have married that dull old Phillimore fellah, why, when you've divorced him, come over and stay at Traynham! I mean, of course, ye know, bring your new husband. There'll be lots of horses to show you and a whole covey of jolly little Cates-Darbys. Mind you come!

With real delicacy of feeling and forgetting his wife.

Never liked a woman as much in my life as I did you!

VIDA, *outside, calling him.* Wilfrid, dear!

SIR WILFRID, *loyal to the woman who has caught him.* Except the one that's calling me!

Re-enter JOHN. SIR WILFRID *nods to him and goes off.* JOHN *shuts the door and crosses the stage. A pause.*

CYNTHIA. So you're not married?

JOHN. No. But I know that you imagined I was.
Pause.

CYNTHIA. I suppose you think a woman has no right to divorce a man—and still continue to feel a keen interest in his affairs?

JOHN. Well, I'm not so sure about that, but I don't quite see how——

CYNTHIA. A woman can be divorced—and still——

JOHN *assents; she hides her embarrassment.*

Well, my dear Karslake, you've a long life before you in which to learn how such a state of mind is possible! So I won't stop to explain. Will you be kind enough to get me a cab?

She moves to the door.

JOHN. Certainly. I was going to say I am not surprised at your feeling an interest in me. I'm only astonished that, having actually married Phillimore, you come here——

CYNTHIA, *indignantly.* I'm not married to him!

A pause.

JOHN. I left you on the brink—made me feel a little uncertain.

CYNTHIA, *in a matter-of-course tone.* I changed my mind— that's all.

JOHN, *taking his tone from her.* Of course.

A pause.

Are you going to marry him?

CYNTHIA. I don't know.

JOHN. Does he know you——

CYNTHIA. I told him I was coming here.

JOHN. Oh! He'll turn up here, then—eh?

CYNTHIA *is silent.*

And you'll go back with him, I suppose?

CYNTHIA, *talking at random.* Oh—yes—I suppose so. I—I haven't thought much about it.

JOHN, *changing his tone.* Well, sit down; do. Till he comes— talk it over.

He places the armchair more comfortably for her.

This is a more comfortable chair!

CYNTHIA, *shamefacedly.* You never liked me to sit in that one!

JOHN. Oh well—it's different now.

CYNTHIA *crosses and sits down near the upset chair. There is a long pause.* JOHN *crosses the stage.*

You don't mind if I smoke?

CYNTHIA, *shaking her head.* No.

JOHN. *He lights his pipe and sits on arm of chair.* Of course, if you find my presence painful, I'll—skiddoo.

He indicates the door. CYNTHIA *shakes her head.* JOHN *smokes pipe and remains seated.*

CYNTHIA, *suddenly and quickly.* It's just simply a fact, Kars- lake, and that's all there is to it—if a woman has once been married—that is, the first man she marries—then—she may quarrel, she may hate him—she may despise him—but she'll always be jealous of him with other women. Always!

JOHN *takes this as if he were simply glad to have the information.*

JOHN. Oh—— Hm! Ah—yes—yes.

A pause.

CYNTHIA. You probably felt jealous of Phillimore.

JOHN, *reasonably, sweetly, and in doubt.* N-o! I felt simply: let him take his medicine.

Apologetically.

CYNTHIA. Oh!

JOHN. I beg your pardon—I meant——

CYNTHIA. You meant what you said!

JOHN *comes a step to her.* Mrs. Karslake, I apologize—I won't do it again. But it's too late for you to be out alone—Philip will be here in a moment—and of course, then——

CYNTHIA. It isn't what you *say*—it's—it's—it's everything. It's the entire situation. Suppose by any chance I don't marry Phillimore! And suppose I were seen at two or three in the morning leaving my former husband's house! It's all wrong. I have no business to be here! I'm going! You're perfectly horrid to me, you know—and—the whole place—it's so familiar, and so—so associated with—with——

JOHN. Discord and misery—I know——

CYNTHIA. Not at all with discord and misery! With harmony and happiness—with—with first love, and infinite hope—and—and—Jack Karslake, if you don't set that chair on its legs, I think I'll explode.

JOHN *crosses the stage rapidly and sets chair on its legs. His tone changes.*

JOHN, *while setting chair on its legs.* There! I beg your pardon.

CYNTHIA, *nervously.* I believe I hear Philip.

Rises.

JOHN, *going up to the window.* N-o! That's the policeman
trying the front door! And now, see here, Mrs. Karslake—
you're only here for a short minute, because you can't help
yourself; but I want you to understand that I'm not trying
to be disagreeable—I don't want to revive all the old unhappy——

CYNTHIA. Very well, if you don't—give me my hat.

JOHN *does so.*

And my sewing! And my gloves, please!

*She indicates the several articles which lie on the small
table.*

Thanks!

CYNTHIA *throws the lot into the fireplace and returns to
the place she has left near table.*

There! I feel better! And now—all I ask is——

JOHN *laughs.* My stars, what a pleasure it is!

CYNTHIA. What is?

JOHN. Seeing you in a whirlwind!

CYNTHIA, *wounded by his seeming indifference.* Oh!

JOHN. No, but I mean a real pleasure! Why not? Time's
passed since you and I were together—and—eh——

CYNTHIA. And you've forgotten what a vile temper I had!

JOHN, *reflectively.* Well, you did kick the stuffing out of the
matrimonial buggy——

CYNTHIA, *pointedly but with good temper.* It wasn't a buggy;
it was a break cart——

She stands back of the armchair.

It's all very well to blame me! But when you married me,
I'd never had a bit in my mouth!

JOHN. Well, I guess I had a pretty hard hand. Do you remember the time you threw both your slippers out of the
window?

CYNTHIA. Yes, and do you remember the time you took my
fan from me by force?

JOHN. After you slapped my face with it!

CYNTHIA. Oh, oh! I hardly touched your face! And do you remember the day you held my wrists?

JOHN. You were going to bite me!

CYNTHIA. Jack! I never! I showed my teeth at you! And I said I would bite you!

JOHN. Cynthia, I never knew you to break your word!

He laughs casually.

And anyhow—they were awfully pretty teeth!

CYNTHIA, *though bolt upright, has ceased to seem pained.*

And I say—do you remember, Cyn——

He leans over the armchair to talk to her.

CYNTHIA, *after a pause.* You oughtn't to call me Cyn—it's not nice of you. It's sort of cruel. I'm not—Cyn to you now.

JOHN. Awfully sorry; didn't mean to be beastly, Cyn.

CYNTHIA *turns quickly.* JOHN *stamps his foot.*

Cynthia! Sorry. I'll make it a commandment: thou shalt not Cyn!!

CYNTHIA *laughs and wipes her eyes.*

CYNTHIA. How can you, Jack? How can you?

JOHN. Well, hang it, my dear child, I—I'm sorry, but you know I always got foolish with you. Your laugh'd make a horse laugh. Why, don't you remember that morning in the park before breakfast—when you laughed so hard your horse ran away with you!

CYNTHIA. I do, I do!

Both laugh. The door opens.

NOGAM *enters.*

But what was it started me laughing?

Laughing, sits down, and laughs again.

That morning. Wasn't it somebody we met?

Laughs.

Wasn't it a man on a horse?

Laughs.

JOHN, *laughing too*. Of course! You didn't know him in those days! But I did! And he looked a sight in the saddle!

NOGAM, trying to catch their attention, comes to right of table.

CYNTHIA. Who was it?

JOHN. Phillimore!

CYNTHIA. He's no laughing matter now.

Sees NOGAM.

Jack, he's here!

JOHN. Eh? Oh, Nogam?

NOGAM. Mr. Phillimore, sir——

JOHN. In the house?

NOGAM. On the street in a hansom, sir—and he requests Mrs. Karslake——

JOHN. That'll do, Nogam.

Exit NOGAM. Pause. JOHN from near the window. CYNTHIA faces audience.

Well, Cynthia?

He speaks almost gravely and with finality.

CYNTHIA, *trembling*. Well?

JOHN. It's the hour of decision; are you going to marry him?

Pause.

Speak up!

CYNTHIA. Jack—I—I——

JOHN. There he is—you can join him.

He points to the street.

CYNTHIA. Join Phillimore—and go home—with him—to his house, and Miss Heneage, and——

JOHN. The door's open.

He points to the door.

CYNTHIA. No, no! It's mean of you to suggest it!

JOHN. You won't marry——

CYNTHIA. Phillimore—no. Never.
Runs to window.
No, never, never, Jack.

JOHN. *He calls out of the window, having opened it.* It's all right, Judge. You needn't wait.
Pause. JOHN *comes down.* JOHN *bursts into laughter.* CYNTHIA *looks dazed. He closes door.*

CYNTHIA. Jack!
JOHN *laughs.*
Yes, but I'm here, Jack.

JOHN. Why not?

CYNTHIA. You'll have to take me round to the Holland House!

JOHN. Of course I will! But, I say Cynthia, there's no hurry.

CYNTHIA. Why, I—I—can't stay here.

JOHN. No, of course you can't stay here. But you can have a bite, though.
CYNTHIA *shakes her head.* JOHN *places the small chair, which was upset, next to table.*
Oh, I insist. Just look at yourself—you're as pale as a sheet and—here, here. Sit right down. I insist! By George, you must do it!
CYNTHIA *crosses to chair beside table and sits.*

CYNTHIA, *faintly.* I am hungry.

JOHN. Just wait a moment.
Exit JOHN.

CYNTHIA. I don't want more than a nibble!
Pause.
I am sorry to give you so much trouble.

JOHN. No trouble at all.
He can be heard off the stage, busied with glasses and a tray.

A hansom of course, to take you round to your hotel?
Speaking as he comes down.

CYNTHIA, *to herself.* I wonder how I ever dreamed I could
marry that man.

JOHN, *by table by this time.* Can't imagine! There!

CYNTHIA. I am hungry. Don't forget the hansom.
She eats; he waits on her, setting this and that before her.

JOHN, *going to door; opens it and speaks off.* Nogam, a hansom at once.

NOGAM, *off stage.* Yes, sir.

JOHN, *back to above table; from here on he shows his feelings for her.* How does it go?

CYNTHIA, *faintly.* It goes all right. Thanks!
Hardly eating at all.

JOHN. You always used to like anchovy.
CYNTHIA *nods and eats.*
Claret?
CYNTHIA *shakes her head.*
Oh, but you must!

CYNTHIA, *tremulously.* Ever so little.
He fills her glass and then his.
Thanks!

JOHN. Here's to old times.
Raising glass.

CYNTHIA, *very tremulous.* Please not!

JOHN. Well, here's to your next husband.

CYNTHIA, *very tenderly.* Don't!

JOHN. Oh well, then, what shall the toast be?

CYNTHIA. I'll tell you—
Pause.
—you can drink to the relation I am to you!

JOHN, *laughing.* Well—what relation are you?

CYNTHIA. I'm your first wife once removed!

JOHN. *Laughing, he drinks.* I say, you're feeling better.

CYNTHIA. Lots.

JOHN, *reminiscent.* It's a good deal like those mornings after the races—isn't it?

CYNTHIA, *nodding.* Yes. Is that the hansom?
Half rises.

JOHN, *going up to the window.* No.

CYNTHIA, *sitting again.* What is that sound?

JOHN. Don't you remember?

CYNTHIA. No.

JOHN. That's the rumbling of the early milk wagons.

CYNTHIA. Oh, Jack.

JOHN. Do you recognize it now?

CYNTHIA. Do I? We used to hear that—just at the hour, didn't we—when we came back from awfully jolly late suppers and things!

JOHN. H'm!

CYNTHIA. It must be fearfully late. I must go.
She rises, crosses to chair where she has left her cloak. She sees that JOHN *will not help her and puts it on herself.*

JOHN. Oh, don't go—why go?

CYNTHIA, *embarrassed and agitated.* All good things come to an end, you know.

JOHN. They don't need to.

CYNTHIA. Oh, you don't mean that! And, you know, Jack, if I were caught—seen at this hour, leaving this house, you know—it's the most scandalous thing anyone ever did my being here at all. Good-by, Jack!
Pause; almost in tears.

I'd like to say, I—I—I—well, I shan't be bitter about you
hereafter, and——
Pause.
Thank you awfully, old man, for the fodder and all that!
She turns to go out.

JOHN. Mrs. Karslake—wait——

CYNTHIA, *stopping to hear.* Well?

JOHN, *serious.* I've rather an ugly bit of news for you.

CYNTHIA. Yes?

JOHN. I don't believe you know that I have been testing the
validity of the decree of divorce which you procured.

CYNTHIA. Oh, have you?

JOHN. Yes; you know I felt pretty warmly about it.

CYNTHIA. Well?

JOHN. Well, I've been successful.
Pause.
The decree's been declared invalid. Understand?

CYNTHIA, *looking at him a moment; then speaking.* Not—
precisely.

JOHN. *Pause.* I'm awfully sorry—I'm awfully sorry, Cynthia,
but you're my wife still.
Pause.

CYNTHIA, *with rapture.* Honor bright?
She sinks into the armchair.

JOHN, *nodding, half laughingly.* Crazy country, isn't it?

CYNTHIA, *nodding. Pause.* Well, Jack—what's to be done?

JOHN, *gently.* Whatever you say.

NOGAM *quietly enters.* Hansom, sir.
Exits. CYNTHIA *rises.*

JOHN. Why don't you finish your supper?
CYNTHIA *hesitates.*

CYNTHIA. The—the—hansom——

JOHN. Why go to the Holland? After all—you know, Cyn, you're at home here.

CYNTHIA. No, Jack, I'm not—I'm not at home here—unless—unless——

JOHN. Out with it!

CYNTHIA, *bursting into tears.* Unless I—unless I'm at home in your heart, Jack.

JOHN. What do you think?

CYNTHIA. I don't believe you want me to stay.

JOHN. Don't you?

CYNTHIA. No, no, you hate me still. You never can forgive me. I know you can't. For I can never forgive myself. Never, Jack, never, never!

She sobs and he takes her in his arms.

JOHN, *very tenderly.* Cyn! I love you!

Strongly.

And you've got to stay! And hereafter you can chuck chairs around till all's blue! Not a word now.

He draws her gently to a chair.

CYNTHIA, *wiping her tears.* Oh, Jack! Jack!

JOHN. I'm as hungry as a shark. We'll nibble together.

CYNTHIA. Well, all I can say is, I feel that of all the improprieties I ever committed this—this——

JOHN. This takes the claret, eh? Oh, Lord, how happy I am!

CYNTHIA. Now don't say that! You'll make me cry more.

She wipes her eyes. JOHN *takes out the wedding ring from his pocket; he lifts a wine glass, drops the ring into it and offers her the glass.*

JOHN. Cynthia!

CYNTHIA, *looking at it and wiping her eyes.* What is it?

JOHN. Benedictine!

CYNTHIA. Why, you know I never take it.

JOHN. Take this one for my sake.

CYNTHIA. That's not benedictine.

With gentle curiosity.

What is it?

JOHN. *He slides the ring out of the glass and puts his arm about* CYNTHIA. *He slips the ring onto her finger and, as he kisses her hand, says,*

Your wedding ring!

PULLMAN CAR
HIAWATHA

A One-Act Play

by

THORNTON WILDER

At the back of the stage is a balcony or bridge or run-way leading out of sight in both directions. Two flights of stairs descend from it to the stage. There is no further scenery.

At the rise of the curtain the STAGE MANAGER is making lines with a piece of chalk on the floor of the stage by the footlights.

THE STAGE MANAGER. This is the plan of a Pullman car. Its name is Hiawatha and on December twenty-first it is on its way from New York to Chicago. Here at your left are three compartments. Here is the aisle and five lowers. The berths are all full, uppers and lowers, but for the purposes of this play we are limiting our interest to the people in the lower berths on the further side only.

The berths are already made up. It is half-past nine. Most of the passengers are in bed behind the green curtains. They are dropping their shoes on the floor, or wrestling with their trousers, or wondering whether they dare hide their valuables in the pillow slips during the night.

All right! Come on, everybody!

The actors enter carrying chairs. Each improvises his berth by placing two chairs facing one another in his chalk-marked space. They then sit in one chair, profile to the audience, and rest their feet on the other. This must do for lying in bed.

The passengers in the compartments do the same.

Reading from left to right we have:

COMPARTMENT THREE: *an insane woman with a male attendant and a trained nurse.*

COMPARTMENT TWO: PHILIP *and*

COMPARTMENT ONE: HARRIET, *his young wife.*

LOWER ONE: *A maiden lady.*

LOWER THREE: *A middle-aged doctor.*

LOWER FIVE: *A stout, amiable woman of fifty.*

LOWER SEVEN: *An engineer going to California.*

LOWER NINE: *Another engineer.*

LOWER ONE. Porter, be sure and wake me up at quarter of six.

PORTER. Yes, ma'am.

LOWER ONE. I know I shan't sleep a wink, but I want to be told when it's quarter of six.

PORTER. Yes, ma'am.

LOWER SEVEN, *putting his head through the curtains.* Hsst! Porter! Hsst! How the hell do you turn on this other light?

PORTER, *fussing with it.* I'm afraid it's outa order, suh. You'll have to use the other end.

THE STAGE MANAGER, *falsetto, substituting for some woman in an upper berth.* May I ask if someone in this car will be kind enough to lend me some aspirin?

PORTER, *rushing about.* Yes, ma'am.

LOWER NINE, *one of these engineers, descending the aisle and falling into Lower Five.* Sorry, lady, sorry. Made a mistake.

LOWER FIVE, *grumbling.* Never in all my born days!

LOWER ONE, *in a shrill whisper.* Porter! Porter!

PORTER. Yes, ma'am.

LOWER ONE. My hot-water bag's leaking. I guess you'll have to take it away. I'll have to do without it tonight. How awful!

LOWER FIVE, *sharply to the passenger above her.* Young man, you mind your own business, or I'll report you to the conductor.

STAGE MANAGER, *substituting for* UPPER FIVE. Sorry, ma'am, I didn't mean to upset you. My suspenders fell down and I was trying to catch them.

LOWER FIVE. Well, here they are. Now go to sleep. Everybody seems to be rushing into my berth tonight.

She puts her head out.

Porter! Porter! Be a good soul and bring me a glass of water, will you? I'm parched.

LOWER NINE. Bill!

No answer.

Bill!

LOWER SEVEN. Ye'? Wha' d'y'a want?

LOWER NINE. Slip me one of those magazines, willya?

LOWER SEVEN. Which one d'y'a want?

LOWER NINE. Either one. *Detective Stories.* Either one.

LOWER SEVEN. Aw, Fred. I'm just in the middle of one of'm in *Detective Stories.*

LOWER NINE. That's all right. I'll take the Western. Thanks.

THE STAGE MANAGER, *to the actors.* All right! Sh! Sh! Sh—

To the audience.

Now I want you to hear them thinking.

There is a pause and then they all begin a murmuring-swishing noise, very soft. In turn each one of them can be heard above the others.

LOWER FIVE, *the lady of fifty.* Let's see: I've got the doll for the baby. And the slip-on for Marietta. And the fountain pen for Herbert. And the subscription to *Time* for George . . .

LOWER SEVEN, *Bill.* God! Lillian, if you don't turn out to be what I think you are, I don't know what I'll do. I guess it's bad politics to let a woman know that you're going all the way to California to see her. I'll think up a song and dance about a business trip or something. Was I ever as hot and bothered about anyone like this before? Well, there was Martha. But that was different. I'd better try and read or I'll go cuckoo. "How did you know it was ten o'clock when the visitor left the house?" asked the detective. "Because at ten o'clock," answered the girl, "I always turn out the lights in the conservatory and in the back hall. As I was coming down the stairs I heard the master talking to someone at the front door. I heard him say, 'Well, good night . . .' "—Gee, I don't feel like reading; I'll just think about Lillian. That yellow hair. Them eyes! . . .

LOWER THREE. *The* DOCTOR *reads aloud to himself from a medical journal the most hair-raising material, every now and then punctuating his reading with an interrogative* "So?"

LOWER ONE, *the maiden lady.* I know I'll be awake all night. I might just as well make up my mind to it now. I can't imagine what got hold of that hot-water bag to leak on the train of all places. Well now, I'll lie on my right side and breathe deeply and think of beautiful things, and perhaps I can doze off a bit.

And lastly:

LOWER NINE, *Fred.* That was the craziest thing I ever did. It's set me back three whole years. I could have saved up thirty thousand dollars by now if I'd only stayed over here. What business had I got to fool with contracts with the goddam Soviets. Hell, I thought it would be interesting. Interesting, what the hell! It's set me back three whole years. I don't even know if the company'll take me back. I'm green, that's all. I just don't grow up.

The STAGE MANAGER *strides toward them with lifted hand, crying* "Hush," *and their whispering ceases.*

THE STAGE MANAGER. That'll do! Just one minute. Porter!

THE PORTER, *appearing at the left.* Yessuh.

THE STAGE MANAGER. It's your turn to think.

THE PORTER *is very embarrassed.*

THE STAGE MANAGER. Don't you want to? You have a right to.

THE PORTER, *torn between the desire to release his thoughts and his shyness.* Ah . . . ah . . . I'm only thinkin' about my home in Chicago and . . . and my life insurance.

THE STAGE MANAGER. That's right.

THE PORTER. . . . well, thank you . . . thank you.

He slips away, blushing violently, in an agony of self-consciousness and pleasure.

THE STAGE MANAGER, *to the audience.* He's a good fellow, Harrison is. Just shy.

To the actors again.

Now the compartments, please.

The berths fall into shadow.

PHILIP *is standing at the door connecting his compartment with his wife's.*

PHILIP. Are you all right, angel?

HARRIET. Yes. I don't know what was the matter with me during dinner.

PHILIP. Shall I close the door?

HARRIET. Do see whether you can't put a chair against it that will hold it half open without banging.

PHILIP. There. Good night, angel. If you can't sleep, call me, and we'll sit up and play Russian bank.

HARRIET. You're thinking of that awful time when we sat up every night for a week . . . But at least I know I shall sleep tonight. The noise of the wheels has become sort of nice and homely. What state are we in?

PHILIP. We're tearing through Ohio. We'll be in Indiana soon.

HARRIET. I know those little towns full of horse blocks.

PHILIP. Well, we'll reach Chicago very early. I'll call you. Sleep tight.

HARRIET. Sleep tight, darling.

He returns to his own compartment. In Compartment Three, the male attendant tips his chair back against the wall and smokes a cigar. The trained nurse knits a stocking. The insane woman leans her forehead against the windowpane; that is, stares into the audience.

THE INSANE WOMAN. *Her words have a dragging, complaining sound but lack any conviction.* Don't take me there. Don't take me there.

THE FEMALE ATTENDANT. Wouldn't you like to lie down, dearie?

THE INSANE WOMAN. I want to get off the train. I want to go back to New York.

THE FEMALE ATTENDANT. Wouldn't you like me to brush your hair again? It's such a nice feeling.

THE INSANE WOMAN, *going to the door.* I want to get off the train. I want to open the door.

THE FEMALE ATTENDANT, *taking one of her hands.* Such a noise! You'll wake up all the nice people. Come and I'll tell you a story about the place we're going to.

THE INSANE WOMAN. I don't want to go to that place.

THE FEMALE ATTENDANT. Oh, it's lovely! There are lawns and gardens everywhere. I never saw such a lovely place. Just lovely.

THE INSANE WOMAN *lies down on the bed.* Are there roses?

THE FEMALE ATTENDANT. Roses! Red, yellow, white . . . just everywhere.

THE MALE ATTENDANT, *after a pause.* That musta been Cleveland.

THE FEMALE ATTENDANT. I had a case in Cleveland once. Diabetes.

THE MALE ATTENDANT, *after another pause.* I wisht I had a radio here. Radios are good for *them.* I had a patient once that had to have the radio going every minute.

THE FEMALE ATTENDANT. Radios are lovely. My married niece has one. It's always going. It's wonderful.

THE INSANE WOMAN, *half rising.* I'm not beautiful. I'm not beautiful as she was.

THE FEMALE ATTENDANT. Oh, I think you're beautiful! Beautiful. Mr. Morgan, don't you think Mrs. Churchill is beautiful?

THE MALE ATTENDANT. Oh, fine lookin'! Regular movie star, Mrs. Churchill.

She looks inquiringly at them and subsides.

HARRIET *groans slightly. Smothers a cough. She gropes about with her hand and finds the bell.*

The PORTER *knocks at her door.*

HARRIET, *whispering.* Come in. First, please close the door into my husband's room. Softly. Softly.

PORTER, *a plaintive porter.* Yes, ma'am.

HARRIET. Porter, I'm not well. I'm sick. I must see a doctor.

PORTER. Why, ma'am, they ain't no doctor . . .

HARRIET. Yes, when I was coming out from dinner I saw a man in one of the seats on *that* side reading medical papers. Go and wake him up.

PORTER, *flabbergasted.* Ma'am, I cain't wake anybody up.

HARRIET. Yes, you can. Porter. Porter. Now don't argue with me. I'm very sick. It's my heart. Wake him up. Tell him it's my heart.

PORTER. Yes, ma'am.

He goes into the aisle and starts pulling the shoulder of the man in Lower Three.

LOWER THREE. Hello. Hello. What is it? Are we there?

The PORTER *mumbles to him.*

I'll be right there. Porter, is it a young woman or an old one?

PORTER. I dono, suh. I guess she's kinda old, suh, but not so very old.

LOWER THREE. Tell her I'll be there in a minute and to lie quietly.

The PORTER *enters* HARRIET'S *compartment. She has turned her head away.*

PORTER. He'll be here in a minute, ma'am. He says you lie quiet.

LOWER THREE *stumbles along the aisle muttering.*

Damn these shoes!

SOMEONE'S VOICE. Can't we have a little quiet in this car, please?

LOWER NINE, *Fred*. Oh, shut up!

The DOCTOR *passes the* PORTER *and enters* HARRIET'S *compartment. He leans over her, concealing her by his stooping figure.*

LOWER THREE. She's dead, porter. Is there anyone on the train traveling with her?

PORTER. Yessuh. Dat's her husband in dere.

LOWER THREE. Idiot! Why didn't you call him? I'll go in and speak to him.

The STAGE MANAGER *comes forward.*

THE STAGE MANAGER. All right. So much for the inside of the car. That'll be enough of that for the present. Now for its position geographically, meteorologically, astronomically, theologically considered.

Pullman Car Hiawatha, ten minutes of ten. December twenty-first, 1930. All ready.

Some figures begin to appear on the balcony.

No, no. It's not time for the planets yet. Nor the hours.

They retire.

The STAGE MANAGER *claps his hands. A grinning boy in overalls enters from the left behind the berths.*

GROVER'S CORNERS, OHIO, *in a foolish voice as though he were reciting a piece at a Sunday School entertainment.* I represent Grover's Corners, Ohio—821 souls. "There's so much good in the worst of us and so much bad in the best of us, that it ill behooves any of us to criticize the rest of us." Robert Louis Stevenson. Thankya.

He grins and goes out right.

Enter from the same direction somebody in shirt sleeves. This is a field.

THE FIELD. I represent a field you are passing between Grover's Corners, Ohio, and Parkersburg, Ohio. In this field there are fifty-one gophers, 206 field mice, six snakes and millions of bugs, insects, ants, and spiders, all in their winter sleep. "What is so rare as a day in June? Then, if ever, come perfect days." *The Vision of Sir Launfal*, William Cullen—I mean James Russell Lowell. Thank you.

Exit.

Enter a tramp.

THE TRAMP. I just want to tell you that I'm a tramp that's been traveling under this car Hiawatha, so I have a right to be in this play. I'm going from Rochester, New York, to Joliet, Illinois. It takes a lotta people to make a world.

> *On the road to Mandalay*
> *Where the flying fishes play*
> *And the sun comes up like thunder*
> *Over China cross the bay.*

Frank W. Service. It's bitter cold. Thank you.

Exit.

Enter a gentle old farmer's wife with three stringy young people.

PARKERSBURG, OHIO. I represent Parkersburg, Ohio—2604 souls. I have seen all the dreadful havoc that alcohol has done, and I hope no one here will ever touch a drop of the curse of this beautiful country.

She beats a measure and they all sing unsteadily:

"Throw out the life line! Throw out the life line! Someone is sinking today-ay . . ."

The STAGE MANAGER *waves them away tactfully.*

Enter a workman.

THE WORKMAN. Ich bin der Arbeiter der hier sein Leben verlor. Bei der Sprengung für diese Brücke über die Sie in dem Moment fahren—

The engine whistles for a trestle crossing.

—erschlug mich ein Felsbock. Ich spiele jetzt als Geist in diesem Stuck mit. "Vor sieben und achtzig Jahren haben unsere Väter auf diesem Continent eine neue Nation hervorgebracht . . ."

THE STAGE MANAGER *helpfully, to the audience.* I'm sorry; that's in German. He says that he's the ghost of a workman who was killed while they were building the trestle over which the car Hiawatha is now passing—

The engine whistles again.

—and he wants to appear in this play. A chunk of rock hit him while they were dynamiting. His motto you know: "Three score and seven years ago our fathers brought forth upon this continent a new nation dedicated," and so on. Thank you, Mr. Krüger.

Exit the ghost.

Enter another worker.

THIS WORKER. I'm a watchman in a tower near Parkersburg, Ohio. I just want to tell you that I'm not asleep and that the signals are all right for this train. I hope you all have a fine trip. "If you can keep your heads when all about you are losing theirs and blaming it on you . . ." Rudyard Kipling. Thank you.

Exit.

The STAGE MANAGER *comes forward.*

THE STAGE MANAGER. All right. That'll be enough of that. Now the weather.

Enter a mechanic.

A MECHANIC. It is eleven degrees above zero. The wind is north-northwest, velocity, 57. There is a field of low barometric pressure moving eastward from Saskatchewan to the eastern coast. Tomorrow it will be cold with some snow in the middlewestern States and northern New York.

Exit.

THE STAGE MANAGER. All right. Now for the hours.

Helpfully to the audience.

The minutes are gossips; the hours are philosophers; the years are theologians. The hours are philosophers with the exception of Twelve O'clock who is also a theologian. Ready, Ten O'clock!

The hours are beautiful girls dressed like Elihu Vedder's Pleiades. Each carries a great gold roman numeral. They pass slowly across the balcony at the back, moving from right to left.

What are you doing, Ten O'clock? Aristotle?

TEN O'CLOCK. No, Plato, Mr. Washburn.

THE STAGE MANAGER. Good. "Are you not rather convinced that he who thus . . ."

TEN O'CLOCK. "Are you not rather convinced that he who sees beauty as only it can be seen will be specially favored? And since he is in contact not with images but with realities . . ."

She continues the passage in a murmur as ELEVEN O'CLOCK *appears.*

ELEVEN O'CLOCK. "What else can I, Epictetus, do, a lame old man, but sing hymns to God? If then I were a nightingale, I would do the nightingale's part. If I were a swan, I would do a swan's. But now I am a rational creature . . ."

Her voice too subsides to a murmur. TWELVE O'CLOCK *appears.*

THE STAGE MANAGER. Good. Twelve O'clock, what have you?

TWELVE O'CLOCK. Saint Augustine and his mother.

THE STAGE MANAGER. So. "And we began to say: If to any the tumult of the flesh were hushed . . ."

TWELVE O'CLOCK. "And we began to say: If to any the tumult of the flesh were hushed; hushed the images of earth; of waters and of air; . . ."

THE STAGE MANAGER. Faster. "Hushed also the poles of heaven."

TWELVE O'CLOCK. "Yea, were the very soul to be hushed to herself."

STAGE MANAGER. A little louder, Miss Foster.

TWELVE O'CLOCK, *a little louder.* "Hushed all dreams and imaginary revelations . . ."

THE STAGE MANAGER, *waving them back.* All right. All right. Now the planets. December twenty-first, 1930, please.

The hours unwind and return to their dressing rooms at the right. The planets appear on the balcony. Some of them take their place halfway on the steps. These have no words, but each has a sound. One has a pulsating, zinging sound. Another has a thrum. One whistles ascending and descending scales. Saturn does a slow, obstinate:

M—M—M—M—

Louder, Saturn—Venus, higher. Good. Now, Jupiter. Now the earth.

He turns to the beds on the train.

Come, everybody. This is the earth's sound.

The towns, workmen, etc., appear at the edge of the stage. The passengers begin their "thinking" murmur.

Come, Grover's Corners. Parkersburg. You're in this. Watchman. Tramp. This is the earth's sound.

He conducts it as the director of an orchestra would. Each of the towns and workmen does his motto.

THE INSANE WOMAN *breaks into passionate weeping. She rises and stretches out her arms to the* STAGE MANAGER.

THE INSANE WOMAN. Use me. Give me something to do.

He goes to her quickly, whispers something in her ear, and leads her back to her guardians. She is unconsoled.

THE STAGE MANAGER. Now sh—sh—sh! Enter the archangels.

To the audience.

THE STAGE MANAGER. We have now reached the theological position of Pullman car Hiawatha.

The towns and workmen have disappeared. The planets, off stage, continue a faint music. Two young men in blue serge suits enter along the balcony and descend the stairs at the right. As they pass each bed the passenger talks in his sleep.

GABRIEL *points out* BILL *to* MICHAEL *who smiles with raised eyebrows. They pause before* LOWER FIVE, *and* MICHAEL *makes the sound of assent that can only be rendered "Hn-Hn." The remarks that the characters make in their sleep are not all intelligible, being lost in the sound of sigh or groan or whisper by which they are conveyed. But we seem to hear:*

LOWER NINE, *loud.* Some people are slower than others, that's all.

LOWER SEVEN, *Bill.* It's no fun, y'know. I'll try.

LOWER FIVE, *the lady of the Christmas presents, rapidly.* You know best, of course. I'm ready whenever you are. One year's like another.

LOWER ONE. I can teach sewing. I can sew.

They approach HARRIET's *compartment.*

THE INSANE WOMAN *sits up and speaks to them.*

THE INSANE WOMAN. Me?

THE ARCHANGELS *shake their heads.*

THE INSANE WOMAN. What possible use can there be in my simply waiting? Well, I'm grateful for anything. I'm grateful for being so much better than I was. The old story, the terrible story, doesn't haunt me as it used to. A great load seems to have been taken off my mind. But no one understands me any more. At last I understand myself perfectly, but no one else understands a thing I say. So I must wait?

THE ARCHANGELS *nod, smiling.*

THE INSANE WOMAN, *resignedly, and with a smile that implies their complicity.* Well, you know best. I'll do whatever is best; but everyone is so childish, so absurd. They have no logic. These people are all so mad . . . These people are like children; they have never suffered.

She returns to her bed and sleeps. The ARCHANGELS *stand beside* HARRIET. *The doctor has drawn* PHILIP *into the next compartment and is talking to him in earnest whispers.*

HARRIET's *face has been toward the wall; she turns it slightly and speaks toward the ceiling.*

HARRIET. I wouldn't be happy there. Let me stay dead down here. I belong here. I shall be perfectly happy to roam about my house and be near Philip. You know I wouldn't be happy there.

GABRIEL *leans over and whispers into her ear. After a short pause she bursts into fierce tears.*

I'm ashamed to come with you. I haven't done anything. I haven't done anything with my life. Worse than that: I was angry and sullen. I never realized anything. I don't dare go a step in such a place.

They whisper to her again.

But it's not possible to forgive such things. I don't want to be forgiven so easily. I want to be punished for it all. I won't stir until I've been punished a long, long time. I want to be freed of all that—by punishment. I want to be all new.

They whisper to her. She puts her feet slowly on the ground.

But no one else could be punished for me. I'm willing to face it all myself. I don't ask anyone to be punished for me.

They whisper to her again. She sits long and brokenly looking at her shoes and thinking it over.

It wasn't fair. I'd have been willing to suffer for it myself, if I could have endured such a mountain.

She smiles.

Oh, I'm ashamed! I'm just a stupid and you know it. I'm just another American. But then what wonderful things must be beginning now. You really want me? You really want me?

They start leading her down the aisle of the car.

Let's take the whole train. There are some lovely faces on this train. Can't we all come? You'll never find anyone better than Philip. Please, please, let's all go.

They reach the steps. The ARCHANGELS *interlock their arms as a support for her as she leans heavily on them, taking the steps slowly. Her words are half singing and half babbling.*

But look at how tremendously high and far it is. I've a weak heart. I'm not supposed to climb stairs. "I do not ask to see the distant scene; one step enough for me." It's like Switzerland. My tongue keeps saying things. I can't control it. Do let me stop a minute: I want to say good-by.

She turns in their arms.

Just a minute, I want to cry on your shoulder.

She leans her forehead against GABRIEL's *shoulder and laughs long and softly.*

Good-by, Philip. I begged him not to marry me, but he would. He believed in me just as you do. Good-by, 1312 Ridgewood Avenue, Oaksbury, Illinois. I hope I remember all its steps and doors and wallpapers forever. Good-by, Emerson Grammar School on the corner of Forbush Avenue and Wherry Street. Good-by, Miss Walker and Miss Cramer who taught me English and Miss Matthewson who taught me biology. Good-by, First Congregational Church on the corner of Meyerson Avenue and Sixth Street and Dr. McReady and Mrs. McReady and Julia. Good-by, Papa and Mama . . .

She turns.

Now I'm tired of saying good-by. I never used to talk like this. I was so homely I never used to have the courage to talk. Until Philip came. I see now. I see now. I understand everything now.

The STAGE MANAGER *comes forward.*

THE STAGE MANAGER, *to the actors.* All right. All right. Now we'll have the whole world together, please. The whole solar system, please.

The complete cast begins to appear at the edges of the stage. He claps his hands.

The whole solar system, please. Where's the tramp? Where's the moon?

He gives two raps on the floor, like the conductor of an orchestra attracting the attention of his forces, and slowly lifts his hand. The human beings murmur their thoughts; the hours discourse; the planets chant or hum. HARRIET's *voice finally rises above them all saying:*

HARRIET. "I was not ever thus, nor asked that Thou
Shouldst lead me on . . . and spite of fears,
Pride ruled my will: remember not past years."

The STAGE MANAGER *waves them away.*

THE STAGE MANAGER. Very good. Now clear the stage, please. Now we're at Englewood Station, South Chicago. See the University's towers over there! The best of them all.

LOWER ONE, *the spinster.* Porter, you promised to wake me up at quarter of six.

PORTER. Sorry, ma'am, but it's been an awful night on this car. A lady's been terrible sick.

LOWER ONE. Oh! Is she better?

PORTER. No'm. She ain't one jot better.

LOWER FIVE. Young man, take your foot out of my face.

THE STAGE MANAGER, *again substituting for* UPPER FIVE. Sorry, lady, I slipped—

LOWER FIVE, *grumbling not unamiably.* I declare, this trip's been one long series of insults.

THE STAGE MANAGER. Just one minute, ma'am, and I'll be down and out of your way.

LOWER FIVE. Haven't you got anybody to darn your socks for you? You ought to be ashamed to go about that way.

THE STAGE MANAGER. Sorry, lady.

LOWER FIVE. You're too stuck up to get married. That's the trouble with you.

LOWER NINE. Bill! Bill!

LOWER SEVEN. Ye'? Wha' d'y'a want?

LOWER NINE. Bill, how much d'y'a give the porter on a train like this? I've been outa the country so long . . .

LOWER SEVEN. Hell, Fred, I don't know myself.

THE PORTER. CHICAGO, CHICAGO. All out. This train don't go no further.

The passengers jostle their way out and an army of old women with mops and pails enters and prepares to clean up the car.

THE MAN
WITH THE HEART
IN THE HIGHLANDS

A One-Act Play
by

WILLIAM SAROYAN

An old white broken-down frame house with a front porch on San Benito Avenue in Fresno, California. There are no other houses nearby, only a desolation of bleak land and red sky. It is late afternoon of a day in August 1914. The evening sun is going down.

Johnny, aged six, but essentially ageless, is sitting, dynamic and acrobatic, on the steps of the porch, dead to the world and deep in thought of a high and holy order. Far away a train whistle cries mournfully. He listens eagerly, cocking his head on one side like a chicken, trying to understand the meaning of the cry and at the same time to figure out everything. He doesn't quite make it and when the cry ends he stops being eager. A fourteen-year-old boy on a bicycle, eating an ice-cream cone and carrying newspaper bags, goes by on the sidewalk in silence, oblivious of the weight on his shoulders and of the contraption on which he is seated because of the delight and glory of ice cream in the world. Johnny leaps to his feet and waves to the boy, smiling in a big humanitarian way, but is ignored. He sits down again and listens to a small overjoyed but angry bird. The bird flies away, after making a brief, forceful speech of no meaning.

From inside the house is heard the somber voice of JOHNNY'S FATHER *reciting poetry of his own composition.*

JOHNNY'S FATHER. The long silent day journeys through the sore solemn heart, and——

Bitter pause.

And——

Quickly.

The long silent day journeys through the sore solemn heart, and——

Pause.

No.

He roars and begins again.

Crippled and weeping, time stumbles through the lone lorn heart.

A table or chair is pushed over in anger. A groan. Silence.

The boy listens. He gets up and tries to stand on his head, fails, tries again, fails, tries again, and succeeds. While he is standing on his head he hears the loveliest and most amazing music in the world: a solo on a bugle. The music is so magnificent he doesn't dare get to his feet or move a muscle. The song is "My Heart's in the Highlands."

The bugler, a very old man, finishes the solo in front of the house. The boy leaps to his feet and runs up to the old man, amazed, delighted, and bewildered.

JOHNNY. I sure would like to hear you play another song.

MACGREGOR. Young man, could you get a glass of water for an old man whose heart is not here, but in the highlands?

JOHNNY. What highlands?

MACGREGOR. The Scotch Highlands. Could you?

JOHNNY. What's your heart doing in the Scotch Highlands?

MACGREGOR. My heart's grieving there. Could you get me a glass of cool water?

JOHNNY. Where's your mother?

MACGREGOR. My mother's in Tulsa, Oklahoma, but her heart isn't.

JOHNNY. Where *is* her heart?

MACGREGOR. In the Scotch Highlands. I'm very thirsty, young man.

JOHNNY. How come the members of your family are always leaving their hearts in the highlands?

MACGREGOR. That's the way we are. Here today and gone to-morrow.

JOHNNY, *aside.* Here today and gone tomorrow?

> *To* MACGREGOR.

How do you figure?

MACGREGOR. Alive one minute and dead the next.

JOHNNY. Where's your mother's mother?

MACGREGOR. She's up in Vermont, in a little town called White River, but her heart isn't.

JOHNNY. Is her poor old withered heart in the highlands, too?

MACGREGOR. Right smack in the highlands. Son, I'm dying of thirst.

> JOHNNY'S FATHER *comes out of the house in a fury, as if he has just broken out of a cage, and roars at the boy like a tiger that has just awakened from evil dreams.*

JOHNNY'S FATHER. Johnny, get the hell away from that poor old man. Get him a pitcher of water before he falls down and dies. Where in hell are your manners?

JOHNNY. Can't a fellow try to find out something from a traveler once in a while?

JOHNNY'S FATHER. Get the old man some water, God damn it! Don't stand there like a dummy. Get him a drink before he falls down and dies.

JOHNNY. *You* get him a drink. You ain't doing nothing.

JOHNNY'S FATHER. Ain't doing nothing? Why, Johnny, you know I'm getting a new poem arranged in my mind.

JOHNNY. How do you figure I know?

JOHNNY'S FATHER, *unable to find an answer.* Well, you ought to know. You're my son. If you shouldn't know, who should?

MACGREGOR. Good afternoon. Your son has been telling me how clear and cool the climate is in these parts.

JOHNNY, *aside.* Jesus Christ, I didn't say anything about the climate. Where's he getting that stuff from?

JOHNNY'S FATHER. How do you do? Won't you come in for a little rest? We should be honored to have you at our table for a bite of supper.

MACGREGOR. Sir, I am starving. I shall come right in.

He moves to enter the house. JOHNNY *gets in his way, looking up at him.*

JOHNNY. Can you play "Drink to Me Only with Thine Eyes"? I sure would like to hear you play that song on the bugle. That song is my favorite. I guess I like that song better than any song in the world.

MACGREGOR. Son, when you get to be my age you'll know songs aren't important, bread's the thing.

JOHNNY. Anyway, I sure would like to hear you play that song.

MACGREGOR *goes up on the porch and shakes hands with* JOHNNY'S FATHER.

MACGREGOR. My name is Jasper MacGregor. I am an actor.

JOHNNY'S FATHER. I'm mighty glad to make your acquaintance. Johnny, get Mr. MacGregor a pitcher of water.

JOHNNY *runs around the house.*

MACGREGOR. Charming boy.

JOHNNY'S FATHER. Like myself, he's a genius.

MACGREGOR. I suppose you're very fond of him?

JOHNNY'S FATHER. We are the same person—he is the heart of my youth. Have you noticed his eagerness?

MACGREGOR. I should say I have.

JOHNNY'S FATHER. I am the same way myself, though older and less brilliant.

JOHNNY, *running, returns with a pitcher of water, which he hands to the old man. The old man throws back his shoulders, lifts his head, his nostrils expand, he snorts, his eyes widen, he lifts the pitcher of water to his lips and drinks all the water in one long swig, while* JOHNNY *and his* FATHER *watch with amazement and admiration. The old man breathes deeply, looks around at the landscape and up at the sky and to the end of San Benito Avenue, where the evening sun is going down.*

MACGREGOR. I reckon I'm three thousand miles from home. Do you think we could eat a little bread and cheese to keep my body and spirit together?

JOHNNY'S FATHER. Johnny, run down to the grocer's and get a loaf of French bread and a pound of cheese.

JOHNNY. Give me the money.

JOHNNY'S FATHER. You know I ain't got a penny, Johnny. Tell Mr. Kosak to give us credit.

JOHNNY. He won't do it. He's tired of giving us credit. He says we don't work and never pay our bills. We owe him forty cents.

JOHNNY'S FATHER. Go on down there and argue it out with him. You know that's your job.

JOHNNY. He says he doesn't know anything about anything, all he wants is the forty cents.

JOHNNY'S FATHER. Go on down there and make him give you a loaf of bread and a pound of cheese. You can do it, Johnny.

MACGREGOR. Go on down there and tell Mr. Kosak to give you a loaf of bread and a pound of cheese, son.

JOHNNY'S FATHER. Go ahead, Johnny. You haven't yet failed to leave that store with provender. You'll be back here in ten minutes with food fit for a king.

JOHNNY. I don't know. Mr. Kosak says we are trying to give him the merry run-around. He wants to know what kind of work you do.

JOHNNY'S FATHER, *furiously*. Well, go ahead and tell him. I have nothing to conceal. I write poetry, night and day.

JOHNNY. Well, all right, but I don't think he'll be impressed. He says you never go out and look for work. He says you're lazy and no good.

JOHNNY'S FATHER, *roaring*. You go on down there and tell him he's crazy, Johnny. You go on down there and tell that fellow your father is one of the greatest unknown poets living.

JOHNNY. He won't care, but I'll go. I'll do my best. Ain't we got nothing in the house?

JOHNNY'S FATHER. Only popcorn. We've been eating popcorn four days in a row now, Johnny. You got to get bread and cheese if you expect me to finish that long poem.

JOHNNY. I'll do my best.

MACGREGOR. Don't take too long, Johnny. I'm *five* thousand miles from home.

JOHNNY. I'll run all the way.

JOHNNY'S FATHER. If you find any money on the way, remember we go fifty-fifty.

JOHNNY. All right.

 JOHNNY *runs down the street.*

SCENE 2

The inside of MR. KOSAK'S *grocery story.* MR. KOSAK *is sleeping on his folded arms when* JOHNNY *runs into the store.* MR. KOSAK *lifts his head. He is a fine, gentle, serious man with a big blond old-fashioned mustache. He shakes his head, trying to waken.*

JOHNNY. Mr. Kosak, if you were in China and didn't have a friend in the world and no money, you'd expect some Christian over there to give you a pound of rice, wouldn't you?

MR. KOSAK. What do you want?

JOHNNY. I just want to talk a little. You'd expect some member of the Aryan race to help you out a little, wouldn't you, Mr. Kosak?

MR. KOSAK. How much money you got?

JOHNNY. It ain't a question of money, Mr. Kosak. I'm talking about being in China.

MR. KOSAK. I don't know nothing about nothing.

JOHNNY. How would you feel in China that way?

MR. KOSAK. I don't know. What would I be doing in China?

JOHNNY. Well, you'd be visiting there, and you'd be hungry and five thousand miles from home and not a friend in the world. You wouldn't expect a good Christian to turn you away without even a pound of rice, would you, Mr. Kosak?

MR. KOSAK. I guess not, but you ain't in China, Johnny, and neither is your Pa. You or your Pa's got to go out and work sometime in your lives, so you might as well start now. I ain't going to give you no more groceries on credit because I know you won't pay me.

JOHNNY. Mr. Kosak, you misunderstand me. I'm not talking about a few groceries. I'm talking about all them heathen people around you in China, and you hungry and dying.

MR. KOSAK. This ain't China. You got to go out and make your living in this country. Everybody's got to work in America.

JOHNNY. Mr. Kosak, suppose it was a loaf of bread and a pound of cheese you needed to keep you alive in the world, would you hesitate to ask a Christian missionary for those things?

MR. KOSAK. Yes, I would. I would be ashamed to ask.

JOHNNY. Even if you knew you would give him back *two* loaves of bread and *two* pounds of cheese instead of one loaf and one pound? Even then, Mr. Kosak?

MR. KOSAK. Even then.

JOHNNY. Don't be that way, Mr. Kosak. That's defeatist talk, and you know it. Why, the only thing that would happen to you would be death. You would die out there in China, Mr. Kosak.

MR. KOSAK. I wouldn't care if I would. You and your Pa have got to pay for bread and cheese. Why don't your Pa go out and get a job?

JOHNNY. Mr. Kosak, how are you anyway?

MR. KOSAK. I'm fine, Johnny. How are you?

JOHNNY. Couldn't be better, Mr. Kosak. How are the children?

MR. KOSAK. They're all fine, Johnny. Stepan is beginning to walk now.

JOHNNY. That's great. How's Angela?

MR. KOSAK. Angela's beginning to sing. How's your grandmother?

JOHNNY. She's fine. She's beginning to sing too. She says she'd rather be an opera singer than Queen of England. How's your wife, Martha, Mr. Kosak?

MR. KOSAK. Oh, swell.

JOHNNY. I can't tell you how glad I am to hear that everything is well at your house. I know Stepan is going to be a great man someday.

MR. KOSAK. I hope so. I'm going to send him to high school and see that he gets every chance I didn't get. I don't want him to open a grocery store.

JOHNNY. I have great faith in Stepan, Mr. Kosak.

MR. KOSAK. What do you want, Johnny, and how much money you got?

JOHNNY. Mr. Kosak, you know I didn't come here to buy anything. You know I enjoy a quiet philosophical chat with you every now and then.
Quickly.
Let me have a loaf of French bread and a pound of cheese.

MR. KOSAK. You got to pay cash, Johnny.

JOHNNY. And Esther? How is your beautiful daughter Esther?

MR. KOSAK. She's all right, Johnny, but you got to pay cash. You and your Pa are the worst citizens in this county.

JOHNNY. I'm glad Esther's all right, Mr. Kosak. Jasper Mac-Gregor is visiting our house. He's a great actor.

MR. KOSAK. Never heard of him.

JOHNNY. And a bottle of beer for Mr. MacGregor.

MR. KOSAK. I can't give you a bottle of beer.

JOHNNY. Sure, you can.

MR. KOSAK. I can't. I'll let you have one loaf of French bread and a pound of cheese, but that's all. What kind of work does your Pa do when he works, Johnny?

JOHNNY. My father writes poetry, Mr. Kosak. That's the only work my father does. He's one of the greatest writers of poetry in the world.

MR. KOSAK. When does he get any money?

JOHNNY. He never gets any money. You can't have your cake and eat it too.

MR. KOSAK. I don't like that kind of work. Why doesn't your Pa work like everybody else, Johnny?

JOHNNY. He works harder than everybody else. My father works twice as hard as the average man.

MR. KOSAK *hands* JOHHNY *a loaf of French bread and a pound of cheese.*

MR. KOSAK. Well, that's fifty-five cents you owe me, Johnny. I'll let you have some stuff this time, but never again.

JOHNNY, *at the door.* Tell Esther I love her.

MR. KOSAK. All right.

JOHNNY. Good-by, Mr. Kosak.

MR. KOSAK. Good-by, Johnny.

JOHNNY *runs out of the store.* MR. KOSAK *swings at a fly, misses, swings again, misses, and, objecting to the world in this manner, he chases the fly all around the store, swinging with all his might.*

SCENE 3

The same as Scene 1. JOHNNY'S FATHER *and the old man are looking down the street to see if* JOHNNY *is coming back with food. His* GRANDMOTHER *is standing on the porch, also eager to know if there is to be food.*

MACGREGOR. I think he's got some food with him.

JOHNNY'S FATHER, *with pride.* Of course he has.

He waves at the old lady on the porch, who runs into the house to set the table. JOHNNY *runs to his* FATHER *and* MACGREGOR.

JOHNNY'S FATHER. I knew you'd do it.

MACGREGOR. So did I.

JOHNNY. He says we got to pay him fifty-five cents. He says he ain't going to give us no more stuff on credit.

JOHNNY'S FATHER. That's his opinion. What did you talk about?

JOHNNY. First I talked about being hungry and at death's door in China. Then I inquired about the family.

JOHNNY'S FATHER. How is everyone?

JOHNNY. Fine. I didn't find any money, though, not even a penny.

JOHNNY'S FATHER. That's all right.

They go into the house.

SCENE 4

The living room. They are all at the table after supper. MACGREGOR *finds crumbs here and there, which he places*

*delicately in his mouth. He looks around the room to see
if there isn't something more to eat.*

MACGREGOR. That green can up there, Johnny. What's in
there?

JOHNNY. Marbles.

MACGREGOR. That cupboard. Anything edible in there,
Johnny?

JOHNNY. Crickets.

MACGREGOR. That big jar in the corner there, Johnny. What's
good in there?

JOHNNY. I got a gopher snake in that jar.

MACGREGOR. Well, I could go for a bit of boiled gopher snake
in a big way, Johnny.

JOHNNY. You can't have that snake.

MACGREGOR. Why not, Johnny? Why the hell not, son? I hear
of fine Borneo natives eating snakes and grasshoppers.
You ain't got a half dozen fat grasshoppers around, too,
have you, Johnny?

JOHNNY. Only four.

MACGREGOR. Well, trot them out, son, and after we've had
our fill, I'll play "Drink to Me Only with Thine Eyes" for
you. I'm mighty hungry, Johnny.

JOHNNY. So am I, but I don't want anybody killing them
poor things.

JOHNNY'S FATHER, *to* MACGREGOR. How about a little music?
I think the boy would be delighted.

JOHNNY. I sure would, Mr. MacGregor.

MACGREGOR. All right, Johnny.

> MACGREGOR *gets up and begins to blow into the bugle.
He blows louder and more beautifully and mournfully than
anybody ever blew into a bugle. Eighteen neighbors gather
in front of the house and cheer when he finishes the solo.*

JOHNNY'S FATHER. I want you to meet your public.

They go out on the porch.

SCENE 5

The same as Scene 1. The crowd is looking up at JOHNNY'S
FATHER, MACGREGOR, *and* JOHNNY.

JOHNNY'S FATHER. Good neighbors and friends, I want you to
meet Jasper MacGregor, the greatest Shakespearean actor
of our day.

MACGREGOR. I remember my first appearance in London in
1867 as if it was yesterday. I was a boy of fourteen from
the slums of Glasgow. My first part was a courier in a
play, the title of which I have unfortunately forgotten. I
had no lines to speak but moved about a good deal, running from officer to officer, and from lover to his beloved,
and back again, over and over again.

RUFE APLEY, *a carpenter.* How about another song, Mr. Mac-
Gregor?

MACGREGOR. Have you got an egg at your house?

RUFE APLEY. I sure have. I've got a dozen eggs at my house.

MACGREGOR. Would it be convenient for you to go and get
one of them dozen eggs? When you return I'll play a song
that will make your heart leap with joy and grief.

RUFE APLEY. I'm on my way already.

He goes.

MACGREGOR, *to the crowd.* My friends, I should be delighted
to play another song for you on this golden-throated bugle,
but time and distance from home find me weary. If you
will be so good as to go, each of you to his home, and
return in a moment with some morsel of food, I shall be
delighted to gather my spirit together and play a song

I know will change the course of each of your lives, and change it, mind you, for the better.

The people go. MACGREGOR, JOHNNY'S FATHER, *and* JOHNNY *sit on the steps and remain in silence, and one by one the people return, bringing food to* MACGREGOR: *an egg, a sausage, a dozen green onions, two kinds of cheese, butter, two kinds of bread, boiled potatoes, fresh tomatoes, a melon, tea, and many other good things to eat.*

MACGREGOR. Thank you, my friends, thank you.

He stands solemnly, waiting for absolute silence, straightens himself, looks about him furiously, lifts the bugle to his lips, and plays "My Heart's in the Highlands, My Heart Is Not Here." The people weep and go away. MACGREGOR *turns to the father and son.*

MACGREGOR. Sir, if it is all the same to you I should like to dwell in your house for some time to come.

JOHNNY'S FATHER. Sir, my house is your house.

They go into the house.

SCENE 6

The same as Scene 4. Eighteen days later. MACGREGOR *is lying on the floor, face up, asleep.* JOHNNY *is walking about quietly in the room, looking at everybody. His* FATHER *is at the table, writing poetry. His* GRANDMOTHER *is sitting in the rocking chair, rocking. There is a knock on the door. Everybody but* MACGREGOR *jumps up and runs to it.*

JOHNNY'S FATHER, *at the door.* Yes?

A YOUNG MAN. I am looking for Jasper MacGregor, the actor.

JOHNNY'S FATHER. What do you want?

JOHNNY. Well, ask him in anyway, Pa.

JOHNNY'S FATHER. Yes, of course. Excuse me. Won't you please come in?

The YOUNG MAN *enters.*

YOUNG MAN. My name is Philip Carmichael. I am from the Old People's Home. I have been sent to bring Mr. Mac-Gregor home.

MACGREGOR, *wakening and sitting up.* Home? Did someone mention home? I'm five thousand miles from home, always have been, and always will be. Who is this young man?

YOUNG MAN. Mr. MacGregor, I'm Philip Carmichael, from the Old People's Home. They've sent me to bring you back. We are putting on our annual show in two weeks and need you for the leading role.

MACGREGOR, *getting up with the help of* JOHNNY'S FATHER *and* JOHNNY. What kind of a part is it? I can't be playing young adventurers any longer.

YOUNG MAN. The part is King Lear, Mr. MacGregor. It is perfect for you.

MACGREGOR, *to* JOHNNY'S FATHER, JOHNNY, *and the* GRAND-MOTHER. Good-by, my beloved friends. Good-by. In all the hours of my life, in all the places I have visited, never and nowhere have I had the honor and pleasure to commune with souls loftier, purer, or more delightful than yours. Good-by.

They say good-by, and the old man and the young man leave the house.

There is a long silence, full of melancholy and loneliness.

JOHNNY'S FATHER. Johnny, go on down to Mr. Kosak's store and get a little something to eat. I know you can do it, Johnny. Get *anything.*

JOHNNY. Mr. Kosak wants eighty-five cents. He won't give us anything more without money.

JOHNNY'S FATHER. Go on down there, Johnny. You know you can get that fine Slovak gentleman to give you a bit of something to eat.

JOHNNY, *with despair.* Aw, Pa.

JOHNNY'S FATHER, *amazed.* What? You, my son, in a mood like that? Come on. I've fought the world this way before you were born, and after you were born we've fought it together, and we're going to keep on fighting it. The people love poetry but don't know it. Nothing is going to stop us, Johnny. Go on down there now and get something to eat. You didn't do so well last time. Remember? I can't write great poetry on bird seed and maple syrup. Go on now.

JOHNNY. All right, Pa. I'll do my best.

He runs to the door.

JOHNNY'S FATHER. Remember, if you find any money on the way, we go fifty-fifty.

GUYS AND DOLLS

A Musical Fable of Broadway

Based on a story and characters by Damon Runyon

Book by JO SWERLING AND ABE BURROWS

Lyrics by FRANK LOESSER

CHARACTERS

(In order of appearance)

NICELY-NICELY JOHNSON

BENNY SOUTHSTREET

RUSTY CHARLIE

SARAH BROWN

ARVIDE ABERNATHY

MISSION BAND

HARRY THE HORSE

LIEUTENANT BRANNIGAN

NATHAN DETROIT

ANGIE THE OX

MISS ADELAIDE

SKY MASTERSON

JOEY BILTMORE

MIMI

GENERAL MATILDA B. CARTWRIGHT

BIG JULE

DRUNK

WAITER

SONGS

ACT ONE

FUGUE FOR TIN HORNS   Nicely-Nicely, Benny, Rusty
     Charlie. 288

FOLLOW THE FOLD   Mission Group. 290

THE OLDEST ESTAB-   Nathan, Nicely-Nicely,
   LISHED   Benny, Ensemble. 295

I'LL KNOW   Sarah and Sky. 309

A BUSHEL AND A PECK   Adelaide and Hot Box
     Girls. 314

ADELAIDE'S LAMENT   Adelaide. 320

GUYS AND DOLLS   Nicely-Nicely and Benny.
     322

IF I WERE A BELL   Sarah. 335

MY TIME OF DAY   Sky. 339

I'VE NEVER BEEN IN   Sky and Sarah. 339
   LOVE BEFORE

ACT TWO

TAKE BACK YOUR MINK   Adelaide and Hot Box
     Girls. 342

REPRISE: ADELAIDE'S   Adelaide. 346
   LAMENT

MORE I CANNOT WISH   Arvide. 347
   YOU

LUCK, BE A LADY   Sky and Crapshooters. 357

SUE ME   Nathan and Adelaide. 362

SIT DOWN, YOU'RE   Nicely-Nicely and Ensemble.
   ROCKIN' THE BOAT   368

REPRISE: FOLLOW THE   Mission Group. 373
   FOLD

MARRY THE MAN TODAY   Adelaide and Sarah. 376

REPRISE: GUYS AND   Entire Company. 380
   DOLLS

ACT ONE

SCENE 1

Broadway. Stage center are TWO SHADY BROADWAY CHAR- ACTERS. MAN *with newspaper crosses and exits.*

BOBBYSOXERS *enter and exit.*

SIGHT-SEEING GUIDE *and* SIGHT-SEERS *enter.*

ACTOR *and* ACTRESS *enter.*
One of the shady Broadway characters is flipping a coin, the other snapping his fingers. They both glance off stage, obviously looking for a pickup.

A NEW YORK POLICEMAN, *swinging a club, enters and exits.*

TWO CHORUS GIRLS *wearing slacks enter. They exit.* TWO VERY ANIMATED BOBBYSOXERS *enter carrying autograph books and pencils. They rush off.*

TWO WELL-DRESSED STREETWALKERS *enter and flirt with the* TWO SHADY CHARACTERS. *One of the shady characters flips the coin. They take* TWO CHORUS GIRLS *by the arms and escort them off.*

A MAN *rushes on and exits hurriedly.*

An ELDERLY WOMAN STREET VENDOR *dressed shabbily and carrying a shoulder tray containing apples, gardenias, and pretzels on sticks enters and slowly exits.*

A SIGHT-SEEING TEXAN *and* HIS WIFE *enter. He is carrying a sight-seeing map and wears a watch and chain across his vest.*

A SIDEWALK PHOTOGRAPHER *enters carrying a camera and order blank. He snaps the* TEXAN *and* HIS WIFE, *who pose for the* PHOTOGRAPHER. PHOTOGRAPHER *hands order blank to* TEXAN *who signs it and gives money to him in payment. The* TEXAN *and* HIS WIFE *exit. The* PHOTOGRAPHER *looks after them, crumples up the order blank, and throws it away.*

An ACTRESS *enters, dressed very elegantly, carrying long cigarette holder. She is escorted by an* ACTOR *dressed in a tuxedo. The* TWO BOBBYSOXERS *have followed them on. They have the* ACTOR *and* ACTRESS *autograph their books.*

As the ACTOR *and* ACTRESS *turn upstage to exit, a sign painted "PESSIMO CIGARS" is revealed. The* BOBBY-SOXERS *exit.*

A MAN PAPER DOLL VENDOR *and* HIS LADY ASSISTANT *enter, pushing a trick convertible vehicle which converts into a baby buggy. They exit.*

A HEAVYWEIGHT PRIZE FIGHTER *with cauliflower ears enters, skipping rope.* HIS MANAGER *enters with him, giving him instructions as they cross the stage and exit.*

PAPER DOLL VENDOR *and* HIS ASSISTANT *enter with vehicle. They set it up at stage center.* LADY ASSISTANT *pulls out black thread, he sets paper doll on thread, she manipulates the paper doll on the black thread. They see the* POLICEMAN *enter. They quickly pull the trigger, which converts the vehicle into a baby buggy. They nod very graciously to the* POLICEMAN *as they pass him. He nods, then suddenly he realizes he has been tricked, rushes off chasing them.*

A SIGHT-SEEING GUIDE *enters, followed by a group of seven or eight* SIGHT-SEERS, *including the* TEXAN *and* HIS WIFE *who are in the rear of the group. The* SIGHT-SEEING GUIDE *is pointing to objects of interest. A* PICKPOCKET *enters, goes to* TEXAN *and points to a tall building and, as the* TEXAN *is looking up, he steals the* TEXAN'S *watch and chain. The* TEXAN *and* HIS WIFE *exit.*

TWO STREETWALKERS *enter. They cross to* PICKPOCKET *and flirt with him and relieve him of the watch and chain he stole from the* TEXAN. *They take the* PICKPOCKET *by the arm and very nonchalantly stroll off with him.*

TEXAN *and* HIS WIFE *rush on. It is very evident that he has suddenly discovered the loss of his watch and is intent upon catching the* PICKPOCKET. *They exit.*

A BLIND MAN *carrying a cane, tin cup in his hand, glasses, and wearing a sign, "BLIND," enters. He feels his way slowly to center stage.*

PAPER DOLL VENDOR *and* HIS LADY ASSISTANT *enter and set up their vehicle at stage center. As they do so, the* MAN VENDOR *flicks his cigarette ashes into* BLIND MAN'S *tin cup.* BLIND MAN *looks at this. At this moment the* PAPER DOLL VENDOR *looks off, sees* POLICEMAN, *motions to* HIS ASSISTANT, *picks up vehicle, and rushes off.* BLIND MAN *runs off.*

PICKPOCKET, SIDEWALK CAMERAMAN *rush on, chased by the* POLICEMAN, TEXAN, *and* HIS WIFE. *They exit. All the characters on stage run off after them very excitedly.*

BENNY SOUTHSTREET *enters, very engrossed in reading a racing scratch sheet.*

PRIZE FIGHTER, *shadow boxing, enters, followed by* HIS MANAGER. *The* PRIZE FIGHTER, *not seeing* BENNY, *runs into him accidentally. He is knocked down by the force of* BENNY'S *head against his solar plexus.* PRIZE FIGHTER, *frightened and not knowing really what happened, runs off, followed by* HIS MANAGER. BENNY *straightens his hat, which has been dented by the collision.*

BENNY *unconcernedly joins* NICELY-NICELY JOHNSON, *who has entered at this moment, finishing a bottle of Coca-Cola, and is at the newsstand buying a scratch sheet from the* NEWSMAN.

RUSTY CHARLIE *enters, reading a scratch sheet. They group together and sing* A FUGUE FOR TIN HORNS.

NICELY.

I got the horse right here, the name is Paul Revere
TWO STREETWALKERS *enter and stand watching* BENNY, NICELY, *and* RUSTY.
And here's a guy that says if the weather's clear
Can do, can do, this guy says the horse can do

If he says the horse can do, can do, can do
Can do, can do, this guy says the horse can do
If he says the horse can do, can do, can do
For Paul Revere I'll bite
I hear his foot's all right
Of course it all depends if it rained last night
Likes mud, likes mud, this X means the horse likes mud
If that means the horse likes mud, likes mud, likes mud
I tell you Paul Revere
Now this is no bum steer
It's from a handicapper that's real sincere
Can do, can do, this guy says the horse can do
If he says the horse can do, can do, can do
Paul Revere! I got the horse right here

BENNY *shows sheet to* RUSTY.

I'm pickin' Valentine, 'cause on the morning line
This guy has got him figured at five to nine
Has chance, has chance, this guy says the horse has chance
If he says the horse has chance, has chance, has chance
I know it's Valentine, the morning works look fine
Besides the jockey's brother's a friend of mine
Needs race, needs race, this guy says the horse needs race
If he says the horse needs race—needs race, needs race
I go for Valentine, 'cause on the morning line
The guy has got him figured at five to nine
Has chance, has chance, this guy says the horse has chance
Valentine! I got the horse right here

CHARLIE.

But look at Epitaph, he wins it by a half
According to this here in the Telegraph
Big Threat, Big Threat,
This guy calls the horse Big Threat
If he calls the horse Big Threat,
Big Threat, Big Threat
And just a minute, boys,
I've got the feedbox noise
It says the great-grandfather was Equipoise
Shows class, shows class,
This guy says the horse shows class

If he says the horse shows class
Shows class, shows class
So make it Epitaph, he wins it by a half
According to this here in the Telegraph
Epitaph! I got the horse right here!

At end of FUGUE FOR TIN HORNS, MISSION BAND *enters,*
playing FOLLOW THE FOLD, SARAH *with tambourine, a*
FEMALE MEMBER *playing the cornet,* ARVIDE ABERNATHY
beating a bass drum and cymbals, a female member carry-
ing a small box which she places on stage. SARAH *steps*
on box and as they finish playing they sing FOLLOW THE
FOLD. TWO BOBBYSOXERS *enter. They stop and listen.*

SARAH *and* MISSION BAND.
Follow the fold and stray no more
Stray no more, stray no more
Put down the bottle and we'll say no more
Follow, follow the fold

DRUNK *enters.*

SIGHT-SEEING GROUP, *including* TEXAN *and* HIS WIFE, *enter.*

SARAH *points at drunk.*
Before you take another swallow

PRIZE FIGHTER *and* HIS MANAGER *enter, listen to singing.*

SARAH *and* BAND.
Follow the fold and stray no more
Stray no more, stray no more
Tear up your poker deck of cards and play no more
Follow, follow the fold

To the meadows where the sun shines
Out of the darkness and the cold

CHORUS GIRLS *enter, stop suddenly, alongside of the drunk.*
SARAH *points at them.*

The sin and shame in which you wallow

Follow the fold and stray no more
Stray no more, stray no more
If you're a sinner and you pray no more
Follow, follow the fold

SARAH. Brothers and sisters, resist the devil and he will flee from you. That is what the Bible tells us.

NICELY, BENNY, RUSTY *cross.*

And that is why I am standing here, in the devil's own city—

The BOBBYSOXERS *exit laughing.*

—on the devil's own street, prepared to do battle with the forces of evil. Hear me, you gamblers!

She points to NICELY, BENNY, *and* RUSTY.

With your dice, your cards, your horses! Pause and think before it is too late!

She is failing to hold her audience and occasionally falters as she notices someone walk out.

You are in great danger! I am not speaking of the prison and the gallows—

SIGHT-SEEING GROUP *exits.*

—but of the greater punishment that awaits you! Repent before it is too late!

PRIZE FIGHTER *and* HIS MANAGER *exit.*

Just around the corner is our little Mission—

DRUNK *exits.*

—where you are always welcome to seek refuge from this jungle of sin.

TWO CHORUS GIRLS *exit.*

Come there and talk to me. Do not think of me as Sergeant Sarah Brown, but as Sarah Brown, your sister.

The TWO STREETWALKERS *slowly exit, showing their wares as they pass* RUSTY CHARLIE, *who is standing at news-stand with* NICELY *and* BENNY. *He follows them off, pointing his finger at them as they exit.* NICELY *and* BENNY *are not conscious of this.*

Join me, brothers and sisters, in resisting the devil, and we can put him to flight forever.

SARAH *looks at* ARVIDE *hopelessly. He motions to her encouragingly.*

Remember, friends, it is the Save-A-Soul Mission—
Slowly stepping down from the box.
—located at 409 West 49th Street, open all day and all
night, with a special prayer meeting this Thursday at——
Looks despairingly at ARVIDE. *Her crowd has disappeared
by this time, except* NICELY *and* BENNY *who are standing
by the newstand reading their scratch sheets.* SARAH *and
the* MISSION BAND *make a disconsolate and disorderly exit.*

NICELY, *looking after them as he crosses, followed by* BENNY.
Poor Miss Sarah! I wonder why a refined doll like her is
mixed up in the Mission dodge.

BENNY. She is a beautiful doll, all right, with one hundred per
cent eyes.

NICELY. It is too bad that such a doll wastes all her time being
good. How can she make any money from that?

BENNY. Maybe she owns a piece of the Mission.

NICELY. Yeah.

HARRY THE HORSE *enters.*

HARRY. Hey! Benny Southstreet!

BENNY. Harry the Horse! How are you? You know Nicely-
Nicely Johnson?

HARRY. Yeah. How goes it?

NICELY. Nicely, nicely, thank you.

HARRY. Tell me, what about Nathan Detroit? Is he got a place
for his crap game?

BENNY *whispers back.* We don't know yet.

NICELY. The heat is on.

BENNY. He's still looking for a place.

HARRY. Well, tell him I'm loaded and looking for action. I just
acquired five thousand potatoes.

BENNY. Five thousand bucks?

NICELY. Where did you acquire it?

HARRY. I collected the reward on my father.

Exits.

BENNY. Everybody is looking for action. I wish Nathan'd find a——

He stops as BRANNIGAN *enters, gets paper at newsstand.*

NICELY. Why, Lieutenant Brannigan! Mr. Southstreet, it is Lieutenant Brannigan of the New York Police Department.

BENNY. A pleasure.

BRANNIGAN. Any of you guys seen Nathan Detroit?

BENNY. Which Nathan Detroit is that?

BRANNIGAN folds his paper with an abrupt movement and faces the two men.

BRANNIGAN. I mean the Nathan Detroit who's been running a floating crap game around here and getting away with it by moving it to a different spot every night.

NICELY. Why are you telling us this—your honor?

BRANNIGAN. I am telling you this because I know you two bums work for Detroit, rustling up customers for his crap game.

NICELY. We do?

BRANNIGAN. Yeah!

NICELY. Oh!

BRANNIGAN. You can tell him for me: I know that right now he's running around trying to find a spot. Well, nobody's gonna give him a spot, because they all know that Brannigan is breathing down their neck!

Starts to exit. NATHAN *enters from above newsstand, not seeing* BRANNIGAN.

NICELY. Hi, Nathan!

NATHAN. Fellows, I'm having terrible trouble. Everybody's scared on account of that lousy Brannigan, and I can't——

BRANNIGAN. Something wrong, Mr. Detroit?

NATHAN, *a sickly grimace.* Oh, hello, Lieutenant. I hope you don't think I was talking about you. There are other lousy Brannigans.

BRANNIGAN. Detroit, I have just been talking to your colleagues about your crap game. I imagine you are having trouble finding a place.

NATHAN. Well, the heat is on, as you must know from the fact that you now have to live on your salary.

BRANNIGAN *glares and exits.*

BENNY *crosses to* NATHAN. Did you find a place?

NATHAN. What does that cop want from me? What am I—a sex maniac? I merely run a crap game for the convenience of those who want a little action, in return for which I take a small cut. Is that a crime? Yeah!

BENNY. Nathan! Did you find a place?

NICELY. Did you find a place for the game?

NATHAN. Did I find a place! Did I find—yes, I found a place! We are holding a crap game tomorrow night in the Radio City Music Hall.

BENNY. How you gonna fix the ushers?

NATHAN. I tried all the regular places. The back of the cigar store, the funeral parlor—

NICELY. Nathan, you said once there might be a chance of the Biltmore Garage.

NATHAN. I was over to the Biltmore Garage. Spoke to Joey Biltmore himself. He says he might take a chance and let me use the place, if I give him a thousand bucks.

BENNY. A thousand bucks!

NATHAN. In cash. He won't take my marker.

BENNY. Your marker's no good, huh?

NATHAN. What do you mean? A marker ain't just a piece of paper that says I O U one thousand dollars signed

NATHAN DETROIT. A marker is like a pledge which a guy can't welch on it. It's like not saluting the flag.

BENNY *and* NICELY *remove hats.*

My marker is as good as gold, only Joey Biltmore don't think so. It don't seem possible. Me without a livelihood. Why, I have been running the crap game ever since I was a juvenile delinquent.

BENNY. Nathan, can't you do something?

NATHAN. What can I do? I'm broke. I couldn't even buy Adelaide a present today, and you know what day today is? It is mine and Adelaide's fourteenth anniversary.

BENNY. Yeah?

NICELY. Yeah?

NATHAN. Yeah. We been engaged fourteen years.

THREE CRAPSHOOTERS *enter, go to newsstand and converse.*

BENNY. Nathan, concentrate on the game. The town's up to here with high players. The Greek's in town!

NICELY. Brandy Bottle Bates!

TWO CRAPSHOOTERS *enter.*

BENNY. Scranton Slim!

NATHAN. I know, I could make a fortune. But where can I have the game?

They sing THE OLD ESTABLISHED.

NICELY.
The Biltmore Garage wants a grand

BENNY.
But we ain't got a grand on hand

NATHAN.
*And they now have a lock on the door
Of the gym at Public School Eighty-four*

NICELY.
There's the stock room behind McClosky's Bar

BENNY.

But Missus McClosky ain't a good scout

NATHAN.

And things bein' how they are
The back of the police station's out

NICELY.

So the Biltmore Garage is the spot

ALL.

But the one thousand bucks we ain't got
SINGERS *enter.*

SINGERS.

Why it's good old reliable Nathan Nathan Nathan Nathan
    Detroit
If you're lookin' for action he'll furnish the spot
Even when the heat is on it's never too hot
Not for good old reliable Nathan for it's always just a
    short walk
To the oldest established permanent floating crap game in
    New York

(*They take off their hats.*)
There are well-heeled shooters ev'rywhere ev'rywhere
There are well-heeled shooters ev'rywhere—

(*Showing money.*)
And an awful lot of lettuce for the fella who can get us
    there

NICELY)
BENNY)   If we only had a lousy little grand we could be a
NATHAN)   millionaire

SINGERS.

There—that's good old reliable Nathan Nathan Nathan
    Nathan Detroit
If the size of your bundle you want to increase
He'll arrange that you go broke in quiet and peace
In a hide-out provided by Nathan where there are no
    neighbors to squawk
It's the oldest established permanent floating crap game
    in New York

SINGERS.

Where's the action, where's the game

NICELY)
BENNY) *Gotta have the game or we'll die from shame*
NATHAN)

ALL.

It's the oldest established permanent floating crap game in New York

All the CRAPSHOOTERS *start to exit.* NATHAN *shouts after them.*

NATHAN. Gentlemen, do not worry. Nathan Detroit's crap game will float again. My boys will let you know where it is.

They exit.

ANGIE THE OX. Okay, Nathan. Say, you know who else is looking for action? Sky Masterson! Sky Masterson's in town.

ANGIE *exits.*

NATHAN. Sky Masterson! There is the highest player of them all!

BENNY. Higher than the Greek?

NATHAN. Higher than anybody. Why do you think they call him Sky? That's how high he bets. I once saw him bet five thousand dollars on a cockroach. And another time he was sick, and he wouldn't take penicillin on account he had bet ten C's that his temperature would go to 104.

NICELY. Did it?

NATHAN. Did it? He's so lucky it went to 106. Good old Sky!

NICELY. Maybe you can borrow the thousand from Sky.

NATHAN. Not Sky. With him that kind of money ain't lending money—it's betting money. So why don't I bet him? Why don't I bet him a thousand on something?

NICELY. You would bet with Sky Masterson?

NATHAN. I ain't scared. I am perfectly willing to take the risk, providing I can figure out a bet on which there is no chance of losing. He likes crazy bets, like which lump of sugar will a fly sit on, or how far can you kick a piece of cheesecake—cheesecake! Ooh! Look—run into Mindy's Restaurant and ask Mindy how many pieces of cheesecake he sold yesterday and also how many pieces of strudel.

BENNY. How much cheesecake, how much strudel—what do you want to know for?

NATHAN. Just find out! Now beat it—here comes Adelaide. If she hears I am running the crap game she will never set foot on me again.

BENNY *and* NICELY *run off as* ADELAIDE *enters, carrying a small box which contains a man's belt and a small card. She is followed by* THREE GIRLS *from the Hot Box.*

ADELAIDE. Hello, Nathan dear.

Embrace.

NATHAN. Adelaide! Pigeon!

ADELAIDE. You go ahead, girls. Order me a tuna fish on rye and a chocolate sundae with tomato ketchup and mayonnaise.

GIRLS. Okay, Adelaide.

They exit.

ADELAIDE. We gotta get back to the Hot Box.

NATHAN. You still rehearsing?

ADELAIDE. Yeah. That slave driver Charlie—he's been working us all day. Finally I says, "Look, Charlie, I'm starving! I gotta get outa here and get something to eat." And he says, "'You don't want to eat. You just want to sneak out and meet that cheap bum, Nathan Detroit!'"

NATHAN, *outraged.* So what did you say to him?

ADELAIDE, *proudly.* I told him. I says, "I'll meet whoever I want!"

NATHAN. Well, don't upset yourself. How's your cold?

ADELAIDE. Oh, it's much better, thank you . . . Nathan! Happy anniversary!

NATHAN. A present! For me?

ADELAIDE. I hope you like it.

NATHAN. A belt!

ADELAIDE. Read the card!

NATHAN. "Sugar is sweet, and so is jelly, so put this belt around your belly." That's so sweet. Look, honey—about your present. I was going to get you a diamond wrist watch with a gold band and two rubies on the side.

ADELAIDE. Nathan, you shouldn't have.

NATHAN. It's all right—I didn't. I'm sorry.

ADELAIDE. No, I kinda like it when you forget to give me presents. It makes me feel like we're married.

NATHAN. Don't worry, honey—one of these days I'll be in the money, and you'll have more mink than a mink.

ADELAIDE. Nathan darling, I can do without anything just so long as you don't start running the crap game again.

NATHAN. The crap game! What an absurd thought!

BENNY *and* NICELY *enter.*

BENNY. Psst! Twelve hundred cheesecake and fifteen hundred strudel.

NATHAN. Huh?

NICELY. Yesterday Mindy sold twelve hundred cheesecake and fifteen hundred strudel.

NATHAN. More strudel than cheesecake. That's great!

ADELAIDE. Nathan! What is this?

NATHAN. Nothing, honey.

HARRY THE HORSE *enters.*

HARRY. Hey! Any news yet?

NATHAN. Not yet, Harry, I'll let you know.

HARRY. O.K., Detroit.

Exit.

ADELAIDE. What was that about?

NATHAN. His wife's having a baby.

ADELAIDE. Why's he asking you?

NATHAN. He's nervous—it's his first wife. Look, Adelaide, I'm expecting a fellow and I know you're hungry . . .

ADELAIDE. Nathan, are you trying to get rid of me?

NATHAN. No, I just don't want your sandwich to get soggy. Fellows . . .

He sees SKY *approaching.*

. . . why don't you take Adelaide to the drugstore?

To her.

You see, honey, you've got a cold, and it's across the street, and there're a lot of open manholes around——

ADELAIDE. *As she is being borne away by* BENNY *and* NICELY, *they raise her up and exit.* Nathan darling, you're so thoughtful. You're just the sweetest person. Good-by.

NATHAN *is alone. He paces a moment, peers off.*

SKY MASTERSON *enters.*

NATHAN. Hey, Masterson! Glad to see you, Sky!

SKY. Nathan! You old promoter, you!

NATHAN. How are you, Sky? You look great!

SKY. *Feel* great, Nathan. Two wonderful weeks out West in Nevada. Great place! Beautiful scenery, healthful climate, and I beat 'em for fifty G's at blackjack.

NATHAN. Fifty G's! Going to be in town long?

SKY. No. Flying to Havana tomorrow.

NATHAN. Havana?

SKY. Yes, there's a lot of action down there. Want to come with me?

NATHAN. No, I got a lot of things to do. Meantime, how about dropping over to Mindy's for a piece of cheesecake? They sell a lot of cheesecake.

SKY. No, I'm not hungry. Tell me, how's Adelaide?

NATHAN. Oh, fine, fine. Still dancing at the Hot Box.

SKY. I suppose one of these days you'll be getting married?

NATHAN. We all got to go sometime.

SKY. But, Nathan, we can fight it. Guys like us, Nathan—we got to remember that, pleasant as a doll's company may be, she must always take second place to aces back to back.

NATHAN, *his mind on other matters.* Yeah. Yeah. Tell me— you hungry yet? Maybe we could go into Mindy's and have a piece of cheesecake or strudel or something?

SKY. No. I think I'll go get the late results.
Takes scratch sheet from pocket.

NATHAN. Oh! But you will admit that Mindy has the greatest cheesecake in the country?

SKY. Yes, I'm quite partial to Mindy's cheesecake.

NATHAN. Who ain't? And yet there are some people who like Mindy's strudel.
SKY *seems uninterested.*
Offhand, which do you think he sells more of, the cheesecake or the strudel?

SKY. Well, I never give it much thought. But if everybody is like I am, I'd say Mindy sells much more cheesecake then strudel.

NATHAN. For how much?

SKY. Huh?

NATHAN. For how much?

SKY. Why, Nathan, I never knew you to be a betting man. You always take your percentage off the top.

NATHAN. Well, for old times' sake I thought I'd give you a little action. I will bet you a thousand bucks that yesterday Mindy sold more strudel than cheesecake.

SKY. Nathan, let me tell you a story.

NATHAN. Oh.

SKY. When I was a young man about to go out into the world, my father says to me a very valuable thing. He says to me like this: "Son," the old guy says, "I am sorry that I am not able to bankroll you to a very large start, but, not having any potatoes to give you, I am now going to stake you to some very valuable advice. One of these days in your travels a guy is going to come to you and show you a nice brand-new deck of cards on which the seal is not yet broken, and this guy is going to offer to bet you that he can make the jack of spades jump out of the deck and squirt cider in your ear. But son, do not bet this man, for as sure as you stand there you are going to wind up with an earful of cider." Now, Nathan, I do not claim that you have been clocking Mindy's cheesecake——

NATHAN. You don't think that . . .

SKY. However, if you're really looking for some action—

Crosses to Nathan, puts his hand across his chest, hiding NATHAN'S *necktie.*

I will bet you the same thousand that you do not know the color of the necktie you have on.

We can tell from NATHAN'S *expression that his entire life is passing before him as he fails to remember the color.* Well?

NATHAN, *dismally.* No bet.

SKY *removes his hand.* NATHAN *looks disgustedly at the color of his tie.*

Blue. What a crazy color.

BENNY *and* NICELY *enter.*

BENNY. Nathan, we took Adelaide to the drugstore . . .

NATHAN. Don't bother me.

He pushes BENNY, *who falls.*

NICELY. Hi ya, Sky!

SKY. Good. How's it with you fellows?

BENNY. Not bad.

NICELY. Nicely, nicely. We took Adelaide to the drugstore, and she says for you to be sure to pick her up after the show at the Hot Box, and don't be late.

NATHAN. Yes, dear. I mean yes.

SKY. Yes, dear. That is husband talk if I ever heard it. Nathan, you are trapped. In Adelaide you have the kind of a girl that is most difficult to unload.

NATHAN. I don't want to unload her; I love Adelaide. And a guy without a doll—well, if a guy does not have a doll—who would holler at him? A doll is a necessity.

SKY. Nathan, I am not putting the rap on dolls. I just say a guy should have them around when he wants them, and they are easy to find.

NATHAN. Not dolls like Adelaide!

SKY. Nathan, figuring weight for age, all dolls are the same.

NATHAN. Oh, yeah?

SKY. Yeah!

NATHAN. Then how come you ain't got a doll? How come you're going to Havana alone without one?

SKY. I like to travel light, but if I wish to take a doll to Havana there is a large assortment available.

MISSION GROUP *is heard singing off stage.*

NATHAN. Not real high class dolls!

SKY. Any doll! You name her!

NATHAN. Any doll? And I name her! Will you bet on that? Will you bet a thousand dollars that if I name a doll you will take her to Havana tomorrow?

SKY. You got a bet!

The MISSION GROUP *enters, singing, headed by* SARAH. NATHAN *points to* SARAH.

NATHAN. I name *her*.

SKY *puts his hand to his ear, then withdraws it.* Her! Cider!

SCENE 2

Interior of Save-A-Soul Mission. The MISSION BAND *files in.* AGATHA, CALVIN, *and* MARTHA *exit.* ARVIDE *places bass drum against window, hat on chair. Standing in center is a painted sign in block letters. It reads* "THERE IS NO PEACE TO THE WICKED——PROVERBS 23.9."

SARAH *puts tambourine on barber chair. Takes hat and coat off.*

SARAH. Someday I'm going to take a pick-ax and rip up Broadway from end to end.

Sits at desk, busies herself with papers.

ARVIDE. They do that every day.

He crosses to armchair, picks up Mission newspaper which is in chair, and sits and reads. SKY MASTERSON *is seen on street through window. He enters, then stops and looks in through window. After a moment he enters through door. He assumes an air of repentance.*

SKY. Do you take sinners here?

ARVIDE, *rising, coming to* SKY. Indeed we do! Sarah!

SARAH *rises.* How do you do?

ARVIDE. My name is Abernathy. Arvide Abernathy.

SKY. Sky Masterson.

And suddenly his head drops into his hands.

SARAH. What's wrong?

ARVIDE. What is the trouble?

SKY. My heart is heavy with sin.

ARVIDE. You poor man!

SKY. I have wasted my life in gambling and evil betting. But I have suddenly realized the terrible things that betting can lead to.

A side glance at Sarah.

ARVIDE, *calling.* Agatha!

AGATHA *sticks her head out of door.*

Coffee!

SARAH. Didn't I see you a little while ago on Broadway?

SKY. Possibly. I have been wandering around, trying to get up the courage to come here.

SARAH. And you're willing to give up gambling?

SKY. Gladly. I would never have become a gambler at all had I not fallen in with evil companions who were always offering me sucker bets.

AGATHA *enters with coffee.*

ARVIDE. Here, young man.

SKY. Thank you. It makes me feel good just to talk to you people.

ARVIDE. You just go right on talking to Sister Sarah, and you'll be all right. I'm glad you found us.

SKY. The Bible says, "Seek and ye shall find."

ARVIDE. Very good! I wish we could reach more sinners like you. We are out every day, trying.

SKY. Maybe you should try the nighttime.

ARVIDE. How's that?

SKY. As a former sinner, I happen to know that the best time to find sinners is between midnight and dawn. You might even try having an all-night session against the devil.

ARVIDE. A very good suggestion indeed! Thank you, Brother Masterson!

SKY. You're welcome.

ARVIDE *drinks coffee.* Coffee is so good I can't understand why it isn't a sin.

Exits.

SARAH *sits at desk.*

SKY, *looking after* ARVIDE. Fine old gentleman. I suppose he sort of—looks after you?

SARAH. We look after each other.

SKY. Uh-huh. I suppose if either of you goes some place, the other goes along?

SARAH. Yes, of course.

SKY. Of course.

SARAH *hands* SKY *pamphlet.* Here are two of our pamphlets I'd like you to read. They will give you a good deal of comfort.

SKY. Thank you.

SARAH. And we're holding a midnight prayer meeting on Thursday, which I'm sure you will wish to attend.

SKY. I'm sure. Miss Sarah, I hope you will not think I am getting out of line, but I think it is wonderful to see a pretty doll—uh—a nice-looking lady like you—sacrificing herself for the sake of others. Staying here in this place—do you ever go any place else? Travel or something?

SARAH. I would like to go to Africa.

SKY. That's a little far. But there are a lot of wonderful places just a few hours from New York, by plane. Ever been in a plane?

SARAH. No.

SKY. Oh, it's wonderful.

SARAH. Here is another pamphlet that I think you should read.
Gives him pamphlet.

SKY. Thank you. Of course I will need a lot of personal help from you. My heart is as black as two feet down a wolf's gullet.

SARAH. I'll be speaking at the Thursday prayer meeting.

SKY. I need private lessons. Why don't we have dinner or something?

SARAH. I think not, Mr. Masterson.

SKY. Sorry, just blossoming under the warmth of your kindness.

Strolling around, looking the place over.

Hey, that's wrong.

SARAH. What's wrong?

SKY. That's not Proverbs—it's Isaiah.

SARAH. It's Proverbs.

SKY. Sorry. "No peace to the wicked." Isaiah, chapter 57, verse 21.

SARAH goes to Bible stand, opens it. Behind his back SARAH looks up quotation in Bible. Slams the book shut.

SKY, *without turning.* Isaiah?

SARAH. Isaiah.

SKY. There are two things been in every hotel room in the country: Sky Masterson and the Gideon Bible. I must have read the Good Book ten or twelve times.

SARAH. You've read the Bible twelve times?

SKY. What's wrong with the Bible? Besides, in my business the strangest information frequently comes in handy. I once won five G's on a parlay, Shadrach, Meshach and Abednego.

SARAH. Tell me, Mr. Masterson, why are you here?

SKY. I told you. I'm a sinner.

SARAH. You're lying.

SKY. Well, lyin's a sin. Look, I'm a *big* sinner. If you get me, it's eight to five the others'll follow. You need sinners, don't you?

SARAH. We're managing.

SKY. Let's be honest. This Mission is laying an egg.
She is silent.
Why don't you let me help you? I'll bet I can fill this place with sinners.

SARAH. I don't bet.

SKY. I'll make you a proposition.
Picks up cardboard from chair, writes marker.
When is this big meeting of yours—Thursday? I will guarantee to fill that meeting with one dozen genuine sinners. I will also guarantee that they will sit still and listen to you.

SARAH. And what's my end of the bargain?

SKY. Have dinner with me.

SARAH. Why do you want to have dinner with *me?*

SKY. I'm hungry. Here!
Gives her marker. She takes it.

SARAH. What's this?

SKY. Sky Masterson's marker for twelve sinners. If you don't think it's good, ask anybody in town. I O U—one dozen sinners.
He hands her red cardboard marker.
I'll pick you up at noon tomorrow, for dinner.

SARAH. At noon?

SKY. It'll take us some time to get there.

SARAH. To get where?

SKY. To my favorite restaurant.

SARAH. Where is that?

SKY. El Cafe Cubana, in Havana.

SARAH. El Cafe Cubana, Havana?

SKY. Where do you want to eat? Howard Johnson's?

SARAH. Havana!

SKY. Why not? The plane gets us there in five hours and back the same night. And the food is great.

SARAH. I now realize, Mr. Gambler, when you were describing the blackness of your heart, you didn't do yourself justice.

SKY. And I now realize, Sister Sarah, that no matter how beautiful a sergeant is, she's still a sergeant.

SARAH. Please go away.

SKY. Why don't you change your pitch, Sarge? "Come to the Mission one and all, except guys. I hate guys!"

SARAH. I don't hate anybody.

SKY. Except me. I am relieved to know that it's just me personally and not all guys in general. It is nice to know that somewhere in the world there's a guy who might appeal to the sergeant. I wonder what this guy will be like?

SARAH. He will *not* be a gambler.

SKY. I am not interested in what he will not be. I am interested in what he will be.

SARAH. Don't worry, I'll know.

They sing I'LL KNOW

SARAH.

> *I've imagined every bit of him*
> *From his strong moral fiber*
> *To the wisdom in his head*
> *To the homey aroma of his pipe*

SKY.

> *You have wished yourself a Scarsdale Galahad*
> *The breakfast-eating Brooks Brothers type*

SARAH.

> *Yes and I shall meet him when the time is ripe*

SKY, *spoken.* You've got the guy all figured out.

SARAH, *spoken.* I have.

SKY, *spoken.* Including what he smokes. All figured out, huh?

SARAH, *spoken*. All figured out.

SARAH *sings*.
> *I'll know when my love comes along*
> *I won't take a chance*
> *For oh, he'll be just what I need*
> *Not some fly-by-night Broadway romance*

SKY.
> *You'll know at a glance*
> *By the two pair of pants*

SARAH.
> *I'll know by that calm steady voice*
> *Those two feet on the ground*
> *I'll know, as I run to his arms*
> *That at last I've come home safe and sound*
> *And till then I shall wait*
> *And till then I'll be strong*
> *For I'll know when my love comes along*

SKY, *spoken*. No, no . . . no . . . you're talking about love. You can't dope it like that. What are you picking, a guy or a horse?

SARAH. I wouldn't expect a gambler to understand.

SKY. Would you like to hear how a gambler feels about the big heart throb?

SARAH. No!

SKY. Well, I'll tell you.

SKY *sings*.
> *Mine will come as a surprise to me*
> *Mine, I leave to chance—and chemistry*

SARAH, *spoken*. Chemistry?

SKY, *spoken*. Yeah, chemistry.
> (*Singing*.)
> *Suddenly I'll know, when my love comes along*
> *I'll know, then and there*
> *I'll know, at the sight of her face*

How I care, how I care, how I care
And I'll stop and I'll stare
And I'll know long before we can speak
I'll know in my heart
I'll know. And I won't ever ask:
"Am I right? Am I wise? Am I smart?"
But I'll stop and I'll stare at that face in the throng
Yes, I'll know when my love comes along

SARAH.

I'll know

SARAH *and* SKY.

When my love comes along

They stand looking at each other as the music continues in the orchestra. SARAH *is standing with her hands at her sides. She has been moved by* SKY's *lyric and is really fascinated by this cobra.* SKY *senses that he has made a dent in her defenses. He puts his arms around her and kisses her tenderly. She submits to this but doesn't respond. He releases her and picks up his hat. She stands, seemingly entranced. He stands watching her. She has been staring off into space. She turns to him. He looks at her in anticipation. She walks towards him, floating on air. He stands confidently, expecting another embrace. She reaches him and hauls off and belts him one across the chops.* SKY *drops his hat. He reaches down and recovers it while rubbing his cheek.*

SKY. I'll drop in again in case you want to take a crack at the other cheek.

He turns and exits.

SARAH *looks at the marker, picks it up from the desk, and throws it into wastebasket in front of desk and sings.*

I won't take a chance
My love will be just what I need
Not some fly-by-night Broadway romance
And till then I shall wait
And till then I'll be strong
For I'll know when my love comes along

SCENE 3

Wall telephone—coin box. We find NATHAN DETROIT *at the phone. During the following conversation,* JOEY'S VOICE *will be heard over the speaker system.*

NATHAN. Hello . . . hello, is this the Biltmore Garage? Let me talk to Joey Biltmore.

JOEY'S VOICE. Who's this?

NATHAN. Nathan Detroit.

JOEY'S VOICE. This is Joey. What do you want?

NATHAN. Joey, I'm calling about the—er—*you*—know.

JOEY'S VOICE. The what?

NATHAN, *whispering.* The crap game.

JOEY'S VOICE. The *what?*

NATHAN, *a shade louder.* The crap game.

JOEY'S VOICE. Wait a minute—I got a customer.

NATHAN. Hurry it up, will you?

Three explosions over the phone, ending in one great big one.

JOEY'S VOICE. That'll be eight dollars . . . What did you say, Nathan?

NATHAN, *loud.* The crap game.

JOEY'S VOICE. Don't say that on the phone—suppose the cops are listening.

NATHAN, *whispering.* I'm sorry, the dice game . . . Look, Joey, is it okay if I use your place tomorrow night?

JOEY'S VOICE. If I get a thousand bucks.

NATHAN. I'll have it tomorrow.

JOEY'S VOICE. Then call me tomorrow.

NATHAN. Listen, Joey, if you're going to take that attitude I'll have the game someplace else.

JOEY'S VOICE. Then have it someplace else.

NATHAN, *shouting*. Where else can I have it?
Softening.
Joey, the dough is guaranteed. Would I lie to you?

JOEY'S VOICE. Yes!

NATHAN. I'm getting it from Sky Masterson.

JOEY'S VOICE. How do you know?

NATHAN. It's a bet—I can't lose. I bet him he could not take a doll to Havana.

JOEY'S VOICE. Why couldn't he?

NATHAN. Because she ain't the kind of doll that *goes* to Havana.

JOEY'S VOICE. Where does she go?

NATHAN. She don't go *no* place. That's why I know I'm gonna win.

JOEY'S VOICE. Don't be so sure. It ain't a horse, it's a doll.

NATHAN. But Joey——

JOEY'S VOICE. Nathan, there will be no crap game here tomorrow unless I get my dough in advance.

NATHAN. Joey, you've known me for a long time.

JOEY'S VOICE. That's why I want it in advance.

NATHAN. Well, I can't talk no more—I got to meet Adelaide at the Hot Box. Look, just one thing. Can I at least tell the guys that the game is gonna be at your place?

JOEY'S VOICE. Not till I get the dough.

NATHAN. Okay, you'll get it. Good-by!

JOEY'S VOICE. Good-by!

NATHAN. I hope you get stabbed by a Studebaker!

SCENE 4

*The Hot Box Night Club. Discovered—*MASTER OF CERE-
MONIES *standing in front of microphone. The place is well
crowded.*

MASTER OF CEREMONIES. And now, for the grand finale of our
Round-the-World Revue, we take you down on the farm
with our star, Miss Adelaide, and the Hot Box Farmer-
ettes.

DANCING GIRLS *enter in abbreviated farmerette costumes
with large hats and carrying rakes, hoes, pitchforks. There
are two large pumpkins, two scarecrows on stage. After
dance by girls,* ADELAIDE *enters, carrying basketful of ears
of corn, throws ears of corn to* TWO SPECTATORS. *They
all sing* BUSHEL AND A PECK

ADELAIDE *sits on pumpkin.*
    I love you a bushel and a peck
    A bushel and a peck and a hug around the neck
    Hug around the neck and a barrel and a heap
    Barrel and a heap and I'm talkin' in my sleep
    About you

GIRLS.
    About you

ADELAIDE.
    About you

GIRLS.
    My heart is leapin', havin' trouble sleepin'

ADELAIDE.
    'Cause I love you a bushel and a peck
    You bet your pretty neck I do

ADELAIDE *and* GIRLS.
    Doodle, oodle, oodle, doodle, oodle, oodle, doodle, oodle,
    oodle, oo

NATHAN *enters, calls to* ADELAIDE. *She crosses to him.* GIRL
DANCER *looks for* ADELAIDE, *runs to her, taps her on the
shoulder, and* ADELAIDE *leaves* NATHAN *to continue song.
She yells "Here chick, chick, chick," throws her ear of
corn to* NATHAN, *which he catches.*

ADELAIDE *and* GIRLS.

I love you a bushel and a peck
A bushel and a peck, tho' it beats me all to heck

ADELAIDE.

Beats me all to heck how I'll ever tend the farm
Ever tend the farm when I want to keep my arms
About you

ADELAIDE *and* GIRLS.

About you
The cows and chickens are going to the dickens
(All of the spectators join in.)
'Cause I love you a bushel and a peck
You bet your pretty neck I do
Doodle, oodle, oodle, doodle, oodle, oodle, doodle, oodle,
    oodle, oo

GIRLS *and* ADELAIDE *exit.*

WAITER *enters with cup of coffee which he places on table
front of* NATHAN. WAITER *enters with push broom and
starts sweeping up petals that were used in number by
dancing girls. Orchestra plays "Home Sweet Home," sig-
nifying the place is closing.*

PATRONS *exit, some a little tight.* NATHAN *hums* BUSHEL
AND A PECK *to himself as the* WAITER *is sweeping up.*

NATHAN, *singing.*

I love you a bushel and a peck—
    (Speaking.)
That lousy Joey Biltmore . . .

ADELAIDE *enters in dressing gown, carrying a cardboard
box with "*SALLY'S WEDDING SHOP*" printed on it, also a
book.*

NATHAN *rises as* ADELAIDE *enters and throws ear of corn
upstage. He turns to* ADELAIDE *who rushes into his arms.*

ADELAIDE. Hello, Nathan.

They embrace.

NATHAN. Hello, pie face.

ADELAIDE. How are you, handsome?

NATHAN. Fine. What have you got there?

ADELAIDE. A book.

NATHAN. A book! You're always reading books. You're becoming a regular bookie.

ADELAIDE. Nathan darling, this is very interesting. The doctor gave it to me. I went to him about my cold.

Sits in chair with book in hand.

NATHAN. How *is* your cold?

ADELAIDE. It's the same. So the doctor asked me how long I had had it, and I told him a long time, and I said I thought it was on account of my dancing with hardly any clothes on, which is what I usually wear, so he said to read this book, because he said it might be due to psychology.

NATHAN. You haven't got that, have you?

ADELAIDE. Nathan, this is the psychology that tells you why girls do certain kinds of things.

NATHAN. Oh! Would it tell you what kind of a doll would go for a certain kind of a guy which you wouldn't think she would do so?

ADELAIDE. What do you mean?

NATHAN. I mean just for instance. There are certain dolls you can almost bet they wouldn't go for certain guys.

ADELAIDE. Nathan, no matter how terrible a fellow seems, you can never be sure that some girl won't go for him. Take us.

NATHAN. Yeah.

ADELAIDE. Nathan darling. Starting with next week, I'm going to get a raise. So with what I'll be making, I wondered what you would think—maybe we could finally get married.

NATHAN, *loosening his collar as he feels the strain.* Well, of course we're going to, sooner or later.

ADELAIDE. I know, Nathan—

Sneeze.

—but I'm starting to worry about mother.

NATHAN. Your mother? What about your mother?

ADELAIDE. Well, Nathan, this is something I never told you before, but my mother, back in Rhode Island—she thinks we're married already.

NATHAN. Why would she think a thing like that?

ADELAIDE. I couldn't be engaged for fourteen years, could I? People don't do that in Rhode Island. They all get married.

NATHAN. Then why is it such a small state?

ADELAIDE. Anyway—I wrote her I was married.

NATHAN. You did, huh?

ADELAIDE, *each word coming through pain.* Uh-huh. Then, after about two years——

NATHAN. *What* after about two years?

ADELAIDE, *in a very small voice.* We had a baby.

NATHAN. You told your mother we had a baby?

ADELAIDE. I had to, Nathan. Mother wouldn't have understood if we hadn't.

NATHAN. What type baby was it?

ADELAIDE. It was a boy. I named it after *you,* Nathan.

NATHAN. Thank you.

ADELAIDE. You're welcome.

NATHAN. And—uh—where is Nathan Jr. supposed to be *now?*

ADELAIDE. He's in boarding school. I wrote mother he won the football game last Saturday.

NATHAN. I wish I had a bet on it.

ADELAIDE. But Nathan—that's not all, Nathan.

NATHAN, *after a pause.* Don't tell me he has a little sister.

ADELAIDE. All those years, Nathan. Mother believes in big families.

NATHAN, *puts hands to ears.* Just give me the grand total.

ADELAIDE, *hardly able to get the word out.* Five.

NATHAN. Your mother must be a glutton for punishment.

ADELAIDE. Anyway, Nathan, now we're finally getting married, and it won't be a lie any more.

NATHAN, *a high moral tone.* Adelaide, how could you do such a thing? To a nice old broad like your mother?

ADELAIDE. But Nathan, you don't even know my mother!

NATHAN. But I'll be meeting her soon, and what'll I tell her? What'll I tell her I did with the five kids? Traded them to the Phillies or something? What are we going to do?

ADELAIDE. We could get married.

NATHAN. But marriage ain't something you jump into like it was a kettle of fish.

Feeling his collar again.

We ain't ready.

ADELAIDE. I'm ready, Nathan.

Picks up box.

What do you think I got in this box? Nathan! What do you think I got in this box?

NATHAN, *reading cover of box:* "SALLY'S WEDDING SHOP." I can't guess.

ADELAIDE. It's a wedding veil. I've had it for three years. I won't show it to you, because it's bad luck . . . Would you like to see it?

NATHAN. It's bad luck.

ADELAIDE. So you see, Nathan darling, I got the veil. All we need now is our license and our blood test.

NATHAN. Our what?

ADELAIDE. Blood test. It's a law.

NATHAN. What a city! First they close my crap game, then they open my veins.

ADELAIDE. Nathan, you're not planning to run your crap game again?

NATHAN. Adelaide, how can you think such a thing! Why do you think I give up the crap game. It's because I love you, and I want us two to be the happiest married couple that there is in the world.

MIMI *enters half undressed.*

MIMI. Anybody see an earring out here?

She is searching the floor.

ADELAIDE, *giving a perfunctory look.* I don't think so.

MIMI, *seeing* NATHAN. You! I'm all dated up tomorrow with Society Max and he breaks it on account of your dopey crap game. Honest, Adelaide, I pity you.

Sees earring on floor and picks it up.

Oh, here it is.

She exits.

ADELAIDE *furiously crosses to* NATHAN. NATHAN *gets down on his knees pleadingly with outstretched arms.*

NATHAN. Adelaide, look at me. I'm down on my knees.

ADELAIDE. Oh, get up. It reminds me of your crap game.

She sneezes.

NATHAN. Look, you're getting yourself upset—you and I are going to be all right—after all, we love each other, and we're going to get married.

ADELAIDE. I don't believe you any more.

NATHAN. But it's true. You'll feel better tomorrow; come on, cheer up, honey.

He crosses to her and chucks her under the chin.

Let's see that old smile.

No response.

That's my girl. See you tomorrow.

She sneezes.

He rushes off.

ADELAIDE *picks up book, and sings* ADELAIDE'S LAMENT.

It says here:

(*Singing.*)

The average unmarried female, basically insecure
Due to some long frustration, may react
With psychosomatic symptoms, difficult to endure
Affecting the upper respiratory tract

(*Looks up from book.*)

In other words, just from waiting around
For that plain little band of gold
A person . . . can develop a cold
You can spray her wherever you figure the streptococci
    lurk
You can give her a shot for whatever she's got but it just
    won't work
If she's tired of getting the fish-eye from the hotel clerk
A person . . . can develop a cold

(*Reads again.*)

It says here:

(*Sings again.*)

The female remaining single, just in the legal sense
Shows a neurotic tendency—see note

(*Looks at note.*)

Chronic, organic syndromes, toxic or hypertense
Involving the eye, the ear, the nose, and throat

(*Looks up, puts book down.*)

In other words, just from wondering whether the wedding
    is on or off
A person . . . can develop a cough
You can feed her all day with the vitamin A and the bromo
    fizz
But the medicine never gets anywhere near where the
    trouble is

*If she's getting a kind of name for herself and the name
    ain't his*
A person . . . can develop a cough
*And furthermore, just from stalling and stalling and stall-
    ing the wedding trip*
A person . . . can develop la grippe
*When they get on the train for Niagara, and she can hear
    church bells chime*
The compartment is air-conditioned, and the mood sublime
Then they get off at Saratoga, for the fourteenth time
A person . . . can develop la grippe
La grippe
La postnasal drip
With the wheezes and the sneezes
And a sinus that's really a pip
*From a lack of community property and a feeling she's
    getting too old*
A person . . . can develop a bad, bad cold

SCENE 5

A street off Broadway. The MISSION BAND *enters. They
are playing* FOLLOW THE FOLD. MARTHA *leads, carrying a
sign, duplicate of the one we saw in Mission interior,
Scene 2, with the exception that it shows that "Proverbs"
has been rubbed off and "Isaiah" substituted.* AGATHA *is
behind* MARTHA, *playing the trombone,* CALVIN *playing
the cornet,* ARVIDE *the bass drum and cymbals,* SARAH *with
her tambourine.* SKY *is patiently following along behind.*
SARAH, *who is aware of his presence, gives an annoyed
flounce.* NICELY *sneaks on following* SKY *and notices the
looks of annoyance that* SARAH *gives* SKY. *He looks after
them as* BENNY *follows on almost immediately.* NICELY *is
still peering off stage as they all exit . . .*

BENNY. Hey! Nicely! What are you looking at?

NICELY, *delighted, turning to* BENNY. Sky was just following
   Miss Sarah, and you should have seen her.

   He gives an imitation of SARAH's *snootiness.*

   She give him a look that would have cooled off a moose
   at mating time.

BENNY. Great! Just so he don't take her to Havana.

NICELY. Havana! He couldn't take this doll to New Rochelle.
   Where's Nathan? He ought to start lining up the game.

BENNY. I don't know—I suppose trying to see Adelaide. She's
   mad at him again.

   Peers off—looks at wrist watch.

NICELY. That Miss Adelaide. She is always taking his mind
   off honest work.

BENNY. Yes, it's too bad that a smart businessman like Nathan
   has to go and fall in love with his own fiancée.

NICELY. Benny, that is his weakness, and we should be tol-
   erant, because I am told that is a world-wide weakness.
   Look.

   They sing GUYS AND DOLLS

NICELY.
   What's playing at the Roxy?
   I'll tell you what's playing at the Roxy
   A picture about a Minnesota man, so in love with a Mis-
      sissippi girl
   That he sacrifices everything and moves all the way to
      Biloxi
   That's what's in the Daily News

BENNY *hits* NICELY *in chest.*
   What's in the Daily News?
   I'll tell you what's in the Daily News
   Shows paper to NICELY.

   Story about a guy who bought his wife a small ruby
   With what otherwise would have been his union dues
   That's what's in the Daily News.

   (*Puts paper in pocket.*)

NICELY.

> What's happening all over?
> I'll tell you what's happening all over
> Guy sitting home by a television set who once
> Used to be something of a rover

BOTH.

> That's what's happening all over
> Love is the thing that has licked 'em
> And it looks like Nathan's just another victim

NICELY.

> Yes sir, when you see a guy reach for stars in the sky
> You can bet that he's doing it for some doll

BENNY.

> When you spot a John waiting out in the rain
> Chances are he's insane as only a John can be for a Jane

NICELY.

> When you meet a gent paying all kinds of rent
> For a flat that could flatten the Taj Mahal

BOTH.

> Call it sad, call it funny, but it's better than even money
> That the guy's only doing it for some doll

BENNY.

> When you see a Joe saving half of his dough
> You can bet there'll be mink in it for some doll

NICELY.

> When a bum buys wine like a bum can't afford
> It's a cinch that the bum is under the thumb of some little
>   broad

BENNY.

> When you meet a mug lately out of the jug
> And he's still lifting platinum folderol

BOTH.

> Call it hell, call it heaven, it's a probable twelve to seven
> That the guy's only doing it for some doll

> A GUY and DOLL enter. She has a long cigarette holder. He
> carries a load of suit boxes and hatboxes. He takes lighter

from pocket and lights her cigarette. She blows smoke in his face. She exits, followed by GUY.

BENNY.

When you see a sport and his cash has run short
Make a bet that he's banking it with some doll

NICELY.

When a guy wears tails with the front gleaming white
Who the hell do you think he's tickling pink on Saturday
      night?

BENNY.

When a lazy slob takes a good steady job
And he smells from Vitalis and Barbasol

BOTH.

Call it dumb, call it clever, ah, but you can give odds for-
      ever
That the guy's only doing it for some doll

SCENE 6

Mission exterior. It is around lunch time. The MISSION BAND *enters, headed by* CALVIN, *who is carrying his cornet by his side. It is very obvious that he is tired and discouraged.* MARTHA *follows carrying the sign that we saw in the previous scene. She is not carrying it erect but at her side.* AGATHA *is carrying her trombone listlessly.* ARVIDE *is carrying his drum by his side, also very discouraged and tired.* SARAH *follows on immediately behind* ARVIDE, *and as she enters she is glancing off stage to see if* SKY MASTERSON *is following her.*

SARAH. Well, we finally lost him.

ARVIDE. I do think you should have paid some attention to him.

AGATHA. Yes, he attended every street meeting we had this morning. He must be interested in our work.

SARAH. Very.

AGATHA. By the way, you spoke beautifully this morning, Sarah.

SARAH. No, I can't reach these people. I should never have volunteered for this post. Well, let's go to lunch.

AGATHA, CALVIN, and MARTHA exit into mission.

And I was going to convert Broadway all by myself. I was going to take these gamblers and have them just begging to come to the Mission.

She sees SKY's marker in trash basket, picks it up. She and ARVIDE are the only ones of the Mission Band who remain outdoors. GENERAL CARTWRIGHT, the head of the Save-A-Soul Mission, enters just as SARAH angrily throws marker back into trash basket. She sees the GENERAL.

SARAH. General Cartwright!

GENERAL. Good morning, Sarah. Arvide!

ARVIDE. Good morning, General.

SARAH. We didn't know you were coming to town, General.

GENERAL. I got in early this morning. I've spent the last hour trying to find you.

AGATHA appears in the Mission doorway.

SARAH. Oh, I'm sorry. We've been holding some extra street meetings, trying to stimulate more interest . . .

AGATHA. Good morning, General.

GENERAL. Good morning. Sarah, there's something I want to talk to you about.

SARAH. Won't you come inside—have some lunch with us?

GENERAL. No, I don't have time, dear. I have several other calls to make . . . Sarah, we at headquarters have come to a definite conclusion. We have decided to close this branch of the Mission.

SARAH. Oh, no!

ARVIDE. Close the Mission!

SARAH. But, General, please! Someone can do good here, even if I can't.

GENERAL. Sarah, there are so many calls on us, so many other places where our work is really needed.

ARVIDE. But we are doing much better now!

AGATHA. We've announced a big meeting for tomorrow night.

GENERAL. You've announced a meeting! But will anyone be here? Will anybody come?

A second's pause, then SKY *enters with quiet dignity.*

SKY. Pardon me—I couldn't help overhearing. General, my name is Sky Masterson, former sinner.

GENERAL. How do you do?

SKY. How do you do? I wish to protest the closing of this Mission. I believe Miss Sarah can be a big success here.

GENERAL. I am glad to hear you say that, but I'm not so certain.

SKY. A dollar will get you ten.

GENERAL. What?

SKY. General, might I make a suggestion?

Goes to trash basket and picks up marker which he conceals in his hat.

GENERAL. Yes.

SKY. Why don't you come to the meeting tomorrow night and find out for yourself?

Crosses to SARAH *and drops marker in her tambourine.*

Don't you think that would be a good idea?

GENERAL. Well, if I thought the Mission had a chance . . .

SARAH, *looking at marker in tambourine.* General, I personally guarantee you one dozen genuine sinners.

GENERAL. Hallelujah!

SKY. Hallelujah!

SCENE 7

Street off Broadway. The CRAPSHOOTERS *walk on.* HARRY
THE HORSE *is in the lead, followed by* BIG JULE. *After they
are all on,* BENNY *enters.*

BENNY. You all got your carnations?
   Ad lib: "Yes."
   Remember, no one will be let in to the game without they
   got red carnations. It's like a password.

HARRY. Okay, but where's the game?
   Exclamations from the mob. NATHAN *enters.*

BENNY. I'll tell you in a minute. Nathan, is it all set? Can I
   tell the guys that it's at the Biltmore Garage?

NATHAN. Not yet. I got to stall 'em for a while. Joey wants
   his dough first.

BENNY. But it's eleven o'clock—they won't stick around much
   longer.

NATHAN. So sue me. I left Nicely at my hotel to wait for the
   money from Sky. It'll be there.
   Enter NICELY, *eating sandwich.* NATHAN *crosses to him.*
   Where's the dough?

NICELY. It hasn't come yet.

NATHAN. I told you to wait for it.

NICELY, *indicating sandwich.* I had to get some groceries. I
   felt a little faint.

NATHAN. Get back to the hotel and wait for the money from
   Sky, and don't come back here without it even if you
   starve to death.

NICELY. Okay, Nathan.
   NATHAN *pushes* NICELY *off.*

HARRY. Where's the game, Detroit?

NATHAN. Hey, Harry the Horse, how are you, Harry? How's everything in Brooklyn?

HARRY. Detroit, if you do not have no place for your game, tell us, and we will seek elsewhere for entertainment.

NATHAN. Now take it easy, Harry.

HARRY. I hope, Detroit, you will not spoil our evening, inasmuch as I happen to be entertaining a very prominent guest tonight. I think you might have heard of him.
He points to a big tough-looking guy.
I would like you to meet Big Jule from Chicago.

NATHAN, *very ingratiating*. Why, how do you do, Big Jule?
Shakes hands perfunctorily.
Welcome to our fair city, in which as you know the heat is on. But just be patient and you'll get some action.
BIG JULE *just stands there looking at* NATHAN.

HARRY. What do you say, Big Jule, shall we stick around or shall we blow?

BIG JULE, *positively*. I came here to shoot crap. Let's shoot crap.

NATHAN. Sure, sure.

HARRY. Nathan, if there is no crap game tonight I am sure Big Jule will be considerably displeased; and Big Jule does not like to be displeased, as you can find out from those citizens who at one time or another displeased him. Although I will admit it is very hard to find such citizens, in view of the fact that they are no longer around and about.

NATHAN. Why, Harry, you don't think I would be so rude as to displease a gentleman like Big Jule here, do you?
He puts his hand on BIG JULE's *arm.*
Big Jule, believe me when I tell you that when Nathan Detroit—Nathan Detroit . . .

He moves his hand and pats BIG JULE *on the chest. His words slow down as he feels* JULE'S *gun. He removes his hand as though he touched a hot stove.*

. . . when Nathan Detroit arranges something . . . you can count on it that . . .

He peters out as BRANNIGAN *enters, and he looks them all over.*

BRANNIGAN. Well! Well! An interesting gathering indeed. The cream of society . . . Angie the Ox, Society Max, Rusty Charlie, Liver Lips Louie.

He goes down the line but nobody says anything.

Hey, Harry the Horse, all the way from Brooklyn, and . . .

Stops in front of BIG JULE.

Pardon me, I'm very bad on names, but your face looks familiar. Mind telling me where you're from?

BIG JULE *chews his cigar a moment.*

BIG JULE. East Cicero, Illinois.

BRANNIGAN. Oh, what do you do there?

BIG JULE. I'm a scoutmaster.

BRANNIGAN. Well, don't ever help my mother across the street.

Smells flower in one of the mugs' lapel.

Mmm, lovely.

Looks over the line-up of flowered lapels.

This looks like the male chorus from *Blossom Time.* What's the occasion?

His eyes travel over the entire group. They finally settle on BENNY.

NATHAN. Well, we . . . er—

BENNY. It's a party.

BRANNIGAN. Indeed! What kind of a party?

At this moment ADELAIDE *backs onto the stage. She is waving at some girls.*

ADELAIDE. Good-by, girls, see you tomorrow.

> BENNY *sees her and immediately gets his idea. He grabs* ADELAIDE *by the waist and leads her over to* BRANNIGAN. It's a bachelor dinner. Nathan's getting married.

ADELAIDE. What?

HARRY, *grabbing* NATHAN *and leading him forcibly to* ADE-LAIDE *and placing him with his arms around* ADELAIDE. NATHAN *is obviously taken by surprise and shows it.* That is correct, Lieutenant! It's a bachelor dinner. Nathan's getting married.

BENNY. Yes, sir!

> (*Sings.*)
> For . . .

GROUP.

> . . . *he's a jolly good fellow*
> *For he's a jolly good fellow*
> *For he's a jolly good fellow*

BIG JULE.

> *Which nobody cannot deny.*
> *Slaps* NATHAN *on back, almost upsetting him.*

ADELAIDE. Nathan darling, I'm so thrilled! Why didn't you tell me?

NATHAN. It was a surprise.

ADELAIDE. But when I saw you standing here with all these— fine gentlemen, I never dreamed it was a bachelor dinner. I thought it was a——

NATHAN. Oh, it's a bachelor dinner.

BENNY. It's a bachelor dinner.

NATHAN. Yes, sir! A bachelor dinner.

ADELAIDE. Just think, after fourteen years I'm finally going to become Mrs. Nathan Detroit. Time certainly does fly.

BRANNIGAN. Tell me, Nathan. When is the happy day?

ADELAIDE. When will it be, Nathan?

NATHAN. Well . . .

BRANNIGAN. Nathan, these good fellows are nice enough to give you a bachelor dinner. You should at least tell them the wedding date.

NATHAN *shouts*. Well, we need time for a license and our blood test.

ADELAIDE *sighs*. Gee, wouldn't it be wonderful if we could be married tomorrow night? Right after the show at the Hot Box.

NATHAN. Adelaide, we need time for a license.

BRANNIGAN. You could elope.

NATHAN. What?

BRANNIGAN. You can drive down to Maryland. What's the name of that town?

BENNY. Pimlico.

BRANNIGAN. Not Pimlico, no, Nathan, Elkton. They'll marry you right away. They don't ask you for a blood test.

NATHAN. Ain't that unhealthy?

HARRY. Nathan, that's a great idea. Elope. I'll lend you my getaway car.
He takes a quick look at BRANNIGAN.
My Buick.

ADELAIDE *throws her arms around his neck*. Oh, Nathan, let's do it.

NATHAN, *long pause; sighs*. Well . . . what the hell?
They embrace.
All congratulate him.

BRANNIGAN. My congratulations too, Nathan. And I only hope there is nothing in heredity.
He exits.

ADELAIDE. Nathan, I got so many things to do before we elope. You'll be at the Hot Box tomorrow night?

NATHAN. I'll have a table reserved, and I'll be all dressed up in whatever you elope in.

ADELAIDE. Oh, Nathan, I'm so happy. I ought to wire my mother. Only what'll I wire her?

NATHAN. Send the telegram and date it back.

ADELAIDE. I'd better wait until we have five children. It won't take us long.

She exits.

HARRY. Nathan, you are indeed a lucky fellow. A most beautiful doll indeed. Do you agree, Big Jule?

BIG JULE. Tell me, how long you know the doll?

NATHAN. Fourteen years.

BIG JULE. Let's shoot crap.

BENNY. Nathan, you'd better find a place!

NATHAN. How can I? The money from Sky ain't come yet.

BENNY. Maybe it won't come. Maybe he took the doll to Havana.

NATHAN. He couldn't have! How could he? She couldn't have gone!

The music of the approaching MISSION BAND *is heard.* NATHAN *is galvanized to attention: he will now find out. The band enters one at a time, with* NATHAN *anxiously counting them as they enter—*MARTHA, *carrying sign,* ALL NIGHT CRUSADE AGAINST THE DEVIL, *then* AGATHA, CALVIN, *and* ARVIDE. *A pause, then* NATHAN *places hand to head and collapses on* BENNY'S *shoulder.*

SCENE 8

Havana, Cuba. A dive. Music is blaring, dances are flaring. SKY *ushers* SARAH *into the place, but it is too much for her. She takes one look and flees.* SKY *must of course follow her.*

*A fashionable couple enter dancing. Immediately fol-
lowing them, a platform unit on casters, with a table and
two chairs, is pushed on stage. This unit represents the
Hotel Nacional.* SARAH *and* SKY *are bowed into the place
by the* HEADWAITER. SARAH *is handed an enormous menu
by the* HEADWAITER.

SARAH. A ham sandwich.

WAITER, SKY, *and* DANCING COUPLE *give her a quick incredulous look.*

The platform unit is pulled off stage with SARAH *and* SKY
on it.

DANCING COUPLE *dance off.*

SARAH *enters with guidebook in her hand, followed by*
SKY. SARAH *looks in guidebook, then points toward audience, supposedly to a monument tablet.*

SARAH. El Santo Cristo, the second oldest mission in Cuba . . .
Come on!

SKY. Where to?

SARAH. To see the oldest.

SARAH *walks on, followed by* SKY. *She points toward audience as she looks in guidebook.*

"Don't miss the dungeons from which prisoners were
thrown to the sharks."

SKY. Sounds like a million laughs.

SARAH *walks on.* SKY *follows her, obviously very tired. She
points toward audience.*

SARAH. Here is buried Christopher Columbus.

SKY. At least he's lying down.

SARAH *starts to walk on again when a very sexy* CUBAN
DANCING GIRL *enters, followed by* TWO CUBAN DANCING
MEN. SARAH *and* SKY *give them a quick glance as they pass
by. A* WAITER *pushes on the platform unit which has been
reset with a mantel and two chairs and a table. This represents a cheap street cafe.* SARAH *and* SKY *walk to table*

and sit. A shoddy-looking WAITER *stands waiting to take their order.*

SKY. How about a drink?

SARAH. A milk shake, please.

SKY, *holding up two fingers to waiter.* Dulce de Leche.

> WAITER *signals back knowingly.* SARAH *goes back to her guidebook, much to* SKY'S *annoyance.* WAITER *returns with two drinks in coconut shells.* SARAH *sips drink, as does* SKY.

SARAH. These are delicious. What did you call them?

SKY. Dulce de Leche.

SARAH. Dulce de Leche. What's in it—besides milk?

SKY. Oh, sugar, and—sort of native flavoring.

SARAH. What's the name of the flavoring?

SKY. Bacardi.

SARAH. It's very good. I think I'll have another one.

> *Black out.*

> *When lights go up several empty coconut shells denote they have had several drinks.* SKY *is tapping the table. He chucks her under the chin. She brushes his hand away.*

SARAH. Doesn't Bacardi have alcohol in it?

SKY. Only enough to act as a preservative.

SARAH, *a little tipsy.* You know—this would be a wonderful way to get children to drink milk.

> *Same* CUBAN DANCING GIRL, *followed by the* TWO CUBAN DANCING MEN *that we saw before, enters. They do the same sexy routine as they pass and exit.* SARAH *rises and imitates their routine as she exits doing bumps.* SKY *rises and places hand to his head in amazement, quite shocked at her. Then he does the same movement as he exits. The lights now come up on the dive.*

> CUBAN GIRL *and* TWO CUBAN MEN *enter, followed by* SARAH *pulling* SKY *on by the hand. She is in a very gay mood.*

SARAH, *shouting as she enters.* Two Dulce de Leche!

A WAITER *places a table.* SARAH *sits.* SKY *sits.* WAITER *brings drinks in coconut shells.*

The solo FEMALE DANCER *begins to make up to* SKY, *much to* SARAH'S *annoyance.* SARAH, *in retaliation, dances with one of the Cuban men.* SKY *forces* SARAH *to sit down. Finally the solo* DANCER *seizes* SKY *and makes him dance with her.* SARAH *takes* CUBAN *by the hand and forces him to dance with her.* SARAH *becomes jealous, leaves* CUBAN *and grabs* SKY, *pulling him away from* DANCER. DANCER *strikes back—a free for all develops. A* CUBAN *gets up on a chair and is about to throw a stool at* SKY. SARAH *sees this, steps up on table, picks up wine bottle, and breaks it over the head of the* CUBAN, *breaking it to bits.* SKY *grabs* SARAH *over his shoulder, rescuing her, and dashes out as the fight becomes a brawl.*

SCENE 9

Havana exterior. SKY *enters carrying* SARAH *in his arms, and she is still struggling. He sets her down, and it is apparent that she is a little tipsy.*

SKY. Take it easy, slugger. It's over and you're still champ.

She kisses him. She staggers after kiss.

Are you all right?

SARAH, *happily.* Am I all right? Ask me how do I feel?

SARAH, *arms around him, sings* IF I WERE A BELL.

Ask me now that we're cozy and clinging
Well, sir, all I can say is
If I were a bell I'd be ringing
From the moment we kissed tonight
That's the way I've just got to behave
Boy, if I were a lamp I'd light
And if I were a banner I'd wave

Ask me how do I feel
Little me with my quiet upbringing
Well, sir, all I can say is
If I were a gate I'd be swinging
And if I were a watch I'd start popping my spring
Or if I were a bell I'd go
(Sky swings his arms over his head.)
Ding, dong, ding, dong, ding
Ask me how I feel
From this chemistry lesson I'm learning

SKY. Chemistry?

SARAH. Yes, chemistry.
Well, sir, all I can say is,
If I were a bridge I'd be burning
Yes, I knew my morale would crack
From the wonderful way you looked,
Boy, if I were a duck I'd quack
Or if I were a goose I'd be cooked
(She falls on his chest.)
Ask me how do I feel
(He straightens her up.)
Ask me now that we're fondly caressing
Pal, if I were a salad
I know I'd be splashing my dressing
Ask me now to describe
This whole beautiful thing
Well, if I were a bell I'd go Ding, dong, ding dong ding
(She falls into his arms.)

SARAH. Havana is so wonderful. Why don't we stay here for a few days so we can see how wonderful it's really like.

SKY *takes a moment.* I think we'd better hurry if we want to catch the plane back to New York.

SARAH. I don't *want* to go back to New York.

SKY. I'm *taking* you back!

SARAH. You're no gentleman.

SKY. Look, a doll like you shouldn't be mixed up with a guy like me. It's no good. I'm no good.

SARAH *puts arms around him; he pushes her away.*

You know why I took you to Havana? I made a bet! That's how you met me in the first place. I made a bet.

SARAH. How else would a girl get to meet a gambler?

SKY. *He picks up* SARAH *in his arms and carries her. She struggles.* Come on!

SARAH. No, no!

SKY. I got to think what's best for *you.*

SARAH. Oh, you talk just like a missionary.

*Black-out. The sound of an airplane is heard through the loud speakers and simultaneously a sign, "*FASTEN SEAT BELTS," *lights up on stage. After a short interval the sound fades out as does the sign.*

SCENE 10

Mission exterior. It is four o'clock the following morning. SARAH *enters. She is minus her uniform coat and hat. She is in a pensive mood.* SKY *follows on almost behind her, also in a thoughtful mood. He is hatless.*

SARAH. Thank you for bringing me back. I must have behaved very badly.

SKY. No, you were fine.

ADELAIDE *enters. She is draped with assorted kitchen utensils given her at a shower. She is followed by* FOUR GIRLS. *They are carrying utensils given to* ADELAIDE *and humming "The Wedding March."*

ADELAIDE. Oh, golly, I don't know how I'll get home with all this stuff. It was wonderful of you to give it to me.

She starts out, sees SKY, *stops.*

Sky, hello!

SKY. How are you, Miss Adelaide?

ADELAIDE. Oh, fine, Sky. Look! The girls just gave me a kitchen shower.

A DRUNK *enters.*

They went to an all-night drugstore and surprised me with a kitchen shower! Look!

She waves utensils in the air. The DRUNK *notices the brightness of the utensils.*

DRUNK. What vulgar jewelry!

He exits.

SKY. That's wonderful, Adelaide! You know Miss Sarah?

There are ad lib greetings.

SARAH. How do you do?

ADELAIDE. Glad to meet you. You know, Sky, we're eloping tomorrow night right after the Hot Box—Nathan and I.

SKY. Good luck!

ADELAIDE. Thank you, Sky.

Crosses to girls.

Gee, I feel just like a housewife, already. I'm going to love being in the kitchen—I've tried all the other rooms.

ADELAIDE *exits, followed by* GIRLS.

SKY. Miss Adelaide certainly seems happy.

SARAH. She's in love.

SKY *turns to* SARAH. Yeah. I guess so.

SARAH. What time is it?

SKY. I don't know. Four o'clock.

SARAH. This is your time of day, isn't it? I've never been up this late before.

SKY. How do you like it?

SARAH. It's so peaceful and wonderful.

SKY. You're finding out something I've known for quite a while.

SKY *sings* MY TIME OF DAY.

My time of day is the dark time
A couple of deals before dawn
When the street belongs to the cop
And the janitor with the mop
And the grocery clerks are all gone
When the smell of the rain-washed pavement
Comes up clean and fresh and cold
And the street lamp light fills the gutter with gold
That's my time of day
My time of day
And you're the only doll I've ever wanted to share it
  with me

SKY. Obediah!

SARAH. Obediah! What's that?

SKY. Obediah Masterson. That's my real name. You're the first person I've ever told it to.

They sing I'VE NEVER BEEN IN LOVE BEFORE.

I've never been in love before
Now all at once it's you
It's you forever more
I've never been in love before
I thought my heart was safe
I thought I knew the score
But this is wine that's all too strange and strong
I'm full of foolish song
And out my song must pour
So please forgive this helpless haze I'm in
I've really never been in love before
(They kiss.)

At end of number, ARVIDE *enters, carrying his drum—he is*
followed by the MISSION BAND. *They are obviously very*
tired from being out all night trying to convert sinners.

SARAH sees ARVIDE as he enters; she goes to him as he is setting his drum down beside the Mission door.

SARAH. Grandfather! I thought you'd be asleep.

ARVIDE. Hello, Sarah dear. Good morning, Brother Masterson.

SKY. Good morning.

ARVIDE. We followed your suggestion and stayed out all night. We spoke to a lot of sinners. Where have you been, Sarah?

SARAH. I've been to Cuba.

ARVIDE. You're even more tired than I am.

Off stage can be heard the clang of a police patrol wagon bell. A GUY dashes on at top speed. He runs across to the Mission entrance, sticks his head in the door, and lets go with a loud piercing whistle, finger-in-mouth, as the MISSIONARIES and SKY express surprise.

SKY. What the hell is this?

BENNY, NICELY, and NATHAN come hurrying out of the door, putting on their coats at the same time. They start off. The LOOKOUT whistles at them and motions for them to go the other way. As they stop and turn, followed by HARRY THE HORSE, the other CRAPSHOOTERS emerge, some with coats off, others just putting them on.

They start off and collide with GUYS coming back, but they all exit. As NATHAN goes by, SKY grabs him but NATHAN doesn't stop.

SKY. Hey! What is this?

NATHAN. Canasta!

He dashes off, followed by some of the GUYS. BIG JULE enters.

BIG JULE, *yelling to NATHAN as he is running off.* Wait a minute! I'm losing ten G's.

He runs off. The sound of the patrol bell has come very close. As the bell stops clanging, BRANNIGAN and TWO COPS rush on. BRANNIGAN realizes they have escaped him.

BRANNIGAN, *to the* TWO COPS. Someone must have tipped them off.

The TWO COPS *rush off.* BRANNIGAN *turns to* SARAH.

I seen a lot of strange things in my time but this is the first time I ever see a floating crap game going full blast in a Mission.

He runs off.

SARAH, *stunned.* Crap game!

SKY. Sarah, you know I had nothing to do with this, don't you?

SARAH *walks slowly toward the Mission entrance.*

Sarah!

She stops.

SARAH *turns away.* This wouldn't have happened if I hadn't . . .

She turns to him.

I never should have gone with you. It was wrong.

SKY. No, it wasn't. You went to help the Mission.

SARAH, *dully.* Did I?

SKY *looks at her a moment.* Will I see you tomorrow?

SARAH. Everyone is welcome at the Mission.

SKY. That's not what I mean.

SARAH. It's no good, Sky. You said it yourself—it's no good.

SKY. Why not? What the hell kind of doll are you, anyway?

SARAH. I'm a Mission doll.

ACT TWO

The Hot Box night club. The place is well crowded with patrons sipping cocktails. The MASTER OF CEREMONIES *is standing in front of a microphone.*

MASTER OF CEREMONIES. And now for the feature number of the evening. The Hot Box proudly presents Miss Adelaide and her Debutantes.

Music strikes up. MASTER OF CEREMONIES *exits, taking microphone with him.* EIGHT DANCING GIRLS *enter, followed by* ADELAIDE. *They all carry long gold cigarette holders with cigarettes and are wearing golden gowns, shoes, hats, pearl necklaces, and mink stoles.*

They sing TAKE BACK YOUR MINK

ADELAIDE.
He bought me the fur things five winters ago
And the gown the following fall
Then the necklace, the bag, the hat, and the shoes
That was late forty-eight I recall
Then last night in his apartment
He tried to remove them all
And I said as I ran down the hall:
Take back your mink
Take back your pearls
What made you think
That I was one of those girls?
Take back the gown, the shoes, and the hat
I may be down but I'm not flat as all that
I thought that each expensive gift you'd arrange

Was a token of your esteem
But now when I think of what you want in exchange
It all seems a horrible dream
So take back your mink
To from whence it came
And tell them to Hollanderize it
For some other dame

ADELAIDE AND GIRLS.

Take back your mink

(They all throw cigarette holders in music pit and take off mink.)

Take back your pearls

(Take off pearls.)

What made you think
That I was one of those girls?

Take back the gown

(Take off gowns.)

Take back the hat

(Take off hats.)

I may be down but I'm not flat as all that
I thought that each expensive gift you'd arrange
Was a token of your esteem
But when I think of what you want in exchange
It all seems a horrible dream—eek!
Take back your mink
Those old worn-out pelts
And go shorten the sleeves
For somebody else

(To the audience.)

Well wouldn't you?

ADELAIDE *and* GIRLS *exit.*

After the number the lights come down and a single table is spotted. SKY *enters, no hat, looks around like a man on the loose. He is unshaven again and a bit crumpled. He drifts over to an empty table and sits down. A* WAITER *comes over.*

WAITER. Will you be with Mr. Detroit's party, sir?

SKY. Is he here?

WAITER. No, sir. Mr. Detroit has not been here all evening.

SKY. Bring me a rye and soda.

WAITER *exits.*

NICELY *enters a bit furtively. Sits at table.*

NICELY *picks up a stalk of celery and starts eating it.* Sky, did you see Miss Adelaide?

SKY. Huh?

NICELY. I bring a message for her from Nathan. I wish Nathan would bring his own messages.

SKY. What's the message? Where is Nathan?

NICELY. It's this way.

He concentrates but still nibbles celery.

Nathan's aunt in Pittsburgh was suddenly taken ill with— er——

SKY, *wryly.* A rare tropical disease.

NICELY. Yeah, that's not bad. Anyway, Nathan has to——

SKY. Nicely, what is the message? Where *is* Nathan?

NICELY *looks around to see if he's overheard, then leans over toward Sky.* The crap game is still going on.

SKY, *casually.* Since last night.

NICELY. Big Jule, being a large loser, does not wish the game to terminate. In fact, he is most insistent. So we find another place and the game goes on.

SKY. Where is the game?

NICELY. Are you looking for some action?

SKY. No, I'm leaving town tonight, but I do want to talk to some of the guys. You see, Nicely, I gave a marker to— well, somebody—and I'd kinda like to clean it up before——

He stops as ADELAIDE *approaches.* NICELY *is quickly on his feet.*

NICELY. I'll meet you outside.

SKY. What about Nathan's message?

NICELY. Oh! Miss Adelaide, Nathan is in Pittsburgh with a rare tropical aunt. Good-by.

Rushes out.

ADELAIDE. What? I don't understand. Sky, Nathan *has* to come here tonight. We're eloping to get married. Is it the crap game again?

SKY. You know Nathan. Why does it surprise you?

ADELAIDE. But he promised to change.

SKY. Change, change. Why is it, the minute you dolls get a guy that you like, you take him right in for alterations?

ADELAIDE. What about you men? Why can't you marry people like other people do and live normal like people? Have a home, with—wallpaper and book ends.

SKY, *sadly.* No, Miss Adelaide.

ADELAIDE. What do you mean—no?

SKY. Guys like Nathan Detroit and—yeah, Sky Masterson—we don't belong in a life like that. So when dolls get mixed up with guys like us, it's no good.

He gets to his feet, places one dollar on table to pay for his drink.

No good. See you in a couple months.

ADELAIDE. Where you going?

SKY. I don't know—Las Vegas, maybe. I got a ticket on the late plane.

ADELAIDE. Will you see Nathan before you go?

SKY. Maybe.

ADELAIDE. Tell him I never want to talk to him again and have him call me here.

Sneezes and sniffles.

SKY. Look! Why don't you get another guy?

ADELAIDE. I can't. I love Nathan. Wait till you fall for some-body! You'll find out.

SKY *looks at her a second.* Yeah.

Exits.

ADELAIDE *sniffles and then sings* ADELAIDE'S LAMENT

*In other words—just from sitting alone at a table reserved
   for two
A person . . . can develop the flu
You can bundle her up in her woollies
And I mean the warmest brand
You can wrap her in sweaters and coats
Till it's more than her frame can stand
If she still gets the feeling she's naked
From looking at her left hand
A person . . . can develop the flu
Huh! the flu!
A hundred and three point two
So much virus inside
That her microscope slide
Looks like a day at the zoo
Just from wanting her memories in writing
And a story her folks can be told
A person . . . can develop a cold
(She sneezes.)*

SCENE 2

*Street exterior. Manhole rail. Edison blinker wagon with
light blinking.*

SARAH *enters at a brisk pace,* ARVIDE *following her, carrying his bass drum and having quite a time keeping up.*

ARVIDE. Not so fast, Sarah, not so fast. Look, suppose we don't have a big meeting tonight. Suppose nobody is there at all. We'll explain to the general.

SARAH. We won't have to explain. It'll be very clear. I just want to get away from this whole place. To go someplace where—where——

ARVIDE. Where the sinners are all respectable and well-behaved?

SARAH. You saw what happened last night. They gambled— in our Mission.

ARVIDE. And some day they'll be praying there. Even a man like Sky Masterson. He came seeking refuge.

SARAH. He came seeking *me*. Did you know that?

ARVIDE. Are you kidding? I knew that the minute he started picking on you. But I didn't know you were going to get stuck on him.

SARAH. I'll get over it.

ARVIDE. What do you want to get over it for? It isn't pneumonia.

SARAH. The man I love will not be a gambler.

ARVIDE. But if you love him enough——

SARAH. He will not be a gambler.

ARVIDE. Sarah, dear. I've always taken care of you. All I want is for you to be happy.

He sings MORE I CANNOT WISH YOU.

Velvet I can wish you
For the collar of your coat
And fortune smiling all along your way
But more I cannot wish you
Than to wish you find your love
Your one true love, this day
Mansions I can wish you
Seven footmen all in red
And calling cards upon a silver tray
But more I cannot wish you
Than to wish you find your love
Your own true love, this day
Standing there

Gazing at you
Full of the bloom of youth
Standing there
Gazing at you
With the sheep's eye
And the lickerish tooth
Music I can wish you
Merry music while you're young
And wisdom when your hair has turned to gray
But more I cannot wish you
Than to wish you find your love
Your own true love, this day
With the sheep's eye
And the lickerish tooth
And the strong arms to carry you away

Kisses SARAH *on cheek.*

SKY *enters with* NICELY.

SKY. Good evening, Miss Sarah. Well, Brother Abernathy, how goes it with the soul-saving? Tonight's the big meeting, isn't it?

ARVIDE. It's supposed to be. The general is coming, and she's expecting—uh . . .

SKY. The general's a tough doll, eh?

ARVIDE. Well, very few people will be there—in fact, nobody. And, uh . . .

SARAH. I don't think Mr. Masterson is interested in our troubles, Grandfather. We've got to hurry.

SKY. Miss Sarah.
She stops.
You've forgotten something, but, being a gambler, I never forget things like this. You hold my marker for twelve sinners tonight.

SARAH. Thank you, Mr. Masterson, but I'd rather you forgot about it.

SKY. I cannot welch a marker.

SARAH. Mr. Masterson, last night the Mission was filled with your friends. Let us say we're even.

She exits.

ARVIDE. If you don't pay off on that marker, I'll tell the whole town you're a dirty welcher.

He exits.

SKY. Nicely! Where's the crap game?

NICELY. Well, Sky, it's about ten minutes' walk from here.

SKY. Which way?

NICELY. This way.

He starts down the manhole.

SCENE 3

Crap game in the sewer. The stage lights come up, revealing the CRAP GAME DANCE.

There is a CRAPSHOOTER *sitting on pipe.* HARRY THE HORSE *and a* CRAPSHOOTER *are standing on a platform.*

TWO CRAPSHOOTERS *are hanging on ladder watching the dance.*

BENNY, ANGIE THE OX, BIG JULE, SOCIETY MAX, *and one other* CRAPSHOOTER *are standing on another platform.* NATHAN DETROIT *is standing in front of it.*

When the dance is finished, all the CRAPSHOOTERS *put their coats on, some even put ties on. They all wear red carnations. Most of them are getting ready to leave the game.*

BIG JULE. Wait a minute. Where you all going? I came here to shoot crap.

PLAYER. We had enough.

ANOTHER PLAYER. Let's go home.

NATHAN. You see, Big Jule, the boys are slightly fatigued from weariness, having been shooting crap for quite a while now, namely twenty-four hours.

Ad libs from the crowd.

BIG JULE. I do not care who is tired. I am out twenty-five G's, so nobody leaves.

He pats his shoulder revolver threateningly.

NATHAN. Gentlemen, I begin to see the logic of Big Jule. It is not that Big Jule is a bad loser; it is merely that he prefers to win. Right, Big Jule?

BIG JULE. Give me the dice. I'm shooting five hundred.

BENNY. Take two hundred.

The players are a little slow in getting their money up and they all groan.

PLAYER. I'm half dead.

HARRY. If you do not shut up, Big Jule will arrange the other half.

Players quickly put their money up.

BIG JULE, *as he rolls.* Hah!

NATHAN. And it's a one and a one. Snake eyes. You lose.

Reaches for his take.

And fifty dollars for the house. But the dice are still yours, and your luck is bound to——

BIG JULE. Shut up! Another five.

BENNY. Two hundred more.

The GUYS *cover him again but very reluctantly.*

NATHAN. And here comes that big lucky roll.

BIG JULE, *as he throws.* Haah!

NATHAN. And it's—snake eyes again.

They all grab their money.

BENNY. Tough luck, Big Jule.

BIG JULE. Well, that cleans me.

General relaxation, even expressions of pleasure.

But I ain't through yet.

General apprehension.

I will now play on credit.

Many moans.

NATHAN. You see, Big Jule, the fellows are pretty tired. Of course me, personally, I am fresh as a daisy.

BIG JULE. Then I will play with *you*.

NATHAN. Me?

BIG JULE. Yeah, you. You been rakin' down out of every pot— you must have by now quite a bundle.

NATHAN. Well, being I assume the risk, it is only fair I should assume some dough.

BIG JULE. Detroit, I am going to roll you, willy or nilly. If I lose, I will give you my marker.

Starts writing.

NATHAN. And if I lose?

HARRY. You will give him cash.

NATHAN. Let me hear from Big Jule.

BIG JULE. You will give me cash.

NATHAN. Now I heard it.

BIG JULE. Here is my marker.

NATHAN *looks at it—then at* BIG JULE.

Put up your dough. Is anything wrong?

NATHAN. No—no. "I O U one thousand dollars," signed "X"! How is it you can write one thousand, but you cannot write your signature?

BIG JULE. I was good in arithmetic, but I stunk in English.

NATHAN. Here! This will put you through Harvard.

BIG JULE. I'm rolling a thousand. And to change my luck I will use my own dice.

NATHAN. Your own dice!

BIG JULE. I had them made for me especially in Chicago.

NATHAN. Big Jule, you cannot interpolate Chicago dice in a New York crap game.

BENNY. That is a breach of etiquette.

HARRY. Show me where it says that in Emily Post.

NATHAN. Not that I wish to seem petty, but could I look at these dice?

All men crowd around looking at dice. BIG JULE *takes them out, gives them to* NATHAN.

But these—these dice ain't got no spots on 'em. They're blank.

BIG JULE. I had the spots taken off for luck. But I remember where the spots formerly were.

NATHAN. You are going to roll blank dice and call 'em from remembering where the spots formerly was?

BIG JULE, *threateningly.* Why not?

Pulls NATHAN *up by coat.*

NATHAN *wipes perspiration from his forehead.* I see no reason.

BIG JULE, *rolling.* A five—and a five. My point is ten.

NATHAN. Well, I still got a chance.

BIG JULE, *shaking the dice.* Tensy! Tensy! Come againsy!

NATHAN. I wish he'd fall down on his endsy.

BIG JULE. Heah!

He rolls.

A ten! I win!

NATHAN. A ten?

BIG JULE, *pointing.* A six and a four.

NATHAN, *looking.* Which is the six and which is the four?

BIG JULE. Either way . . .

Picks up dice.

Now I'm shooting two thousand. Get it up!

NATHAN *looks at his watch.* I just remembered. I'm eloping tonight. Adelaide is waiting for me.

Starts to exit. BIG JULE *grabs him and pulls him back.*

BIG JULE. Get up the two thousand.

NATHAN. How about letting some of the other chaps in on the fun?

Ad lib: "Ah no."

BIG JULE. After I'm through with you! Two thousand!

NATHAN *puts it up reluctantly.* BIG JULE *shakes dice, rolls.*

Haah! Seven! I win.

NATHAN, *swallowing hard.* What a surprise!

BIG JULE *picks up dice.* Detroit, I think I will take it easy this time.

NATHAN. What do you mean?

BIG JULE. I am shooting one dollar.

NATHAN. I'll take all of it.

BIG JULE *puts it down.*

BIG JULE *rolls.* How do you like that? Snake eyes! I lose.

NATHAN. For this I got to bend down.

BIG JULE. Now I will give you a chance. I will roll for you three thousand.

NATHAN. Three G's?

BIG JULE *picks up dice—firm.* I am rolling you for three G's. Put it down there.

NATHAN *counts out the money. Puts his hands over his eyes as* BIG JULE *starts to roll.*

NATHAN. Wouldn't it be more convenient if I put it right into your pocket?

BIG JULE. Get it up!

Rolling.

Haaah! Eleven. I win.

NATHAN. That cleans me.

BIG JULE, *to the others, picks up dice and money.* Now I will play with *you* guys.

NATHAN. Wait a minute! You gotta give me a chance to get even. I will roll *you,* with my dice.

BIG JULE. All right, Detroit, that's fair. What are you gonna use for money?

NATHAN. I will give you my marker.

HARRY. And you want Big Jule to put up cash?

BENNY. Nathan done it.

NATHAN. Sure I done it. What kind of a deal is this, anyway?

BENNY. Take it easy, Nathan.

NATHAN. Him and his no-spot dice! Somebody ought to knock the spots off *him!*
Stands right up to BIG JULE.

HARRY. Nathan, don't make Big Jule have to do something to you.

BIG JULE. Yeah, I am on my vacation.

NATHAN. Go ahead—shoot me. Put me in cement. At least I would know where I am. Here I risk my neck to set up a crap game. I even promise to get married on account of it. So look how I wind up. Broke in a sewer. Believe me, my tough friend from Chicago, there is nothing you could do to me that would not cheer me up.
NICELY *comes down the stairs.*

NICELY, *motioning to someone.* Here they are.
SKY *comes down.*

SKY. Good evening, gentlemen.

BIG JULE *crosses to* SKY. Well, fresh blood. You looking for some action?

SKY. Not at the moment. I would like to talk to some of you guys.

BIG JULE. We ain't talking. We're shooting crap.

SKY, *quietly.* I am asking for only one minute.

BIG JULE. We are shooting crap.

SKY. It has to do with Miss Sarah Brown's Mission.

BIG JULE. Say, who is this guy?

HARRY. It's the fellow I was telling you—took the Mission doll to Havana.

BIG JULE. Oh, I get it. Look, fellow, why don't you go back to your praying tomato? You're slowing up the action around here.

SKY, *smoothly.* If you want action, would you care to make a small wager on a proposition?

BIG JULE. What's the proposition?

SKY. Am I right-handed or left-handed?

BIG JULE. How would I know a thing like that?

SKY. I'll give you a clue.

Socks BIG JULE *with a right.* BIG JULE *goes down. Staggers to his feet, reaching groggily for his gun.* SKY *gets it first —tosses it to* NATHAN *who catches it gingerly.*

HARRY. Heh!

NATHAN, *handing gun to* BENNY. Kindly return this to Sears Roebuck.

SKY. Look, you guys. Tonight in Miss Sarah Brown's Mission at 409 West 49th Street they are holding a midnight prayer meeting. I promised I would deliver to them some sinners, and when it comes to sinning most of you guys are high up among the paint cards.

Everyone looks uncomfortable.

HARRY. I don't want to waste no evening in a hallelujah joint.

SKY. If you won't do it as a favor to me, do it as a favor to yourselves. I guarantee you the air in the Mission smells cleaner than down here. And maybe it would not hurt you guys to learn something else besides the odds on making a four the hard way.

HARRY. You been reading the Bible too much.

SKY. So what? Maybe the Bible don't read as lively as the scratch sheet, but it is at least twice as accurate.

They only mumble with heads hung low.

Well, I tried. See you around, Nathan.

NATHAN. Okay, Sky. About that Havana business, I regret I temporarily do not have the one thousand to pay you.

SKY. You don't have to pay me.

Pulls out a bill.

You won.

NATHAN. But I thought you took Miss Sarah to Havana.

SKY. You thought wrong.

Giving money to NATHAN *he starts up the ladder.*

NATHAN. Come on, Big Jule, get up. I have now got dough to roll you again. But with my dice.

HARRY, *on his feet again.* Nothing doing. With those dice he cannot make a pass to save his soul.

SKY *stops dead on ladder.* What'd you say?

HARRY, *belligerently.* I says with them dice he cannot make a pass to save his soul.

SKY. Well, maybe I can make a pass to save his . . .

Pointing to one, then another.

And yours! . . . and yours . . . and his . . .

From the group: "Huh? . . . What are you talking about?" *Ad lib.*

I am going to roll the dice. I will bet each of you a thousand dollars against your souls. One thousand cash against a marker for your souls.

BIG JULE *rises. Ad lib.*

If I win, you guys all show up at the Mission tonight.

There is a buzz of interest. Ad lib.

Is it okay?

Ad lib.

HARRY. Let me get this. If you lose, we each get a thousand bucks, and if you win we gotta show up at the Mission doll's cabaret?

SKY, *tight-lipped.* If I win, you show up at the Save-A-Soul Mission. One meeting.

HARRY *thinks a minute.* Okay by me.

BENNY, *taking the lead.* By me too.

The others agree, as they all start writing markers. BENNY *also writes.*

SKY, *as the others hand him their markers.* You too, Nathan. A thousand dollars against your soul.

NATHAN. Me? I don't even know if I got one.

SKY. You got one some place.

NATHAN. How do you spell "soul"?

BENNY, *spelling.* So—o—

SKY. All right, put down your markers.

They do so. SKY *covers them all with a one-thousand-dollar bill.*

Give me the dice.

He gets them.

And give me room.

He hesitates nervously. Tosses the dice in his hand once or twice.

PLAYER. Come on—quit stallin'—roll.

HARRY. What's the matter, Sky, turning chicken?

SKY. You've seen me roll for a hundred G's. But I've got a little more than dough riding on this one.

He sings LUCK, BE A LADY TONIGHT

They call you Lady Luck
But there is room for doubt
At times you have a very unladylike way of running out
You're on this date with me
The pickings have been lush

And yet before this evening is over
You might give me the brush
You might forget your manners
You might refuse to stay and so
The best that I can do is pray
Luck, be a lady tonight
Luck, be a lady tonight
Luck, if you've ever been a lady to begin with
Luck, be a lady tonight
Luck, let a gentleman see
How nice a dame you can be
I know the way you've treated other guys you've been with
Luck, be a lady with me
A lady doesn't leave her escort
It isn't fair, it isn't nice
A lady doesn't wander all over the room
And blow on some other guy's dice
So let's keep the party polite
(Takes roll of money out of pocket.)
Never get out of my sight
Stick with me, baby, I'm the fellow you came in with
Luck, be a lady
(Throws money on floor.)
Luck, be a lady
(Throws more money on floor.)
Luck, be a lady tonight

ENSEMBLE.

Luck, be a lady tonight
Luck, be a lady tonight.
Luck, if you've ever been a lady to begin with
Luck, be a lady tonight

SKY.

Luck, let a gentleman see

ENSEMBLE.

Luck, let a gentleman see

SKY.

How nice a dame you can be

ENSEMBLE.

>*How nice a dame you can be*

SKY.

>*I know the way you've treated other guys you've been with*

ENSEMBLE.

>*Luck, be a lady, a lady, be a lady with me*

SKY.

>*Luck, be a lady with me*
>*A lady wouldn't flirt with strangers*
>*She'd have a heart, she'd have a soul*
>*A lady wouldn't make little snake eyes at me*

ENSEMBLE.

>*Roll 'em, roll 'em, roll 'em, snake eyes*
>*When I've bet my life on this roll*

ENSEMBLE.

>*Roll 'em, roll 'em, roll 'em*

SKY.

>*So let's keep the party polite*

ENSEMBLE.

>*So let's keep the party polite*

SKY.

>*Never get out of my sight*

ENSEMBLE.

>*Never get out of my sight*
>*Stick here, baby, stick here, baby*

SKY.

>*Stick with me, baby, I'm the fellow you came in with*
>*Luck, be a lady*

ENSEMBLE.

>*Luck, be a lady*

SKY.

>*Luck, be a lady*

ENSEMBLE.

>*Luck, be a lady, roll with you, what's the matter, roll the*
>*dice*

SKY.
> *Luck, be a lady, a lady tonight*

ENSEMBLE.
> *Coming out, coming out, coming out*

SKY *and* ENSEMBLE.
> *Right, huh!*

SCENE 4

A street off Broadway. TWO CRAPSHOOTERS *enter. One is putting on his tie. They exit.* BIG JULE *and* HARRY THE HORSE *enter.*

BIG JULE. I tell you I don't want to go to no prayer meeting.

HARRY. Big Jule, you give your marker, and if you welch it will cause me no little embarrassment. I am sure you do not wish to cause me embarrassment?

BIG JULE. But if it ever gets back to Chicago that I went to a prayer meeting, no decent person will talk to me.

They exit. THREE CRAPSHOOTERS *enter.* ADELAIDE *enters, reading a newspaper. She looks around, obviously looking for* NATHAN. NATHAN *enters.* ADELAIDE *sees him and drops the newspaper and purposely bumps into* NATHAN. CRAP-SHOOTER *picks up newspaper as* CRAPSHOOTERS *exit.*

NATHAN. Adelaide!

ADELAIDE, *Lady Windermere.* Oh! What a coincidence!

NATHAN. Adelaide, did Nicely explain to you about tonight? I hope you ain't sore about it?
Tries to embrace her. She pulls away.

ADELAIDE. Please! Let us not have a vulgar scene. After all, we are civilized people. We do not have to conduct our-selves like a slob.

NATHAN. Adelaide! What is this? You are my doll.

ADELAIDE. Your doll! Please, if that weren't so amusing one could laugh at it.

NATHAN. Sweetheart! Baby! How can you carry on like this over one lousy elopement? Adelaide, please!

ADELAIDE. It's no use, Nathan. I have succeeded in your not being able to upset me no more. I have got you completely out of my——

Sneezes. Then throws herself into NATHAN'S *arms, weeping.*

Oh, Nathan!

NATHAN. Adelaide, baby! Don't ever do that to me again! I can't stand it. We'll get married. We'll have a home, a little white house with a green fence—just like the Whitney colors.

ADELAIDE, *through her tears.* Nathan, we got to do it soon. I had another letter from my mother today asking a lot of questions. And she put in a letter for you, too.

Hands it to him.

NATHAN. A letter for me? From your mother? Well——

Opens it and reads.

"Dear Son Nathan: This is my first letter to you, although you have now been married to my daughter for twelve years. But I feel like I know you from Adelaide's letters, and in my mind's eye I can see you as you go down to work every morning at seven. What a responsibility it must be, to be the assistant manager of an A. & P."

He breaks off.

I'm not even the manager?

ADELAIDE. I was going to promote you for Christmas.

NATHAN. "I know how hard you have to work to take care of your family—Adelaide and the five children and the one that's on the way."

ADELAIDE. Mother wanted me to visit her, so I had to tell her that.

NATHAN. Don't she know I can't have six kids on what they pay me at the A. & P.?

Reads quickly to himself, then slows up as he reads it aloud.

"I am very proud to have you as a son-in-law. You are a good man, and I know you will always take care of Adelaide." I feel like a heel.

ADELAIDE. Look, Nathan darling, we can still make everything all right. Look, it's not even midnight yet. Five minutes to twelve—let's elope right now.

NATHAN. Okay, Adelaide.

Embrace.

BENNY *and* NICELY *enter.* NATHAN *sees them.*

No, I can't.

ADELAIDE. Why not?

BENNY. Come on, Nathan—we'll be late.

NICELY. Come on!

They exit.

ADELAIDE, *in measured tones.* Nathan, *why* can't we elope now?

NATHAN. Because—well, I got to go to a prayer meeting.

ADELAIDE. Nathan. This is the biggest lie you ever told me.

NATHAN. But I promise you it's true.

ADELAIDE *takes letter from* NATHAN, *tears letter up, throws it on floor.* NATHAN *kneels, picks up pieces.*

They sing SUE ME

ADELAIDE.
You promise me this
You promise me that
You promise me anything under the sun
Then you give me a kiss
And you're grabbin' your hat
And you're off to the races again
When I think of the time gone by

NATHAN.
Adelaide, Adelaide

ADELAIDE.
And I think of the way I try

NATHAN.
Adelaide

ADELAIDE.
I could honestly die

NATHAN.
Call a lawyer and
Sue me, sue me
What can you do me
I love you
Give a holler and hate me, hate me
Go ahead and hate me
I love you

ADELAIDE.
The best years of my life I was a fool to give to you

NATHAN.
All right already I'm just a no-good-nik
All right already, it's true, so nu
So sue me, sue me
What can you do me?
I love you
(Tries to take her in his arms. She backs away.)

ADELAIDE.
Gamble it here
You gamble it there
You gamble on everything all except me
And I'm sick of you keeping me up in the air
Till you're back in the money again
When I think of the time gone by

NATHAN.
Adelaide, Adelaide

ADELAIDE.
And I think of the way I try

NATHAN.

Adelaide

ADELAIDE.

I could honestly die

NATHAN.

Serve a paper and sue me, sue me
What can you do me
I love you
(She sneezes.)
Give a holler and hate me, hate me
Go ahead and hate me
I love you

ADELAIDE.

When you wind up in jail don't come to me to bail you out

NATHAN.

All right already so call a policeman
All right already it's true, so nu
(She goes to him.)
So sue me, sue me
(They embrace.)
What can you do me?
I love you

BENNY *and* NICELY *enter. They beckon to* NATHAN. NATHAN
waves them away. ADELAIDE *turns and sees them. They
see the anger in her eyes and hurriedly exit.*

ADELAIDE.

You're at it again.
You're playing the game
I won't play second fiddle to that
And I'm sick and tired of stalling around
And I'm telling you now that we're through
When I think of the time gone by

NATHAN.

Adelaide, Adelaide
(She waves him away.)

ADELAIDE.
   And I think of the way I try
   I could honestly die

NATHAN.
   Sue me, sue me,
   Shoot bullets through me
   I love you!

SCENE 5

Interior of Mission. The MISSION GROUP—SARAH, ARVIDE,
AGATHA *and* CALVIN—*sits expectantly at a long table. An-*
other figure is present: the GENERAL. *She is pacing the*
room, looking at the group who are momentarily growing
more uneasy.

GENERAL. It is now several minutes past midnight. Isn't anyone coming?
   They all sit glumly.

GENERAL. Sergeant Sarah, something is very wrong.

ARVIDE. Maybe your watch is fast.

SARAH. General, I know what's wrong. *I'm* wrong. I've failed.
   I've spoken to these people day after day, but my words
   haven't reached them . . . I think you had better . . .
   Mugs enter. SARAH *turns to them as they enter.*

ARVIDE. Welcome, brothers. Welcome.

   A few little grunts from the boys. Then SKY *enters.*

SKY. Everybody here? Where's Nathan Detroit?

   NATHAN *enters.*

NATHAN. Present.

SKY. Miss Sarah, here you are. One dozen or more assorted
   sinners. Sorry we didn't have time to clean 'em up.

ARVIDE. Won't you gentlemen sit down?

They shuffle their feet a little.

SKY. Sit down! All of you!

They do.

ARVIDE. I would like to welcome you gentlemen to the Save-A-Soul Mission.

A loud Bronx cheer from one of the gang.

SKY. Just a minute, you guys. This is a Mission, not Roseland, and I suggest that you do not indulge in any unpleasantness. Since I am required to depart for points West tonight, I am appointing Nathan Detroit major-domo in my place. Nathan, anybody who does not conduct himself according to Hoyle will answer to Sky Masterson personally, and that means in person.

He gives them a final glance, then goes.

GENERAL. What a remarkable young man!

SARAH *looks at her but says nothing.*

NATHAN *rises—confronts them, clears his throat, and shouts.* So remember that, you guys.

Turns to ARVIDE.

Brother Abernathy, your dice.

He sits.

ARVIDE *rises.* Gentlemen, we are honored tonight. The meeting will be conducted by the head of our organization, General Cartwright.

Sits.

NATHAN *starts the applause.*

GENERAL *rises.* It is wonderful to see our Mission graced by the presence of so many evil-looking sinners.

NATHAN *starts to applaud, but realizes he may be wrong.* Now, who would like to testify? Who would like to start the ball rolling by giving testimony?

They are silent and hang their heads.

NATHAN. Benny! Give testimony.

BENNY. I ain't no stool pigeon.

GENERAL. Come, brothers—I know it is difficult. But let one of you give testimony to the sin that is in his heart.

NATHAN. Benny! Tell 'em what a bum you are!

BENNY *rises*.

Benny!

BENNY, *forced to it*. I always was a bad guy and a gambler, but I ain't going to do it no more. I thank you.

Sits, quickly.

GENERAL. There! Don't you feel better now?

BENNY. I'm all right.

GENERAL. Anyone else?

NATHAN. Big Jule.

BIG JULE. What's the pitch?

NATHAN. Just tell them about all the terrible things you did but ain't going to do no more.

BIG JULE *rises*. Well, I used to be bad when I was a kid, but ever since then I have gone straight as I can prove by my record—thirty-three arrests and no convictions.

Sits.

NATHAN, *pointing*. Harry!

HARRY. Oh no!

NATHAN, *louder this time*. Harry the Horse!

HARRY, *getting reluctantly to his feet*. Ah, well, like when Sky was rolling us for our souls—

GENERAL. I beg your pardon?

HARRY. Sky Masterson. He rolled us a thousand dollars against our souls. That's why we're here.

GENERAL. I don't think I understand.

SARAH. I do, General. He means that they are only here because Mr. Masterson won them in a dice game.

GENERAL. How wonderful! This whole meeting the result of gambling! It shows how good can come out of evil. Sergeant Sarah, you have done remarkable work.

ARVIDE. Hasn't she, though?

SARAH, *a small voice.* Thank you.

HARRY. Hey! I ain't finished my testimony. My sins is that when Sky rolled us I wished I would win the thousand dollars instead of having to come here, but now that I'm here I still wish it.

Sits.

GENERAL. Anybody else?

BRANNIGAN *plunges in, ready for anything: he points to* NATHAN. NATHAN *raises a warning finger to his lips.* BRANNIGAN *subsides.* NATHAN *removes* BRANNIGAN'S *hat.*

NATHAN, *in a new voice of piety.* We will now hear testimony from——

He looks them over.

Brother Nicely-Nicely Johnson——

NICELY *forces a smile—then* NATHAN *says sweetly:*

Brother Nicely-Nicely Johnson——

BIG JULE. Get up, you fat water buffalo.

NICELY *slowly rises.*

NICELY. Well. It happened to me kind of funny. Like a dream. That's it, a dream.

GENERAL. Tell us, in your own words.

NICELY *sings* SIT DOWN, YOU'RE ROCKIN' THE BOAT.
*I dreamed last night I got on a boat to heaven
And by some chance I had brought my dice along
And there I stood
And I hollered "Someone fade me"
But the passengers, they knew right from wrong
For the people all said sit down, sit down, you're rockin'
the boat*

ENSEMBLE.
People said sit down, sit down, you're rockin' the boat

NICELY.

> And the devil will drag you under
> By the sharp lapel of your checkered coat
> Sit down, sit down, sit down, sit down

ENSEMBLE.

> Sit down, you're rockin' the boat

NICELY.

> I sailed away on that little boat to heaven
> And by some chance found a bottle in my fist

ENSEMBLE.

> Ooo——

NICELY.

> And there I stood

ENSEMBLE.

> Ooo——

NICELY.

> Nicely passin' out the whisky
> But the passengers were bound to resist

ENSEMBLE.

> Ooo——

NICELY.

> For the people all said beware, you're on a heavenly trip

ENSEMBLE.

> People all said beware

NICELY.

> People all said beware, beware, you'll scuttle the ship

ENSEMBLE.

> People all said beware

NICELY.

> And the devil will drag you under
> (*They all rise.*)

ENSEMBLE *sit*.

> Down——

NICELY.

> By the fancy tie around your wicked throat

ENSEMBLE *sit.*
> *Down——*

NICELY.
> *Sit down, sit down, sit down, sit down*

ENSEMBLE.
> *Sit down, sit down, sit down*
> (*They all sit down.*)

NICELY.
> *Sit down, you're rockin' the boat*

ENSEMBLE.
> *Sit down, you're rockin' the boat*

NICELY.
> *And I laughed at those passengers to heaven*

ENSEMBLE.
> *Down——*

NICELY, *gasping.*
> *A great big wave came and washed me overboard*

ENSEMBLE.
> *Ooo——*

NICELY.
> *And as I sank*

ENSEMBLE.
> *Ooo——*

NICELY.
> *And I hollered "Someone save me"*

ENSEMBLE.
> *Ooo——*

NICELY.
> *That's the moment I woke up*

ENSEMBLE.
> *Ooo——*

NICELY.
> *Thank the Lord*

ENSEMBLE. MISSION BAND *rises.*
> *Thank the Lord, thank the Lord*

NICELY.
> *And I said to myself, sit down, sit down, you're rockin'*
>   *the boat*

ENSEMBLE.
> *And he said to himself sit down, sit down*

NICELY.
> *Said to myself, sit down, sit down, you're rockin' the boat*

ENSEMBLE. MISSION BAND *sits.*
> *Said to himself sit down*

NICELY.
> *And the devil will drag you under*

ENSEMBLE.
> *And the devil will drag you under*

NICELY.
> *With a soul so heavy you'd never float*
> *Sit down, sit down, sit down*

ENSEMBLE.
> *Sit down, sit down*

NICELY.
> *Sit down*

ENSEMBLE.
> *Sit down, sit down*

NICELY.
> *You're rockin' the boat*
> (*They all rise.*)

ENSEMBLE.
> *You're rockin' the boat, sit down you're rockin'*

NICELY *and* ENSEMBLE.
> *Sit down, sit down, sit down, you're rockin' the boat*
> (*They all sit.*)
> *At the end of this number* NATHAN *and* BRANNIGAN *rise.*

NATHAN. Anything we can do for you, Brother Brannigan? Maybe you would care to testify?

BRANNIGAN. I'll do my testifying in court, where I will testify that you ran a crap game here in this Mission last night. Miss Sarah, you were standing there when they came out. You saw them. Aren't these the fellows?

SARAH *slowly looks at them; takes her time.* I never saw them before in my life.

BIG JULE. There's a right broad!

ARVIDE. Now if you would excuse me, Officer, we would like to go on with our meeting.

BRANNIGAN. I never saw crapshooters spend so much time in a Mission. Maybe that's what they mean by Holy Rollers.

He puts his hat on and exits. HARRY THE HORSE *rises indignantly.* NATHAN *waves him down as* BIG JULE *pulls* HARRY *down by the sleeve.*

NATHAN. Thank you, Miss Sarah. People, I also have a confession to make, and I got to get it off my chest. We *did* shoot crap here last night, and we're all sorry. Ain't we, boys?

He turns to the mob. They mumble assent, hanging their heads.

BIG JULE. I'm really sorry.

NATHAN, *turning to* SARAH. But I did another terrible thing. I made a bet with a certain guy that he could not take a certain doll away with him on a trip, and this I should not have done, although it did not do any harm as I won the bet.

SARAH. You won the bet?

NATHAN. Sure. The guy told me that he didn't take the doll. Well, that makes me feel a lot better.

GENERAL. Hallelujah!

NATHAN. Hallelujah!

The mob all say "Hallelujah." The GENERAL *picks up a handful of songbooks and passes them out.*

GENERAL. Gentlemen, we will now sing No. 244, FOLLOW THE FOLD.

She stands in front of them and raises her hand to conduct. Music begins. SARAH *quietly picks up her cape and quickly makes an exit.*

SCENE 6

Night. Street off Broadway. Two roped-together bundles of newspaper tabloids on which two people can sit.

ADELAIDE *enters disconsolately. Drops onto one newspaper bundle—sneezes. A passing* MALE *enters, stops to look at her—to flirt if encouraged—*

ADELAIDE, *angrily.* Oh, go away!

He hurries off. ADELAIDE *starts to sing softly as* SARAH *enters, singing softly. She is wearing a cape. She sits on the other newspaper bundle not noticing* ADELAIDE.

ADELAIDE, *singing.*	SARAH, *singing simultaneously.*
Keep the Vicks on your chest	So please forgive this
And get plenty of rest	Helpless haze I'm in
You can wisely warn her	I've never really been in love before
But in spite of the quiet	
Massages and diet	
She's still a goner	
Once she gets the idea that the little	
Church will always be around the corner	
A person . . . can develop a cold	
Looks at SARAH.	

ADELAIDE, *noticing* SARAH *and not caring much.* Oh hello.

SARAH, *uncertainly.* Good evening.

ADELAIDE. I'm Adelaide, the well-known fiancée.

SARAH. Oh yes. When are you getting married?

ADELAIDE. The twelfth of never.

SARAH. Oh, I'm sorry.

ADELAIDE. I didn't even get close enough to a church to be left at it . . .
Half to herself.
Gee, what'll I ever tell my mother?

SARAH. Oh, your mother will understand. Just tell her your engagement is broken.

ADELAIDE. I'm afraid that might confuse her. Maybe I'll tell her Nathan is dead, and then see *to* it.

SARAH. You mustn't carry hate in your heart, Miss Adelaide. Try to be forgiving and understanding, and the pain will go away. In the Bible it tells us in Isaiah . . . Isaiah . . .
The thought is too much for her.
. . . Isaiah . . .

ADELAIDE. You've got a boy friend named Isaiah, huh?

SARAH, *through her tears.* Isaiah was an ancient prophet.

ADELAIDE. Don't tell me. Nobody cries like that over an old guy. Whoever it is, you got it bad. You know, when I saw you with Sky Masterson the other night——
SARAH *goes into a fresh outburst of tears.* ADELAIDE *looks at her.*
Oh no! Not Sky! You're not in love with Sky?
No answer, which is its own confirmation.
You poor thing!

SARAH, *low-voiced.* I thought I hated him.

ADELAIDE. I thought I hated Nathan. I still think I hate him. That's love.

SARAH. Adelaide—can't men like Sky ever change?

ADELAIDE *shakes her head.* For fourteen years I've tried to change Nathan. I've always thought how wonderful he would be, if he was different.

SARAH. I've thought about Sky that way, too.

ADELAIDE. I've sat and pictured him by the hour. Nathan—my Nathan—in a little home in the country . . . happy . . .

Lights go on behind her, revealing a NATHAN *in overalls and farmer's hat, standing beside a trellis of beautiful roses. With a spray gun he is tenderly treating each bud with loving care. He picks off a bug, removes his hat to wipe his brow. The lights go down again.*

ADELAIDE *sighs as picture fades.* Gee, wouldn't it be wonderful!

SARAH. Wouldn't it—if only Sky . . .

On the other side SKY *appears. He appears, as in* SARAH's *imagination, wearing a dainty bib-type kitchen apron, holding wicker laundry basket filled with diapers. With clothespins in his mouth, he is hanging diapers on line. The vision fades.*

ADELAIDE. But they just can't change.

SARAH. A little while ago at our prayer meeting there were a lot of gamblers who acted as though maybe they could change.

ADELAIDE. Yes, but that doesn't mean . . . gamblers at your prayer meeting . . . Was Nathan Detroit there?

SARAH. I'm sure I heard that name.

ADELAIDE. A darling little fellow with a cute mustache?

SARAH. I think so.

ADELAIDE. How do you like that rat! Just when he should have been lying, he's telling the truth! I'm glad I'm through with *him.* And you ought to be glad you're through with Sky, too.

SARAH, *thoughtfully.* I am.

ADELAIDE *crosses to* SARAH—*sits on same bundle of newspapers.*
What are we—crazy or something?

They sing MARRY THE MAN TODAY.

ADELAIDE.

> At Wanamaker's and Saks' and Klein's
> A lesson I've been taught
> You can't get alterations on a dress you haven't bought

SARAH.

> At any vegetable market from Borneo to Rome
> You mustn't squeeze a melon till you get the melon home

ADELAIDE.

> You've simply got to gamble
> You get no guarantee
> Now doesn't that kind of apply to you and I?

SARAH.

> You and me

ADELAIDE.

> Why not?

SARAH.

> Why not what?

ADELAIDE.

> Marry the man today
> Trouble though he may be
> Much as he loves to play
> Crazy and wild and free

SARAH *and* ADELAIDE.

> Marry the man today
> Rather than sigh and sorrow

ADELAIDE.

> Marry the man today
> And change his ways tomorrow

SARAH.

> Marry the man today
> Maybe he's leaving town
> Don't let him get away
> Hurry and track him down

ADELAIDE, *simultaneously.*

> Marry the man today
> Maybe he's leaving town
> Don't let him get away
> Counterattack him and

SARAH *and* ADELAIDE.
> *Marry the man today*
> *Give him the girlish laughter*

SARAH.
> *Give him your hand today*
> *And save the fist for after*

ADELAIDE.
> *Slowly introduce him to the better things*
> *Respectable, conservative, and clean*

SARAH.
> *Reader's Digest*

ADELAIDE.
> *Guy Lombardo*

SARAH.
> *Rogers Peet*

ADELAIDE.
> *Golf*

SARAH.
> *Galoshes*

ADELAIDE.
> *Ovaltine*

BOTH.
> *But marry the man today*
> *(Shaking their fists.)*
> *Handle it meek and gently*

ADELAIDE.
> *Marry the man today*
> *And train him subsequently*

SARAH.
> *Carefully expose him to domestic life*
> *And if he ever tries to stray from you*
> *Have a pot roast*

ADELAIDE.
> *Have a headache*

SARAH.
  Have a baby

ADELAIDE.
  Have two

SARAH.
  Six

ADELAIDE.
  Nine

SARAH.
  Stop!

BOTH.
  Marry the man today
  Rather than sigh and sorrow
  Marry the man today
  And change his ways tomorrow

SCENE 7

Broadway. The TWO BROADWAY CHARACTERS *we saw in opening scene are discovered doing the same routine. The* TWO STREETWALKERS *are at the newsstand and cross over to the* TWO BROADWAY CHARACTERS, *who turn them down and exit, followed by the* TWO STREETWALKERS.

All the mugs march on. They have been cleaned up, and each one is wearing a big white gardenia. HARRY *is in the lead, followed by* NICELY, BENNY. *They stand in line.*

The PAPER DOLL VENDOR *and* HIS ASSISTANT *enter and set up their pitch. The* PRIZE FIGHTER *and* HIS MANAGER *watch the bouncing doll and the* PRIZE FIGHTER *motions to* HIS MANAGER *to buy one, which he does. The* DOLL SALESMAN *and* HIS ASSISTANT *quickly exit. The* PRIZE FIGHTER *places the doll on the stage to watch it bounce, but it collapses. He picks it up in disgust.*

SIGHT-SEEING CROWD *enter.* BRANNIGAN *enters and goes to newsstand, which is strung with Christmas tree lights, and stands in front of it looking at the lights.*

ADELAIDE *enters, followed by* GIRLS. *She is dressed in a wedding outfit and carries a bouquet in her hands. She is very nervous and calls offstage.*

ADELAIDE. Nathan! Nathan! Where are you? Nathan!

BRANNIGAN, *at newsstand.* Gimme a late paper.

ADELAIDE. Nathan darling, come on, we're waiting for you.

NATHAN *sticks his head out of the newsstand. He is wearing a red turtle-neck sweater.*

NATHAN. Just a minute! I'm waiting on the lieutenant. Thank you, Lieutenant.

ADELAIDE. Nathan, close up the newsstand. We're getting married.

NATHAN *pulls down shade on newsstand—on it is painted* NATHAN DETROIT'S NEWSSTAND.

HARRY. Look, is this wedding going to take place or ain't it? I paid half a buck for this mesantheorum.

ADELAIDE, *shouting to newsstand.* Nathan! Come on.

NATHAN *emerges through a small door at end of newsstand. He is carrying a top hat and cane in his hand and is now seen to be wearing a very elegant cutaway outfit.*

NATHAN. Gee, Adelaide, you picked the busiest time of the day.

HARRY. Let's go. Where's the wedding?

NATHAN. Holy smoke!

ADELAIDE. What's the matter?

NATHAN. I didn't get a place for the wedding.

ADELAIDE. Oh, Nathan!

NICELY. How about the Biltmore Garage?

MISSION BAND *enters, playing—all five of the* MISSION BAND, *for who is now a member but* SKY MASTERSON, *and*

in uniform, too. He is ripping out FOLLOW THE FOLD *with
the rest of them, swinging his big drumstick lustily.* AR-
VIDE, *meanwhile, has shifted to the cymbals.*

SKY, *starting the pitch.* Brothers and sisters! Life is one big
crap game, and the devil is using loaded dice!

BIG JULE. Where's the crap game?

NATHAN *hits drum with cane.* Brother Masterson?

SKY. Yes, Brother Detroit?

NATHAN. Can we get married in your Mission—Adelaide and I?

SKY *looks at* SARAH, *who looks at* ARVIDE.

ARVIDE. Certainly, I married Brother Masterson and Sister
Sarah. Glad to do the same for you.

SKY. Congratulations, Nathan! I'll lay you eight to five you'll
be very happy.

SARAH. What Obediah means is—

NATHAN. Obediah?

SARAH. —he wishes you every happiness, and so do I.

ADELAIDE. Thank you very much. I *know* we're going to be
happy. We're going to have a little place in the country,
and Nathan will be sitting there beside me every single
night.

An enormous sneeze from NATHAN; *her expression changes
as she realizes what it means.*

They all sing GUYS AND DOLLS.

NOTES

CAPTAIN JINKS OF THE HORSE MARINES opened in Philadelphia on January 7, 1901, and at the Garrick Theatre, New York, a month later. Ethel Barrymore played Madame Trentoni. The first edition of the play (published by Doubleday, Page, and Company in 1902) contains pictures of the first production, in which Miss Barrymore stands revealed as one of the great beauties of all stage history.

THE NEW YORK IDEA opened at the Lyric Theatre, New York, on November 19, 1906. It was produced by Mrs. Fiske, who played the part of Mrs. Karslake. The author's wife, Marion Lea, played Vida Phillimore. Also in the cast were George Arliss and Dudley Digges.

THE MAN WITH THE HEART IN THE HIGHLANDS, 1938, is not to be confused with the longer and more celebrated *My Heart's in the Highlands,* produced in New York in 1939 under the direction of Robert Lewis. Both scripts are adaptations of a story written by Mr. Saroyan in 1935. It was William Kozlenko who suggested to Mr. Saroyan that the story contained a play and who printed the above one-act version, first in the *One Act Play Magazine* and then in *Contemporary One-Act Plays* (Scribner's). The first edition of the longer play (Harcourt, Brace, 1939) contains the music to Burns's poem, *My Heart's in the Highlands,* air by J. M. Courtney, arrangement by Paul Bowles.

PULLMAN CAR HIAWATHA is taken from the volume *The Long Christmas Dinner and Other Plays in One Act,* published jointly by Coward-McCann Inc. and the Yale University Press in 1931.

GUYS AND DOLLS is derived from a story in Damon Runyon's collection, *Runyon à la Carte* (1944), entitled "The

Idyll of Sarah Brown." This story did not appear in the original collection entitled *Guys and Dolls* (1931) but is found in the Pocket Book reprint of that title (1955). The musical, from which the book is first published in the present volume, opened on Broadway in November 1950, and ran there until November 1953; the movie had its première in November 1955. The "cast recording" of the Broadway show was made by Decca Records; there are many different recordings of various individual numbers.